DATE DUE

OCT 11 2012	
Jan. 29, 2013	

Problem-Solving Courts

Problem-Solving Courts

JUSTICE FOR THE TWENTY-FIRST CENTURY?

Edited by

Paul Higgins

and

Mitchell B. Mackinem

PRAEGER

An Imprint of ABC-CLIO, LLC

ABC CLIO

Santa Barbara, California • Denver, Colorado • Oxford, England

Library of Congress Cataloging-in-Publication Data

Problem-solving courts : justice for the twenty-first century? / edited by Paul Higgins and Mitchell B. Mackinem.
p. cm.
Includes bibliographical references and index.
ISBN 978–0–313–35284–3 (hard copy : alk. paper) – ISBN 978–0–313–35285–0 (ebook)
1. Courts of special jurisdiction—United States. I. Higgins, Paul C. II. Mackinem, Mitchell B.
KF8759.P76 2009
347.73'28—dc22 2009010077

13 12 11 10 09 1 2 3 4 5

This book is also available on the World Wide Web as an eBook.
Visit www.abc-clio.com for details.

ABC-CLIO, LLC
130 Cremona Drive, P.O. Box 1911
Santa Barbara, California 93116-1911

This book is printed on acid-free paper ♾

Manufactured in the United States of America

Contents

Introduction

MITCHELL B. MACKINEM and PAUL HIGGINS

In thousands of courtrooms in every state in America and in a growing number of countries throughout the world, defendants stand before the bench in a court—a different court, one concerned about their well-being. The rooms may be richly paneled courtrooms with all the symbols of judicial authority, or they may be industrial concrete conference rooms. The defendants may be grizzled drug addicts with long criminal records or wide-eyed truants caught for the first time. In all these courts, human service professionals, lawyers, police officers, judges, and others work together to enable the defendants to change behavior, to help the defendants manage successfully their problems that led them to court. Despite the familiar trapping of traditional courts, the participants are involved in a new, perhaps revolutionary, approach to the court system: problem-solving courts.[1,2,3]

Problem-solving courts are local courts that seek to remedy detrimental community conditions through sustained attention and through possible therapeutic interventions with individual offenders who experience debilitating personal conditions. Problem-solving courts, also called specialized courts or specialized docket courts, address a wide range of individual conditions and behaviors, including mental illness, truancy, domestic violence, homelessness, teen drug use, and prostitution. As we will see in Chapter 1 by Greg Berman, while no one model of problem-solving courts exists, several basic principles inform problem-solving courts. Each problem-solving court adapts the basic principles to address the individual problems in specific local conditions.

The American court system has changed throughout its history. Problem-solving courts are one of three main movements changing today's court system. Proponents of problem-solving courts, along with proponents of restorative justice and therapeutic jurisprudence, are discontented with the traditional court system. Proponents of each seek to remedy perceived shortcomings in the traditional court. While distinct from restorative justice and therapeutic jurisprudence, problem-solving courts draw support from these other two movements.

Let us first look at problem-solving courts. Problem-solving courts are different from traditional courts. Traditional courts use the "adversarial process" to come to a "legal resolution" in "cases." Judges are "arbiters" in the application of "laws" and "precedent." Problem-solving courts use the "collaborative process" to come to a "therapeutic outcome" for "people." Judges are "coaches" in the application of "social science principles" through deliberate "planning." While traditional courts are formal and legalistic, problem-solving courts are often comparatively informal. Traditional courts aim to move many cases as fast as can be reasonably done. Problem-solving courts work with offenders and others for months, even years, in order to manage successfully complex problems.[4]

The change from retributive justice to restorative justice is the second movement. Restorative justice, also called community justice or transformative justice, differs in several ways from retributive justice, upon which traditional courts have typically been based. In retributive justice, crime is a violation against the state. The courts attribute blame and then provide the appropriate punishment. Victims and communities serve as witnesses for the state. Conversely, restorative justice maintains that crime concerns the victim, the offender, and the community. Crime creates an obligation to make things right. The court ensures that the victim, offender, and community find mutually acceptable means to restore that which had been damaged. To the traditional court response of punishment, restorative justice adds other potential responses, including restitution and community service. These options allow for the violation to be resolved, for the victim to receive compensation, and for the community to be improved. Problem-solving courts and restorative justice can complement each other. Of the problem-solving courts discussed in this book, youth courts rely most significantly on restorative justice principles.

Therapeutic jurisprudence, the third movement, began in courts that dealt with mentally ill defendants.[5] Therapeutic jurisprudence developed into an organized legal philosophy that approaches the law and courts as tools for promoting social and individual welfare through the application of social science within a legal setting.[6] Courts based on therapeutic jurisprudence operate within an ethic of caring. These courts, as compared to traditional courts, explicitly focus on helping the defendant because the court leaders believe that a healthier defendant is less likely to commit future crime. "Therapeutic Jurisprudence concentrates on the law's impact on emotional life and psychological well-being. It is a perspective that regards the law itself as a social force that often produces therapeutic or anti-therapeutic consequences."[7]

Problem-solving courts do not derive from therapeutic jurisprudence. Problem-solving courts develop from pragmatic local concerns about specific problematic community conditions. Therapeutic jurisprudence is a more abstract approach to criminal justice. Problem-solving courts vary in their use of therapeutic jurisprudence as a guide and rationale for their operations. For example, family addiction courts use a full range of therapeutic interventions to change the participants. In contrast, community courts do not look to therapeutic jurisprudence as a guide. While distinct, problem-solving courts and therapeutic jurisprudence agree that traditional courts must change to meet the needs of society.

Since the beginning of problem-solving courts in 1986, they have experienced significant growth. As of December 31, 2007, there were 3,204 problem-solving courts.[8] Of these 3,204 courts, 2,147 are drug courts and 1,057 are other problem-solving courts. This number is up 94 percent from 2004. Nationally, problem-solving courts are not evenly distributed and range from the common to the unusual. As we will see in Chapter 9, youth courts are very common and found in every state. Mental health courts are common, numbering over 300 and found in most states. Truancy courts number over 300, but are limited to three states. Despite the extensive scholarship and promotion on community courts, they are limited to only 30 courts in a few states. Prostitution, gun, and gambling courts are all quite rare and number fewer than five.

Problem-solving courts are an exciting and potentially significant change to the American system of justice. While critics are not so convinced, advocates believe that the effectiveness of problem-solving courts will restore the public's confidence and will promote increased cooperation among all agencies involved in criminal justice. However, the future of problem-solving courts is uncertain. The number of participants in these courts remains quite modest, despite the strong potential for improving the lives of participants. The growth of problem-solving courts is not guaranteed. Substantial federal funding is provided for tribal courts, for example, but very little federal funding is allocated for others, such as juvenile drug courts. While adult drug courts have been highly researched and evaluated, others such as domestic violence courts are almost unstudied. Public awareness for some courts appears robust, as with DWI courts, while homeless courts, for example, are nearly invisible.

Problem-solving courts have the potential to change the American court system and perhaps the court systems in other countries. The addition of problem-solving courts to the range of courts and, more importantly, the integration of problem-solving court approaches into the traditional court system have begun to change the court system. Problem-solving courts and the resulting changes from them may be significant for justice in the twenty-first century.

PLAN OF THE BOOK

Problem-solving courts, according to Greg Berman in Chapter 1, grew out of the increasing realization of and frustration felt by judges, attorneys, and others in the 1980s and 1990s regarding the shortcomings of the traditional criminal court and criminal justice system. Criminal cases were processed, but offenders continued to experience serious problems that interfered with their successful functioning, citizens were not necessarily any safer, and communities were still unhealthy. That was the first "moment of truth" that Berman mentions. While critics raise important concerns about problem-solving courts, Berman notes that these concerns apply to traditional courts too. Instead of a costly reliance on incarceration or a despair that nothing works, which characterized previous criminal justice policy, problem-solving courts offer approaches that have been shown to be more effective than "business-as-usual." The next "moment of truth," Berman argues, is whether society and the criminal justice system will or will not increase the reach of problem-solving courts so that they become ever-more central to justice in the twenty-first century.

Richard Boldt looks carefully at problem-solving courts and some of their potential problems in Chapter 2. While advocates champion the development of problem-solving courts to address the social ills of people and their communities, others offer concerned criticism. Drawing particularly on commentary and evaluations of drug courts, but applying that work to problem-solving courts in general, Boldt raises a variety of concerns. Among these concerns are the following: How well does the merger of punishment and treatment work? Are treatment and social services effectively allocated through the court system? Does therapy become subservient to punishment within problem-solving courts? Do problem-solving courts maintain the procedural fairness that is expected in criminal courts? Are problem-solving court judges able to be unbiased in their new role? Boldt's chapter asks society to examine thoroughly the assumptions and practices of problem-solving courts before any greater commitment is made to them.

Adult drug courts, as Mitch Mackinem and Paul Higgins explore in Chapter 3, continue America's historical mix of punishment and treatment toward problem drug users. Drug courts developed in the United States out of the concern in the late 1980s that the criminal justice system was ineffective in managing the increasingly large number of drug-abusing offenders. With more than 1,000 adult drug courts operating in the United States and others throughout the world, drug courts are one of the most prevalent problem-solving courts. While they vary, the professionals and their supporters understand drug court to be a demanding, comprehensive team- and community-oriented approach to enabling drug-using offenders to stop their drug use and their criminal behavior. Evaluations generally show that adult drug courts are more effective and less costly than the traditional alternatives in reducing the criminal behavior of drug-abusing offenders. Even though concerns about drug court, such as those presented by Boldt in Chapter 2, may not apply to specific courts, they should be taken seriously in order to protect the rights and welfare of drug-court clients. The hope underlying the development of drug courts remains to be realized.

Juvenile drug courts, as Caroline Cooper explains in Chapter 4, cannot succeed if they merely follow the adult drug court approach. Juvenile drug courts must address the particular needs of youth who have a drug problem. These youth are not "little adults." Juvenile drug courts began from a strong foundation. The juvenile justice system has a rehabilitative mission. Adult drug courts have been successful. This strong foundation gave rise to the hope that juvenile drug courts would enable communities to address successfully the growing problem of juvenile drug abuse. However, implementing juvenile drug courts that reach the large number of youth with drug abuse problems has been more difficult than imagined. Less than 10 percent of the approximately 475 existing juvenile drug courts have been opened within the past 2 years. Enrollments in the programs appear to be decreasing. Juvenile drug courts have been found to reduce successfully drug use among the participants compared to comparable youth who are not in such programs. Further, much has been learned about how to operate effectively juvenile drug programs from the experience of the past 15 years. However, without renewed support, juvenile drug courts may not make a significant impact in the twenty-first century on the population of youth who use and abuse drugs.

In Chapter 5, David Hanson argues that the need for DWI (driving while intoxicated) problem-solving courts that handle those persons who constitute a threat to the community due to their addiction to alcohol and their history of impaired driving is obvious. Every injury and death from drunken driving is preventable. Further, the traditional approach of punishing without treating repeat offenders has generally not been effective. Hanson presents ten basic principles for how DWI courts should be organized. The coercive treatment in DWI courts for those addicted to alcohol is a complex matter. Specific practices, including court monitoring and staggered sentencing, can improve DWI courts, as Hanson explains. While DWI courts have not been extensively evaluated, studies of specific DWI courts show them to be effective in reducing drunken driving compared to traditional judicial handling of drunk drivers. DWI courts can be an important and effective means to handle the threat of drunk driving. How important they become in the twenty-first century will depend on how widely legislators, judicial officials, and the community embrace them.

Approximately half of jail and prison inmates in the United States report mental health symptoms, as Patricia Griffin and David DeMatteo note in Chapter 6. Mental health courts rose as a response to the increasingly visible cycle of arrest, incarceration, release, and rearrest of offenders with mental health needs. Approximately 180 mental health courts existed in the United States in 2008, a doubling from three years earlier. Another dozen juvenile mental health courts have also been established in the United States, with more being planned. Other countries, including Canada and the United Kingdom, have also established mental health courts. Based on the philosophy of therapeutic jurisprudence, mental health courts operate on the belief that by treating the mental health needs of offenders, the offenders' functioning will improve and their criminal behavior will decrease. Evaluation studies provide cautious optimism that mental health courts can be effective. While the need for mental health services for offenders is accepted, some observers are concerned that the voluntary nature of participation in mental health courts may not be as well protected as it needs to be. Mental health courts are presently a small component within the criminal justice system, but with increasing understanding of what works best with offenders with mental health needs, mental health courts may increase their impact in the twenty-first century.

Comprehending the complexity of domestic violence is the foundation for understanding domestic violence courts, as Angela Gover makes clear in Chapter 7. Domestic violence courts developed out of changes in the law enforcement and judicial response to domestic violence, which in the latter decades of the twentieth century began to handle domestic violence as a serious crime, not merely a family matter. The philosophy of therapeutic jurisprudence, which underlies domestic violence courts, leads to the primary goals of domestic violence courts being the safety of the victim and the accountability of the offender. While no single model for domestic violence courts has emerged, a close look at the domestic violence court in Lexington County, South Carolina, shows how one domestic violence court works. While many specific domestic violence courts have worked well, the movement toward using domestic violence courts to handle intimate partner violence faces the uncertainty of sufficient funding and other challenges in the twenty-first century.

Community courts, as Victoria Malkin explains in Chapter 8, are intended to focus on the local problems of the neighborhoods that they serve and in which they may be located. While the fewer than 40 community courts in the United States vary by locale, they have increasingly become focused on quality-of-life problems such as excessive noise, drinking in public, urinating in public, graffiti, walking a dog without a leash, and misdemeanor and less serious drug-related crimes. Ironically, community courts may be a misnomer. Even when they are located within the local communities they serve, they may not be significantly of the community, with little meaningful participation by community residents in deciding the focus and operation of the court. Community courts may operate primarily through the actions of the judge of the court and access of residents to that powerful individual. Further, the needs of struggling communities, which, according to Malkin, are not being met by the insufficient attention from the government, are addressed through the legal power of the state that focuses on the disruptive behavior of individuals, not the development of the communities. Whose problems are being solved through community courts, wonders Malkin.

Youth courts, which are not courts per se, try to empower youth to solve problems due to the criminal or unacceptable behavior of other teenagers, as Tracy Mullins discusses in Chapter 9. The more than 1,000 youth courts operating in the United States focus on less serious offenses that youth may commit such as theft, shoplifting, curfew violations, possession of alcohol, truancy, vandalism, and school disciplinary cases. Youth courts vary throughout the country in what offenders they accept, in how they operate, in what agency they are located, in how they are funded, and in other ways. Youth courts have increasingly turned to principles of restorative justice as a guide for their operations. Consequently, youth courts rely heavily on schools and the community in order to be effective. Although the effectiveness of youth courts needs to be more carefully evaluated, they appear to be a useful alternative to the traditional juvenile justice system. While obtaining sufficient funding for youth courts is often a challenge, the future for youth courts is promising.

Problem-solving courts continue the long history of court innovation in the United States and elsewhere. Problem-solving courts today are not the same as they were 15 or 20 years ago when they began to emerge. For many, they hold great promise. For others, they are a cause for caution. Whether problem-solving courts will continue to develop, spread, and become a more integral and significant component of justice in the twenty-first century remains to be determined.

NOTES

1. Huddleston et al.
2. Berman et al.
3. Mackinem and Higgins.
4. Rottman and Casey.
5. Wexler (1990).
6. Hora et al.
7. Wexler (2008).
8. Huddleston et al.

REFERENCES

Berman, G., Feinblatt, J., & Glazer, S. (2005). *Good courts: The case for problem-solving justice.* New York: New Press.

Hora, P., Schma, W., & Rosenthal, J. (1999). Therapeutic jurisprudence and the drug court movement: Revolutionizing the criminal justice system's response to drug abuse and crime in America. *Notre Dame Law Review, 74,* 439–537.

Huddleston, C. W., Marlowe, D. B., & Casebolt, R. (2008). *Painting the picture: A national report card on drug courts and other problem solving court programs in the United States.* Alexandra, VA: National Drug Court Institute.

Mackinem, M. B., & Higgins, P. C. (2008). *Drug court: Constructing the moral identity of drug offenders.* Springfield, IL: C. C. Thomas.

Rottman, D., & Casey, P. (2000). Therapeutic jurisprudence and the emergence of problem-solving courts. *Alternatives to Incarceration,* 27–30.

Wexler, D. B. (1990). *Therapeutic jurisprudence: The law as a therapeutic agent.* Durham, NC: Carolina Academic Press.

Wexler, D. B. (2008). Welcome. International Network on Therapeutic Jurisprudence.

1

Problem-Solving Justice and the Moment of Truth

GREG BERMAN

When the Midtown Community Court opened its doors in New York City in the early 1990s, it was the first community court in the country. It is fair to say that the project, with its goal of reengineering how the justice system responds to misdemeanor crime, was widely viewed as a radical experiment. There were many who expected it to fail—indeed, there were many who actively hoped it would go belly up.

Midtown has defied these dire expectations. Located in the heart of Manhattan just a few blocks from Times Square, the Midtown Court combines punishment and help, sentencing low-level offenders to visible community restitution projects (sweeping the streets, painting over graffiti, cleaning local parks) and linking them to on-site social services, including drug treatment, job training, and counseling. According to independent evaluators, Midtown helped to reduce local street crime, improve compliance with court orders, enhance judicial access to information, and improve public attitudes towards courts.[1]

Now well into its second decade, the Midtown Community Court continues to thrive. Each year, the Court is visited by hundreds of curious criminal justice officials, many of whom go on to adapt elements of the Midtown model when they return home. Indeed, at Midtown's tenth anniversary celebration the guest of honor was the lord chancellor of Britain, who came to announce that he was going to import the community court concept to England and Wales.

I was fortunate to be part of the team that helped to plan and implement the Midtown Community Court. Since then, from my perch as the director of the Center for Court Innovation, I have watched as the ideas that Midtown embodies—engaging new partners in the work of the courts, reaching out to the public in new ways, testing new approaches to crime problems—have spread across the United States and around the world.

Today, there is a growing movement towards what has become known as "problem-solving justice." There are now thousands of problem-solving courts in the United States. In addition to community courts, these include drug courts, mental health courts, domestic violence courts, and others. Problem-solving courts have tapped into a desire on the part of judges, prosecutors, defense attorneys, court managers, and other justice system players to respond more creatively and effectively to local crime problems as well as the kinds of individual problems (addiction, mental illness, etc.) that often fuel crime.

UNDERLYING PRINCIPLES

Problem-solving courts operate in both politically conservative states and liberal states and in big cities and small towns. Some address low-level offending. Others tackle serious, felony-level crime. In some, the focus is on rehabilitation, attempting to provide therapeutic interventions to change the lives of defendants in a positive direction. In others, the focus is on accountability, making sure that offenses (such as domestic violence) that might have received scant attention in the past are given the scrutiny they deserve.

While each individual type of problem-solving court has its own unique history, underlying philosophy, and organizational structure, it is possible to tease out some common underlying principles that most problem-solving courts share.

Enhanced Information: In an effort to improve the quality of decision-making, problem-solving courts seek to provide justice system officials with enhanced training (about complex issues like domestic violence and drug addiction) as well as better information about litigants, victims, and the community context of crime. For example, in Clackamas County, Oregon, a community court developed a simple psychosocial assessment that collects information on defendants' educational history, employment status, health, and mental illness. The results are provided to the judge, who can use this information to better understand each defendant—and tailor a sentencing mandate accordingly.

Community Engagement: Problem-solving courts believe that citizens and neighborhood groups have an important role to play in helping the justice system identify, prioritize, and solve local problems. The theory is that actively engaging citizens will help to improve public trust in justice and foster law-abiding behavior. One example of problem-solving courts' emphasis on community engagement can be found in San Diego, where a community court convenes community impact panels that bring together local residents and low-level offenders for facilitated conversation about the impact of quality-of-life crime on the surrounding neighborhood.

Collaboration: By bringing justice agencies together and reaching out to potential partners beyond the courthouse (e.g., social service providers, victims groups, block associations), problem-solving courts seek to improve interagency communication and foster new responses to public safety problems. For example, the Seattle Community Court has a community advisory board composed of government and nonprofit partners that is responsible for brainstorming solutions to local problems. A community advisory board is hardly a revolutionary idea in other fields, but in criminal justice circles it amounts to a significant departure from business as usual.

Individualized Justice: Problem-solving courts seek to move away from an assembly-line approach to justice. In particular, they seek to link offenders to individually tailored community-based services (e.g., job training, drug treatment, mental health counseling) where appropriate. In doing so—and by treating defendants with dignity and respect—problem-solving courts seek to reduce recidivism, improve community safety, and enhance confidence in justice. Problem-solving courts also attempt to link victims to services in an effort to improve their safety and help restore their lives. In Athens, Ohio, a court that serves defendants suffering from dual disorders of mental illness and substance abuse carefully assesses each individual and then matches him or her with appropriate community-based service providers. In New York, the Brooklyn Domestic Violence Court applies a similarly thoughtful approach to victim services, ensuring that every individual is linked to an advocate who can assist with safety planning and access to benefits.

Accountability: Problem-solving courts seek to send the message that all criminal behavior should have meaningful consequences. By insisting on regular and rigorous compliance monitoring—and quickly responding to noncompliance—problem-solving courts seek to improve the accountability of offenders. For example, the Atlanta Community Court holds low-level offenders accountable by requiring them to participate in visible community restitution projects in the neighborhood where they offended. The Brooklyn Treatment Court, like other drug courts across the country, uses a system of graduated sanctions and rewards to respond to participants' setbacks and achievements in treatment.

Outcomes: Problem-solving justice encourages courts to look at what works and what does not. By collecting data about both outcomes and process, problem-solving courts seek to evaluate their effectiveness and make midcourse improvements. One example of this can be found at New York City's Bronx Community Solutions, where a researcher routinely measures compliance rates and provides feedback to staff. Among other things, the researcher found that approximately 15 percent of the defendants sentenced to alternative sanctions never made it from the courtroom to the program's intake office. Based on this information, program administrators instituted an escort system to reduce the drop-out rate.

Problem-solving courts have emerged in a more-or-less organic fashion, from the grass roots up. There is no single foundational document, no unified theory, that summoned problem-solving courts into existence.[2] Instead, the growth of problem-solving justice has been incremental, starting with the opening of the first drug court in Dade County, Florida, in 1989. Since then, the idea of problem-solving justice has gradually become a standard feature of the judicial landscape in this country as judges, attorneys, and administrators have looked for new ways to improve the performance of local courts.

All 50 states now have at least one problem-solving court. The concept of problem-solving justice has been officially endorsed by the Conference of Chief Justices, the Conference of State Court Administrators, and the American Bar Association. The U.S. Congress has repeatedly authorized funds to support drug courts. The U.S. Justice Department, under both President William Clinton and President George W. Bush, has also effectively endorsed the concept of problem-solving justice, providing seed grants and technical assistance to encourage states and localities to open problem-solving initiatives.

"THE TRADITIONAL APPROACH YIELDS UNSATISFYING RESULTS"

In less than 20 years, the idea of problem-solving justice has come a long way—from a handful of experiments to broad replication and endorsement by some of the most important justice agencies in the country. What has driven this progress? The answer can be found by taking a look at the realities of how the criminal justice system works in this country rather than the idealized version that gets taught in civics classes.

For many people, the best articulation of the American criminal court system can be found in the rights enshrined in the Sixth Amendment to the U.S. Constitution: "In all criminal prosecutions, the accused shall enjoy the right to a speedy and public trial, by an impartial jury . . . and to be informed of the nature and cause of the accusation; to be confronted with the witnesses against him; to have compulsory process for obtaining witnesses in his favor, and to have the Assistance of Counsel for his defense."

Translating these lofty goals into practice is no simple task. Compare the idealized vision of criminal case processing inscribed in the Constitution with Malcolm Feeley's description of "low-stakes, high-volume" American criminal courts in his seminal work, *The Process Is the Punishment*:

> In the lower courts trials are rare events, and even protracted plea bargaining is an exception . . . These courts are chaotic and confusing; officials communicate in a verbal short-hand wholly unintelligible to accused and accuser alike . . . by conventional standards nearly all of the defendants are failures, both in life and in crime. They are poor, often unemployed, usually young and from broken homes . . . A great many of them have come to rely on alcohol and drugs . . . The solemnity that the words "crime" and "criminal court" imply aside, lower court officials—judges, prosecutors and public defenders alike—feel frustrated and belittled. Trained to practice law, they are confronted with the kinds of problems that social workers face.[3]

The movement towards problem-solving justice begins here, in the spirit of legal realism, with a long, hard look at the realities of life in American criminal courts. New York State Chief Judge Judith S. Kaye takes up this baton when she writes:

> Let's face facts: many of the cases in state courts today are not complicated legal matters. But they do involve people with complicated lives . . . In many of today's cases, the traditional approach yields unsatisfying results. The addict arrested for drug dealing is adjudicated, does time, then goes right back to dealing on the street. The battered wife obtains a protective order, goes home and is beaten again. Every legal right of the litigants is protected, all procedures followed, yet we aren't making a dent in the underlying problem. Not good for the parties involved. Not good for the community. Not good for the courts.[4]

What Kaye is describing is a moment of truth that many problem-solving reformers have experienced—the moment when they realize that standard operating procedure in American criminal courts might be efficient, might dot all the i's and cross all the t's, but that it fails to see the big picture, to truly make a difference in the lives of the people it is supposed to serve.

This, in a nutshell, is why so many judges and attorneys across the country have begun to think of themselves as problem solvers and not just case processors. The tremendous growth of problem-solving courts over the past 20 years has been driven by a relatively simple premise: that problem-solving courts have the potential to focus the energies of courts more effectively on both process (ensuring that the system is fair) and outcomes (helping protect victims, change the behavior of offenders, and enhance public safety).

SKEPTICS

Of course, there have always been those who have been skeptical about problem-solving courts' ability to achieve these goals. In the early 1990s, there was concern, primarily among local prosecutors and policy makers with one eye on the politics of criminal justice, that problem-solving courts, particularly drug courts, were "soft on crime." These critics focused on the use of alternatives to incarceration to argue that the problem-solving approach was not punitive enough. Over the years, problem-solving courts have worked hard to inoculate themselves from this line of argument, emphasizing the principle of accountability through judicial monitoring of defendants.

One sign of the success of these efforts is that the most intense criticisms of problem-solving courts today come not from prosecutors but from the defense bar and their allies in academia. Professors such as Mae Quinn at the University of Tennessee Law School and Tamar Meekins at Howard Law School have written eloquently about these issues. According to Meekins, "the specialty court model may encourage a culture of underzealous representation by some defenders that may set a dangerous precedent for the overall professional role of the defender in our criminal justice system . . . [I] have called for a careful review of the impractical goals, due process shortcuts, and great potential for ethical challenges that exist in specialty courts."[5]

Leaving aside the hypothetical nature of this argument (note the use of the conditional tense: "problem-solving courts *may* have the *potential* to create a problem for *some* defenders"), Meekins's concerns are still worthy of investigation. Meekins identifies a number of problems faced by defense attorneys who practice in problem-solving courts, including heavy caseloads, insufficient time to investigate cases and devise strategy, and pressure to plead guilty to dispose of cases quickly.

Unfortunately, these problems are, as Malcolm Feeley would attest, part and parcel of the American justice system and have been for quite some time. As a thought experiment, let us imagine a world where problem-solving courts have been abolished. What has Meekins won? Have the caseloads of defenders been reduced? Has the coercive authority of judges and prosecutors diminished? Would there be more trials? Would the life trajectories of defendants be any better? The answer to all of these questions is a resounding no.

But look at what would be lost if we were to eliminate problem-solving courts. There is a growing body of evidence that documents that drug courts reduce both substance abuse and recidivism. For example, researchers at the Center for Court Innovation examined six drug courts, including courts located in urban areas, rural jurisdictions, and the suburbs. When comparing drug court participants to defendants who received conventional prosecution, they found statistically significant reductions in reoffending at all sites.[6] These results have been confirmed by numerous studies across the country, including several randomized trials, the so-called gold standard of social science research.

It is worth pausing a moment to highlight the stories behind these statistics.[7] Drug court graduates are not just numbers on a page. They are formerly homeless individuals who now have stable housing. They are career criminals who have become solid employees and regular taxpayers. They are mothers who have reconnected with children lost to the foster care system. These transformations have far-reaching implications not just for the individual families involved, but for the health and well-being of our society. Several studies have documented significant cost savings from drug courts, particularly in avoided jail and prison costs. But the human savings are literally beyond calculation. They include reductions in victimization, welfare cases, and emergency room admissions—not to mention the damage done to children raised in broken homes.

While there are fewer studies investigating community courts, mental health courts, domestic violence courts, and other models of problem-solving justice, here too there is encouraging news to report.[8] The available research suggests that community courts are capable of reducing neighborhood crime and improving public confidence in courts, that mental health courts can improve psychosocial functioning and reduce rearrests among mentally ill defendants, and that domestic violence courts can improve not only victim satisfaction with the criminal justice process but access to services as well.

DEBUNKING "NOTHING WORKS"

Is there a need for more research into the efficacy of problem-solving courts? Absolutely. There is still a lot to learn about what makes a drug court effective. We do not have many randomized trials that compare mental health courts and community courts to conventional prosecution. And we are still in the early stages of discovering what, if any, interventions are effective with domestic violence offenders.

However provisional our current knowledge of problem-solving courts may be, it is important to understand the political and intellectual context from which these projects have emerged. For at least a generation, if not longer, the politics of criminal justice have been dominated by concerns about "law and order." Plagued by crime and disorder, many American cities were viewed as "ungovernable."[9] Starting in the 1960s and continuing up until fairly recently, local and national policy makers advanced a series of proposals that essentially sought to promote more punitive responses to crime (e.g., mandatory minimums, "three strikes and you're out" laws, the "truth in sentencing" movement).

At the same time, the intellectual climate had grown exceedingly skeptical, if not downright hostile, to the idea of rehabilitation. The signature moment here was the publication of sociologist Robert Martinson's influential 1974 article in *The Public Interest*, "What Works?—Questions and Answers About Prison Reform." The essay is credited with popularizing the idea that "nothing works"—that all efforts to change the behavior of offenders, however well-intentioned, are essentially doomed to failure.

Problem-solving courts are, in many respects, a reaction against these two interrelated trends—on the one hand a political drive toward increasingly punitive solutions to crime and on the other a despairing social policy environment that offered little succor for those interested in advancing the rehabilitative ideal. By documenting that it is, in fact, possible to reduce crime and change the behavior of offenders, problem-solving courts have helped create space, both political and operational, for a balanced approach to justice that emphasizes both punishment and rehabilitation.[10] This represents a significant shift in the policy landscape that will reverberate for years to come.

Before we leave the subject of research and problem-solving courts, it is worth returning to the question of fairness. Do problem-solving courts undermine the principle of fairness that is at the very heart of the American legal system? In an effort to introduce some empirical evidence into this debate, researchers from the Center for Court Innovation surveyed hundreds of defendants at the Red Hook Community Justice Center, a community court in southwest Brooklyn.[11] Eighty-six percent reported that their case was handled fairly. These results were consistent regardless of the race, gender, or socioeconomic status of the defendant.

This single study does not, of course, mean that we have answered all of the concerns that defense attorneys have raised about problem-solving courts—there is a need for more research here as well.[12] But it does suggest that the problem-solving approach has the potential to improve the procedural fairness of criminal courts.

THE FUTURE

So where does problem-solving justice go from here? I would argue that problem-solving courts have reached another moment of truth. It is clear by now that problem-solving justice cannot be dismissed as a fad that is going to go the way of the hula hoop or New Coke. Problem-solving courts have proven that they can outlive the initial cadre of judicial leaders that helped give them birth. They have proven that they can make the transition from one presidential administration to the next. (The transition from Clinton to Bush was a particularly important one, given the visible leadership that Attorney General Janet Reno provided to the field.) It remains an open question, however, whether problem-solving courts will fulfill their potential to transform the way that justice is administered in the United States.

A significant obstacle stands in the way. That obstacle is volume. The truth of the matter is that many potentially appropriate cases are not making their way to problem-solving courts. This reality was highlighted by a recent report from the Urban Institute, which estimated that American taxpayers would save more than $46 billion dollars if all of the estimated 1.5 million addicted defendants in the criminal justice system were linked to treatment instead of incarceration. As provocative as this conclusion may be, it is worth reading the small print of the report, which goes on to state that only 3 percent of arrested addicts currently find their way into drug court.[13]

Put simply, the next challenge for problem-solving courts is scale. How do we ensure that every litigant, every victim, and every community that might benefit from the problem-solving approach has access to it? In addition to addicted arrestees who do not receive drug treatment, there are still thousands of mentally ill offenders who would benefit from community-based counseling and strict judicial monitoring but do not have access to a mental health court. And there are still many families in crisis that find themselves shuttled from court to court and decision maker to decision maker without the benefit of an integrated domestic violence court, to cite another example.

In order to address this challenge, there is a need for a national push to expand the capacity of problem-solving courts and to spread the principles of problem-solving justice beyond specialized courtrooms. The National Association of Drug Court Professionals has seized on the issue of scale—"going to scale" with drug court has been a recurring theme at their annual conference, attended by thousands of criminal justice officials, for the past several years. It is also worth noting that the U.S. Department of Justice has for the first time made an investment in identifying domestic violence courts across the country and building a national network to support their development. A similar architecture exists for mental health courts.

How this new emphasis on expanding the reach of problem-solving courts will play out is anybody's guess. But there are reasons to be optimistic about the chances of success. The conversation about justice in this country is markedly different today than it was when the Midtown Community Court started in the early 1990s. Crime reductions have taken a lot of the heat out of criminal justice policy debates at the national level. New York and other major urban areas are no longer viewed as ungovernable. The idea that "nothing works" has been thoroughly debunked.

Amidst all of these developments, two seemingly contradictory policy lessons seem to be emerging within the field of criminal justice. The first is the value of taking all criminal behavior seriously. The "broken windows" theory, first advanced by James Q. Wilson and George Kelling, posits that minor crime and disorder, if left unchecked, can encourage more serious offending.[14] This idea holds tremendous sway at the local level; hundreds of mayors and police chiefs have embraced "broken windows" as an effective crime-fighting strategy. At the same time, there is a growing movement of scholars, foundation executives, journalists, and policy makers that looks at the exponential growth in the American prison population over the past few decades and argues that we need to rethink our reliance on incarceration.

Problem-solving justice is a ready-made solution capable of reconciling these two conflicting impulses. Problem-solving courts are, at the end of the day, a vehicle for offering a meaningful and proportionate response to criminal behavior that does not rely on incarceration as a default setting. While predicting the future is a fool's game, it is not difficult to imagine a growing demand, among the public and policy makers of all political stripes, for problem-solving justice in the years ahead.

If this comes to pass, there are signs that the judiciary will be ready. According to a recent survey of more than a thousand trial court judges across the country, 76 percent of respondents approved of problem-solving methods of judging (only 10 percent disapproved).[15] This is a far cry from the early days of the Midtown Community Court, when it was difficult to find a judge to sit in the court because it was viewed as such a risky proposition.

It all adds up to a sea change, not just in how judges think of themselves, but in how courts work and how they are perceived by the public. These are the accomplishments of the first generation of problem-solving reformers. It is a legacy well worth building upon in the days to come.

NOTES

1. Sviridoff et al., 2000.
2. Berman and Feinblatt, 2005.
3. Feeley, 1992, p. 3.
4. Kaye, 1999, p. 13.
5. Meekins, 2007.
6. Zeilbauer, 2003.
7. Wolf and Berman, 2007.
8. Berman and Feinblatt, 2005, p. 151.
9. Cannato, 2001.
10. Not all problem-solving courts see themselves as being in the business of rehabilitation. Certain problem-solving courts, including domestic violence courts, integrated domestic violence courts, and sex offender management courts, are focused less on rehabilitation and more on strengthening the accountability of participants.
11. Frazer, 2007, p. 36.
12. It is worth noting, however, that a similar study, examining the perceptions of litigants in a community court that focuses on handling housing court cases, found similar results (Abuwala and Farole 2008).
13. Ratcliffe, 2008.
14. Kelling and Wilson, 1982.
15. Farole et al., 2008.

REFERENCES

Abuwala, R., & Farole, D. J., Jr. (2008). *The effects of the Harlem Housing Court on tenant perceptions of justice*. New York: Center for Court Innovation.

Berman, G., & Feinblatt, J. (2005). *Good courts: The case for problem-solving justice*. New York: The New Press.

Cannato, V. (2001). *The ungovernable city: John Lindsay's New York and the crisis of liberalism*. New York: Basic Books.

Farole, D., Rempel, M., Byrne, F., and Chang, Y.-W. (2008). *Problem-solving and the American bench: A national survey of trial court judges*. New York: Center for Court Innovation.

Feeley, M. (1992). *The process is the punishment: Handling cases in a lower criminal court*. New York: Russell Sage Foundation.

Frazer, M. S. (2007, July–August). Examining defendant perceptions of fairness in the courtroom. *Judicature*.

Kaye, J. S. (1999, October 11). Making the case for hands-on courts. *Newsweek*.

Kelling, G., & Wilson, J. Q. (1982, March). Broken windows. *Atlantic Monthly*.

Meekins, T. M. (2007). Risky business: Criminal speciality courts and the ethical obligations of the zealous criminal defender. *Berkeley Journal of Criminal Law, 12*, 75.

Ratcliffe, H. (2008, May 31). Drug courts touted for savings. *St. Louis Post-Dispatch*.

Sviridoff, M., Rottman, D. B., Ostrom, B., & Curtis, R. (2000). *Dispensing justice locally: The implementation and effects of the Midtown Community Court*. New York: Harwood Academic Publishers.

Wolf, R. V., & Berman, G. (2007). *Drug courts: Personal stories—narratives from across New York State*. New York: Center for Court Innovation.

Zeilbauer, P. (2003, November 9). Court treatment system is found to help drug offenders stay clean. *New York Times,* Metro section, New York edition.

2

A Circumspect Look at Problem-Solving Courts

RICHARD C. BOLDT

Drug treatment courts have become commonplace in virtually every jurisdiction in the United States and have been established in Canada, Australia, the United Kingdom, and elsewhere.[1] The success of these courts has combined with at least two other factors to spur the creation of a new generation of therapeutic or problem-solving courts. One factor has been the growing influence of "therapeutic jurisprudence" and "restorative justice," theoretical perspectives that offer consequentialist critiques of existing legal regimes and that identify alternative practices thought to be capable of producing more positive outcomes for participants.[2] A second, intersecting dynamic is the growing recognition by judges and others that traditional judicial processes are ill-suited to dealing effectively with the multiple social pathologies that have found their way inevitably into courthouses as a consequence of the failure of other institutions that in the past have helped to socialize individuals, construct communities, and perform basic functions related to social control.[3]

The result of this confluence of practice (the hundreds of operating drug treatment courts around the country), perception (the growing recognition that judges increasingly are being required to manage cases in which litigants bring to court a broad range of often intractable underlying pathologies), and theory (the spread of therapeutic jurisprudence and restorative justice from a few academics to scores of influential judges and other policy makers) has been the creation of a number of other problem-solving courts, including community courts, mental health courts, domestic violence courts, and others.

The claim that drug treatment courts have a solid theoretical grounding and demonstrable efficacy has been central to advocates, academics, and others who have worked to develop a "second generation" of problem-solving courts built on the foundation of the drug treatment court experiment.[4] The project of this chapter is to provide a circumspect assessment of this claim, and to suggest that the problem-solving court model, like the drug treatment court model upon which it is based, while useful in some circumstances, has important limitations.

Advocacy in support of drug treatment courts in particular and problem-solving courts more generally is part of a broader "post-welfarist crime control" narrative.[5] This narrative places strong emphasis on pragmatic efficacy, and on the construction of "the offender as a 'responsibilized' and 'accountable' agent who is given privileged 'opportunities' for rehabilitation" through his or her participation in the court process.[6] A central feature of this narrative is that the criminal justice system is understood as an appropriate site for the building of institutional and professional partnerships between law-trained actors oriented toward adjudication and punishment and others whose primary goals are to provide treatment and other social services. This narrative of collaboration between and integration of the justice and human services systems generally takes as a given that the harmonization of these disparate worlds is both desirable and practicable.

In a variety of ways, however, the melding of justice and treatment is potentially problematic. This uneasy partnership can be explored by examining the ways in which individual defendants are conceptualized in drug treatment courts and other problem-solving courts, and by examining the roles assumed by judges, defense lawyers, and other actors in these hybrid settings. At least with respect to defendants who have substance use disorders, the group that is the principle focus of drug treatment courts and a significant subset of all the defendants in problem-solving courts, the problems of coherent conceptualization are considerable. On the one hand, these actors are understood as suffering from a chronic, relapsing disorder that requires the intervention of therapeutic measures in order to interrupt a pathological pattern over which they are unable to exercise meaningful control. On the other hand, these same individuals are constructed as responsible moral agents who are capable of autonomous decision making and who are to be held responsible for their choices. The mechanism that mediates this apparent tension is the use of "legal coercion," the threat of legally sanctioned punishment as a device for encouraging treatment readiness and treatment retention.[7]

A close consideration of the role played by legal coercion in the context of problem-solving courts is warranted because it presses focus on a series of concerns that have been raised by critics. First is the concern that the mandated treatment and supervision typical of these courts represents an unnecessary expansion and dispersal of behavior control and surveillance. A second concern is that problem-solving courts too often cause a misallocation of scarce social services resources. A third concern is that the therapeutic objectives animating practice in these courts sometimes become debased and are lost within the broader punitive norms of the criminal justice system. Finally, some critics suggest, the attempt to deliver therapeutic interventions in problem-solving courts risks undermining the values of procedural fairness and open justice that ordinarily attach to our formal criminal justice blaming practices. Each of these concerns is considered below.

THE MERGING OF TREATMENT AND PUNISHMENT

While there are research data suggesting that legal coercion may be effective in getting substance-abusing defendants into treatment and lengthening their retention in treatment,[8] there are questions about both the longer term benefits and the costs of such a regime. In addition to an examination of these costs and benefits from the defendants' point of view, it is worth considering as well the costs that a reliance on legally coercive practices places on other actors in the system and on the system itself.

The argument for leveraging the compulsory elements of the criminal system as a means of improving treatment outcomes, and its embedded critique of voluntary treatment, has been very influential. In 1999, two early drug treatment court judges, Peggy Hora and William Schma (along with a third co-author), published a detailed article in the *Notre Dame Law Review* that explicitly made the case for drug treatment courts on the basis of the therapeutic value of criminal system coercion.

> The question of whether coerced treatment provides an individual with the proper incentives to successfully complete a treatment program stands as a traditional point of concern with treatment providers. Through the years, many experts in the drug treatment field have questioned the effectiveness of legally coerced treatment due to a belief that individuals must enter a program voluntarily in order to have the requisite state of mind for recovery ... Recent studies and findings by several researchers and treatment specialists serve to dispel and debunk this notion ... "[T]he 'coercion' actually improves the substance abusers' chances of overcoming their addiction."[9]

The sharp elbows approach of the drug treatment court model is grounded in a research literature that seeks to demonstrate that outcomes related both to substance abuse relapse and to criminal recidivism are correlated with a client's length of stay in treatment, and that individuals who are coerced into treatment by the criminal system tend to remain longer than do voluntary patients.[10] As others have pointed out, however, "a body of literature on the psychology of choice suggests that if the defendant experiences [the choice to enter treatment] as coerced, his or her attitude, motivation, and chances for success in the treatment program may be undermined."[11] Consistent with this more skeptical view of coerced treatment, other researchers have found mixed results with respect to the therapeutic pressure employed by drug treatment courts.[12]

At bottom, the question whether to force treatment compliance through the threat of criminal punishment is framed by a larger tension between two distinct public policy approaches to drug use disorders. One perspective, the strict prohibition model, is reflected in the federal Controlled Substances Act and most corresponding state statutes, and is operationalized primarily through the criminal enforcement process. "Under the paradigm of strict prohibition, proscribed drugs and their use are subject to control by the criminal justice system and only complete abstinence is permissible under the law." [13] The drug treatment court movement, although in some respects a hybrid practice standing between traditional criminal punishment and a pure public health strategy, is still, on these terms, squarely within the prohibition framework.

These courts are innovative because their design and operation acknowledge the chronicity of drug use disorders and the frequency with which persons in treatment suffer relapse on the road toward recovery. Thus, by employing graduated sanctions to respond to treatment setbacks, this approach avoids the on/off switch of probation or parole revocation proceedings characteristic of more traditional settings. Nevertheless, the drug treatment court approach is still squarely within the strict prohibition framework because it operates on the premise that abstinence from drug use is the only acceptable outcome and that clients should seek to become abstinent under a schedule driven by underlying criminal justice system benchmarks.[14]

> The drug court model, however, while stressing rehabilitation over retribution, still does not represent a fundamental departure from the federal legal framework. The use and sale of selected psychoactive substances, which are prohibited and punished under federal law, continue to be uniformly prohibited and punished in all of the states, and the federally-subsidized drug courts use the threat of criminal sanctions to coerce abstinence, sanctions which are often imposed; many, if not most, drug court participants are still confined to jail or prison for failure to complete treatment requirements.[15]

The alternative approach, although not necessarily incompatible with prohibition, focuses less on abstinence and the strict enforcement of controlled substances provisions and relies instead on the voluntary involvement of individuals in treatment. This alternative is guided by the principle of "harm reduction," and adopts "a non-judgmental and non-coercive approach, rendering services to assist drug users in reducing the attendant harm from drug use and often in reducing drug use itself." [16]

Supporters of the drug treatment court model point to extraordinarily high attrition rates for most voluntary treatment programs and argue that an addict's involvement with the criminal system through arrest creates a unique window of opportunity, and that his or her continuing potential criminal liability creates treatment leverage that should be exploited to ensure satisfactory treatment outcomes. By contrast, supporters of more voluntary approaches who start with the premises of the harm reduction perspective point out that many persons with drug use disorders require several attempts at treatment before accomplishing a sustained recovery. From their point of view, arguments based upon the high attrition rates associated with drug treatment facilities potentially are misleading because they fail to acknowledge this clinical reality.[17] Thus, a program with an attrition rate of 50 percent may not, in fact, be experiencing a one-half failure rate, if some or most of its clients return for second, third, or fourth attempts at treatment at a later time (or enroll successfully in a different program at a later date).

At stake in this choice between these two alternative approaches is the question whether it is wise to maintain a regime of comprehensive surveillance and behavior control for this population of defendants. Although the architects of drug treatment courts and many other problem-solving courts frame their interventions in therapeutic language, the range and intensity of measures that are coercively imposed in order to create "positive lifestyle change,"[18] which run the gamut from alcohol and other drug treatment obligations, to parenting classes, to employment monitoring and the like, are considerable. Regular urine testing, frequent and periodic court appearances, and detailed reporting to the court and to prosecutorial officials from treatment providers all serve to control and monitor the individual's daily routine in a fashion potentially more invasive and coercive than a traditional sentence of incarceration.[19] As one writer has explained, drug treatment courts (as well as other problem-solving courts) present "an instructive illustration of a dispersed, yet comprehensive and pervasive regime of behavioural 'discipline' acting upon the offender from many sides ... As such, D[rug] T[reatment] C[ourts] may be viewed as a microcosm of late modern governmentality, in which singular expressions of punishment have been replaced with a dispersed regime of disciplinary tools and technology."[20]

Notwithstanding this dispersion of coercive control, problem-solving courts still employ traditional forms of criminal punishment as well. Offenders who fail to comply with one or more of the requirements that the court has imposed may receive short jail sentences, and others who fail more fundamentally and are discharged from the program may end up serving full sentences in jail or prison. In the end, from the point of view of the defendant, drug treatment courts and other problem-solving courts may be "more difficult to complete, more onerous and far more intrusive on liberty" than traditional criminal court dispositions.[21]

In addition, drug treatment courts and many other problem-solving courts serve to extend the reach of the criminal system, by retaining in the system defendants who otherwise might not be subject to criminal justice control and by failing to divert a significant number of other offenders—often those facing more serious changes—into alternative treatment-based dispositions. Drug treatment courts thus may produce a "net widening" effect by channeling into the system defendants who would otherwise have avoided a criminal justice system disposition. According to one writer, treatment courts in many jurisdictions engage in "cherry picking the low-risk candidates who would have been screened out of a traditional diversion system and channeling up and into the criminal justice system the high-risk candidates they were originally designed to serve."[22] As a consequence, these courts and others based on the treatment court model do not necessarily function as diversion mechanisms limiting the impact of the prohibition approach; rather, they sometimes serve as adjuncts of that social control system, extending and diversifying the range of measures available to support that policy and expanding the pool of individuals enmeshed in it.

COMMUNITY COURTS AND THE PROBLEM OF ALLOCATING SCARCE SOCIAL SERVICES RESOURCES

Both of the tendencies noted above, the dispersion of surveillance and behavior controls and the widening of the criminal justice system's net, are especially present in the case of community courts. Like many other problem-solving courts, community courts seek to provide responses to a wide range of problems, including child neglect, mental illness, drug abuse, and domestic violence. They employ many of the same mechanisms for monitoring and controlling defendants' behavior that were developed by drug treatment courts, and, like drug treatment courts, transform detention and surveillance functions, often moving them outside the jail and into community-based settings.[23]

Beginning with the first community court, which was established in New York City through the collaborative efforts of the Center for Court Innovation and the Chief Judge of the New York Court of Appeals, Judith Kaye, it has been clear that these courts were designed to implement the "zero tolerance" and "quality-of-life" policing tactics at the heart of the "broken windows" theory of law enforcement, under which police are encouraged to increase the number of arrests for minor criminal offenses.[24] The first New York community court and others like it have been designed to handle a wide range of low-level misdemeanor offenses that generally were not prosecuted at all prior to the adoption of the broken windows philosophy and the establishment of these new courts. As Anthony Thompson has explained, "[t]he types of cases addressed in these new courts have come to include those 'victimless' crimes once considered outside the jurisdiction of traditional criminal courts. What had once been minor infractions or low-level misdemeanors became the principal focus of this new judicial effort."[25]

Thompson makes it clear that a central goal of many community courts has been to address the persistent problem of homelessness, and the related problem of undertreated mental disabilities, through the provision of much needed social services. He argues, however, that this approach is flawed both because its focus on individual defendants fails to address "the structural and systemic causes of homelessness" and because "the root causes of many of the perpetual problems in low-income areas and communities of color a[re] far too nuanced to be addressed by means of court adjudication." He suggests that, while underserved communities often are quite attracted to the array of social services made available through community courts, community members might well prefer to gain access to those resources "without the threat of the criminal justice system hanging in the balance."[26]

This critique about the allocation of scarce social services resources has been made by a number of other observers, and even some participants, in the problem-solving court movement. Victoria Malkin, for example, has noted that the communities typically served by community courts are those most in need of new services and programs. She ponders whether problem-solving courts are "the proper arena to develop" these resources, in light of the mainstream institutional affiliations and political power of the actors who establish and direct these courts. Malkin's concern is that these affiliations and power dynamics give community courts and their supporters "advantages over smaller grassroots organizations in terms of their political and cultural capital," thereby steering resources away from these smaller community-based entities.[27]

A related set of concerns have been raised in the context of mental health courts and domestic violence courts. Mental health courts are a direct response to the problem of large numbers of persons with mental disabilities coming into the criminal justice system as a consequence of a history of deinstitutionalization and the failure of the community mental health system. Some experts have observed that these problem-solving courts, while essential in dealing with this influx in the short term, absorb resources that could be directed toward ameliorating the problems more systematically. Indeed, some writers have suggested that "effective community intervention could prevent the need to find and treat mentally ill citizens in the criminal justice system" altogether.[28] The reservations expressed by some about the allocation of treatment resources to defendants in domestic violence courts are even more focused. These observers are especially concerned about "the use of valuable domestic violence resources on services for perpetrators . . . when doing so diverts limited funds away from services for battered women."[29]

THE PREDOMINANCE OF PUNISHMENT

The effort to meld punishment and treatment in the problem-solving court model risks reinforcing the "hegemony of punishment over therapeutic values and practices" in the broader effort to manage problems related to substance use disorders and other, related social pathologies.[30] In part, this risk is inherent in the well-documented tendency of rehabilitative regimes that rely on coercion to devolve over time into increasingly punitive enterprises. As the liberal critics of the rehabilitative ideal pointed out more than a quarter century ago, "the natural progression of any program of coercion is one of escalation."[31] As a consequence, and without regard to the good intentions of court officials, therapeutic problem-solving courts are always at risk of becoming debased over time.[32]

Additionally, the very design of these courts tends to reinforce the primacy of the criminal justice components over the therapeutic/helping elements. Although the judge, attorneys, probation and parole officials, and service providers often are described as functioning as a "treatment team,"[33] it is significant that the team is headed by the judge, who, by training, professional culture, and role definition, is bound to enforce legal norms. Thus, unlike treatment services provided voluntarily in the community, fundamental decisions made in problem-solving courts, including decisions about whether a violation of conditions should be met with a therapeutic response or a more punitive imposition of shock incarceration or expulsion from the program, are made authoritatively by an actor bound to a larger institutional system that takes as its goals deterrence, retribution, and incapacitation.

An interesting observational study of drug treatment courts in Las Vegas provides some perspective on this problem of the debasement of rehabilitative impulses in problem-solving courts.[34] The authors of the study were attempting to explain the relatively high recidivism rates for drug court participants that they had observed and that have been documented by a number of other researchers.[35] Their observations were framed by the theoretical work of John Braithwaite, an Australian criminologist and leading restorative justice theorist, whose work on "reintegrative shaming" is well known.[36] The researchers found that the drug treatment courts they observed actually were more stigmatizing than conventional courts, and were insufficiently reintegrative to overcome the punitive effects produced by their structure and processes.

Braithwaite's theory has several elements. First, it contemplates the use of an initial public proceeding or ceremony designed to certify the offender's deviance, which is followed eventually by a termination ceremony intended to decertify that deviance and return the offender to his or her community. The theory also requires that the offender's conduct be met with disapproval communicated within a relationship of respect and social interconnectedness, and finally, it requires that expressions of disapproval be directed at the offender's conduct and not at the offender himself or herself.[37] The study authors' initial hypothesis was that the drug treatment court model would contain many of the features required by Braithwaite's theory, and thus would function well as a reintegrative shaming process. Unfortunately, their observational data suggested just the contrary.

While the initial appearance of participants before the drug treatment court judge was clearly a public degradation ceremony, as the theory would expect, the "field observations of [subsequent] court sessions revealed a clear preponderance of stigmatizing rather than reintegrative comments directed at most offenders. The individual defendant, not the act itself, was clearly the focal point of the judge's common 'tongue lashings.' These comments were usually of the type, 'Don't you know what this stuff does to your brain!', 'I'm tired of your excuses,' and 'I'm through with you.' " In addition, upon graduation, little effort was made by the court to reintegrate participants into the broader community. Although graduates did receive a T-shirt and key chain stating that they were "2 smart 4 drugs," the decertification ceremony was "largely symbolic and perfunctory," and the provision of ongoing transition help was limited or nonexistent. Thus, "[b]y moving from a rigid and highly structured environment to a potentially chaotic and unstable environment in a matter of weeks, it should not be surprising that drug court graduates experience[d] high rates of relapse and recidivism." Finally, and perhaps most importantly, the researchers found that the defendants' relationship with the drug treatment court judge was not marked by respect and interdependence, as Braitwaite's theory requires. Their research demonstrated instead that because of the rough handling they had experienced along the way, these defendants "did not generally regard court officials, including the judge, as persons they highly respect[ed]."[38]

In light of these findings with respect to defendants' perceptions of drug treatment court judges, it is instructive to look at other research that focuses specifically on the defendant-judge interactions that are at the center of the problem-solving court process. This research is part of a larger effort to open up the "black box" of treatment courts in order to begin learning what effects the specific design features of these courts have on identified subgroups of clients.[39] In one series of studies researchers randomly assigned one cohort of drug court clients to be intensively supervised by judges at regularly scheduled status hearings, while a comparison group of clients was monitored by nonjudicial treatment personnel and received judicial status hearings only in response to "sustained noncompliance or serious infractions."[40] Regularly scheduled judicial status hearings, it should be noted, are a virtually nonnegotiable feature of the drug treatment court model as it has evolved, and of virtually all other problem-solving courts designed on the drug treatment court template.

The researchers found that for the clients as a whole regularly scheduled status hearings had no impact on retention in treatment, rates of alcohol or other drug use, or criminal activity. When the researchers categorized the study subjects by "risk factors" such as prior exposure to drug treatment or having received a diagnosis of Antisocial Personality Disorder, however, they found that the use of regular judicial status hearing had a positive effect on "high risk" clients and a negative effect (that is it increased drug use and recidivism) among "low risk" clients. The researchers explained that "[t]he not-so-simple fact is that drug courts are neither successful nor unsuccessful. They 'work' for some clients under some circumstances but are ineffective or contraindicated for others."[41]

This research only examined the impact of one feature typically found in problem-solving courts, judicial status hearings, and only measured outcomes in relationship to two variables, prior treatment and Antisocial Personality Disorder. It is likely that variations in outcomes depend not only on participants' exposure to judges in regular status hearings, but also upon other features that could be dialed up or down to have greater or lesser coercive force and punitive impact. Moreover, these features could be, but generally are not currently, tailored to a whole range of characteristics that determine clients' risk levels, including gender, employment status, and pattern of substance misuse.

Recent research has raised troubling questions about the universal need for intensive addiction treatment services for all the defendants assigned to drug treatment courts. Indeed, one published paper has suggested that "roughly one third of drug court clients do not have a clinically significant substance use disorder." [42] The existing treatment court model is animated by a conception of substance use disorders that has been termed the "dispositional disease" perspective. Although this perspective has been extremely useful in terms of encouraging the development of effective treatments for persons with alcohol and other drug dependency, it is not especially effective in identifying and providing needed interventions to the much larger group of persons who may suffer from intermittent or mild-to-moderate problems with substances of abuse.

In the context of drug treatment courts and other problem-solving courts that emulate them, the coercive imposition of intensive addictions treatment and monitoring in the case of defendants whose drug use problems do not call for such services is not only contraindicated and a waste of limited resources but is also likely to be experienced as unnecessarily punitive. The package of treatment and monitoring obligations typically required in the treatment court setting may not be punitive in the same way that traditional incarceration is, but it is still "inherently incapacitatory and require[s] the offender to remain under observation in a designated place, such as a probation center or drug clinic, for more or less extended periods of time." [43] Thus, to the extent that individuals who do not need intensive treatment are forced into receiving therapeutic services and submitting to compliance monitoring regimes, this set of practices is a perfect example of treatment collapsing into punishment.

PROCEDURAL FAIRNESS AND OPEN JUSTICE

Although there is considerable variation among different problem-solving courts, there are certain features that characterize virtually all of these undertakings and that raise questions of procedural fairness and challenge the values of open justice. These features include the integration of treatment services with close and ongoing judicial monitoring and case management of defendants, the use of a multidisciplinary or team-based approach to provide both treatment to and supervision of participants, the use of decision-making processes that are characterized by flexibility and role informality, and an emphasis on measuring the success of outcomes pragmatically rather than by reference to notions of formal justice.

Traditional criminal courts in the United States, by contrast to those that have adopted the problem-solving approach, are organized according to an adversarial system paradigm, under which the judge is assigned a more passive and neutral role, the prosecution and defense assume a greater responsibility for setting the forensic agenda by presenting facts and legal arguments, and the interactions that take place between the parties and the judge are governed by highly stylized formal procedural rules. From a theoretical point of view, these features have been adopted out of a recognition that the interests of the state and the individual criminal defendant are adverse and that both the perception and the concrete reality of fairness are advanced by a decision-making process that is characterized by openness and transparency. Finally, to a greater or lesser degree depending on the precise sentencing approach adopted within a given jurisdiction, the imposition of coercive measures (criminal punishments) by judges in traditional criminal courts is the result of the exercise of limited judicial discretion bounded at the outside by principles of desert and proportionality.[44]

There is little doubt that the structural and procedural characteristics of problem-solving courts confer greater power on judges than they enjoy within the traditional criminal justice setting. Indeed, in their study of drug treatment courts, Kassebaum and Okamoto found that the authority and range of discretion held by drug court judges is "unprecedented" in the criminal justice system.[45] The flexibility and informality of practice in these courts is coupled with a shift in the nature of the judicial role. Instead of functioning as a neutral facilitator, the judge is now a social services coordinator and the leader of a treatment team that may include the prosecutor, public defender, human services professionals, probation and parole officials, and others. Instead of overseeing an adversarial process between parties with competing interests, the judge is now charged with ensuring that all team members work together to further the therapeutic interests of the defendant (and perhaps the interests of individual and community victims as well). This shifted role carries risks, and judges who practice in these courts are not unaware of these risks. One has written about her experience in the following terms:

> I'm not sitting back and watching the parties and ruling. I'm making comments. I'm encouraging. I'm making judgment calls. I'm getting very involved with families. I'm making clinical decisions to some extent, with the advice of experts . . . [Consequently,] I have much greater opportunities, I think, to harm someone than I would if I just sat there, listened, and said guilty or not guilty.[46]

The lack of procedural formality and professional distance in problem-solving courts, their replacement of the retributive justice principles of desert and proportionality with therapeutic and pragmatic goals, and their assumption that the various actors all have consistent interests conspire together to increase the chances of procedural irregularity and of the perception of unfairness. The informality of the interactions between judges, defendants, and others in open court is especially troubling. As Judge Jelena Popovic, a problem-solving court judge in Australia, has explained, there are at least three reasons to insist on some degree of formality in court proceedings. First, she writes, formality emphasizes the "solemnity and seriousness of what is occurring." This feature is especially important in the setting of a therapeutic court, because the very fact that treatment and punishment are intermixed raises the possibility that defendants will not sufficiently appreciate the legal and practical jeopardy they face. The second feature of procedural formality observed by Popovic is its role in lending predictability to the proceedings, so that lawyers and defendants "know what to expect and are not taken by surprise." Finally, Popovic explains, formality helps to ensure that defendants in problem-solving courts do not perceive themselves as "second class citizens" receiving a watered-down form of justice.[47]

The degree of discretion that characterizes judicial decision making in problem-solving courts only adds to the procedural and substantive risks. The judge quoted above reports that she is not "sitting back," she is "making judgment calls."[48] The problem here is that the expanded duties and broad discretion accorded judges in these courts raise legitimate concerns about both the appearance and the impact of bias. Popovic worries, for example, about the practice in many problem-solving courts of conducting *in camera* meetings or "case conferences," where members of the treatment team meet to discuss the progress of defendants scheduled for upcoming status hearings. For Popovic, these closed meetings, which take place without the defendant in attendance, are inconsistent with the principles of open justice because they provide the judge with information that has not been subject to the rigorous adversarial testing that ordinarily accompanies the presentation of evidence in formal court proceedings, and yet that may be determinative in the judge's exercise of broad discretion.[49] Anthony Thompson has raised a parallel set of worries about bias infecting the discretionary judgments of community court judges. "As community court judges participate in community meetings," he writes, "they are subject to influence by various constituencies. Some judges have raised concerns about the potential for making decisions based in part on community sentiment, something the judicial oath prohibits."[50] Finally, even if problem-solving court judges do not gain access to untested or improper information, their discretionary judgments may still be influenced by, perhaps unconscious, personal considerations triggered by the characteristics of an individual defendant or the interpersonal dynamics of an ongoing relationship with a defendant. As one scholar has explained:

> [D]rug court is fertile ground for the unfolding of psychological drama. Perhaps, for example, the judge is a recovering alcoholic or has loved a one who is addicted to drugs. This could stir up inappropriately strong feelings of sympathy, impatience or even hostility toward a participant who happens to remind him of his or her former self (or his or her loved one). Consider the participant who casts the judge in the parental role. He or she may elicit deep feelings in the judge, rooted in the latter's own experience as a parent or a once-needed child. Or consider the participant who related to the judge in a provocative manner—or, more precisely, in a manner that the judge finds provocative—stemming from an unconscious desire to be punished or controlled or to elicit concern through censure.
>
> These kind of psychodynamic scenarios are more likely to get played out in a drug court, with its somewhat relaxed structure, than in a standard court where proceedings, expectations and personnel roles are clear, traditional and fairly predictable.[51]

All of these forms of potential bias are troubling in the context of problem-solving courts because of the nature of the authority exercised by the judge. In addition to the ability to mandate formal control measures such as prison or probation, and in addition to structuring and overseeing the coercive imposition of treatment and monitoring, these judges also exercise psychological authority. As one community court judge has explained:

> I've found that we as judges have enormous psychological power over the people in front of us. It's not even coercive power. It's really the power of an authority figure and a role model. You have power not only over that person, but over their family in the audience, over all the people sitting in that courtroom.[52]

The augmented judicial power, broad discretion, and informality of problem-solving courts likely would raise questions of procedural fairness and challenge the values of open justice even under ordinary circumstances, but these courts are characterized by an institutional culture that intensifies such risks by weakening the external checks against arbitrary decision making that do remain. This institutional culture, a shared psychology that begins with problem-solving court judges and works its way throughout these institutions, is very much a product of the history under which these courts were conceived and developed. The genesis of the drug treatment court movement is a complex story, but the important protagonists in this story were the "hardworking and charismatic" judges who pushed for the development of these institutions in response to the overwhelming impact of the War On Drugs upon the day-to-day functioning of the criminal justice system, and the systematic effects of mandatory minimum sentencing policies and the like.[53] A similar story can be told about the entrepreneurialism of the founders of the first community courts, including those in midtown Manhattan and in Red Hook, New York, and about the roots of the mental health courts movement in the innovations of individual judges worried about the problems of homelessness, deinstitutionalization, and the flood of defendants with mental disabilities coming into the criminal justice system.[54]

Eric Miller, borrowing the provocative vocabulary of Charles Ogletree, has characterized this institutional culture as both "heroic" and "empathetic."[55] Ogletree originally deployed these terms in his work on the motivation of public defenders to persist in their advocacy efforts notwithstanding enormous contrary systemic pressures, explaining that heroism is a self-directed psychological feature that supports "the desire to take on 'the system' and prevail, even in the fact of overwhelming odds." Empathy, he explained, is an other-directed psychological dynamic in which the actor "[identifies] with another person in distress," the criminal defendant clients in the case of Ogletree's defenders.[56] In Miller's creative transposition, drug treatment courts are described as both heroic and emphatic undertakings, in which the judicial leaders and other supporters of these enterprises see themselves as intervening to rescue addicts and other defendants weighed down with an array of social pathologies. In his telling, this is an

> expressly empathetic and heroic enterprise. The therapeutic posture of the drug court permits the judge[s] to envision themselves as risk-taking administrators at the forefront of the struggle to undo the damage of both drug abuse and the War on Drugs . . . In all of these courts, as a hero of the oppressed, the legal agent finds reasons for attacking or disregarding social or legal norms that prevent her succeeding in this mission; as an empathic individual, she justifies such reasons in terms of her client's needs or goals, as a necessary component of ensuring that the client succeeds against the system.[57]

Importantly, this transposition has moved the heroic and empathic actors from "the context of an adversarial contest in which the legal agent is pitted, on behalf of his or her client, against another legal agent"[58] to a relatively informal, nonadversarial context where the most heroic and most empathic actors are the judges, decision makers who have no significant formal restraints on their exercise of discretionary authority. Their heroic efforts extend beyond their conduct in the courtroom and include going into the community to raise private funds for their efforts, soliciting support from health care providers, job training organizations, and educational institutions, and pressing the case for these innovative undertakings in the media.[59] The empathic elements in their practice are evident both in the courtroom and beyond. Thus, one problem-solving judge has described his relationship with the defendants before him as akin to "parenting."[60] Another judge reports that "[w]e smile and laugh at them [defendants]. We have them turn around in the courtroom and give speeches. I read the poems they write for me. I play the songs that they record for me. I show pictures."[61]

But empathy is more than friendliness and cheerleading, it involves the adoption of the other's interests, and an identification with his or her distress.[62] For some problem-solving court judges, this empathic response takes them out of the courtroom and into the spaces where the defendants under their jurisdiction live. Because of the psychology of empathic heroism, this judicial reaching out can be relatively unmodulated and unrestrained. Indeed, this is one of the ways in which coercion and control becomes dispersed and expanded into the community. For example, social scientist James Nolan has described an instance in which a drug court judge arranged a job for a defendant backed by the threat of jail:

> A participant in Judge McKinney's Syracuse, New York drug court lost his job. McKinney called the employer and learned that the client was regarded as a "damn good employee" and that the boss would "hire him back in a heartbeat" if the judge could guarantee that he was drug free and wouldn't miss any work. So the judge made a deal with the employer. He said to him: "Okay, I'll make a deal with you, you take him back and I'll add another weapon to your arsenal. If he doesn't come to work when he is supposed to, doesn't come to work on time, if he comes to work under the influence . . . , I'll put him in jail, on your say so." [The judge told the client about the deal.] "I'll get your job back for you, but you've got to promise you'll be at work when you are supposed to and not take any drugs. Your employer is now

on the team of people who are reporting to me. When he calls up and tells me that you are late or that you're not there, I'm going to send the cops out to arrest you."[63]

In these circumstances it is crucial to understand that problem-solving court judges acting heroically and empathically exercise enormous power to "solve problems," even if their actions do not comport with due process or other notions of formal justice. There is an ongoing discussion among academics who write in the fields of therapeutic jurisprudence and restorative justice about just what role considerations of due process and natural justice should play in limiting therapeutic or restorative judicial decision-making processes,[64] but the practitioners in these courts tend to be more attentive to the pragmatic needs of individual cases than to the broader implications of theory or justice. In the end, the combination of heroic and empathic dynamics in the person of judges who are situated in these informal and highly discretionary settings leads them to prioritize "getting the drug court client well" over the competing goals of "consistency and impartiality."[65] As Miller puts it: "problems arise when the self-directed and other-directed aspects of the legal agent's reconstituted identity do not check each other, but combine to provide justifications for bending or ignoring rules of behavior, legal practice or ethics."[66]

CONCLUSION

The proliferation of problem-solving courts has been driven by the claimed successes of drug treatment courts, by a pragmatic sense on the part of judges and other advocates that courts must offer practical solutions to the myriad social pathologies that have found their way into the criminal justice system as a consequence of the failure of other institutions of social control, and by the growing influence of therapeutic jurisprudence and restorative justice. Rhetorically, supporters have sought to make the case for expanding the number and range of problem-solving courts by arguing that the criminal justice system will suffer a loss of legitimacy if it fails to adjust by becoming more pragmatic and more therapeutic.

Generally, the legitimacy of legal institutions that deploy the power of the state depends upon the perception that they operate according to established legal principles and formal legal rules, that they are founded on the basis of consent, and that they are transparent and procedurally fair.[67] Timothy Casey has argued that drug treatment courts and the second generation of problem-solving courts that have built upon the treatment court model derive their legitimacy not from their claims of pragmatic efficacy but from the fact that they are courts thought to be characterized by "neutrality, procedural justice, fairness, and ritualism."[68] Casey suggests that, to the extent these courts undermine these claims to neutrality, due process, and open justice, they are likely to exhaust and not enhance the legitimacy of the system. In this sense, he argues, problem-solving courts are operating on "borrowed legitimacy." From this perspective, "[a]s soon as the smoke clears," these courts

> will have to justify their exercise of authority without reference to the traditional courts. This will be a difficult, perhaps impossible, task. The problem-solving courts change the basic nature of the courts. They demonstrate none of the characteristics that would ordinarily add to the rational basis of legitimacy. They are not fair. They are not neutral. In some instances, they are not legislatively enacted. Without a rational basis to exercise authority, the tradition of following the authority of the court, merely because it is a court, will deteriorate. The problem-solving courts are headed for a crisis of legitimacy.[69]

The procedural fairness and open justice concerns that Casey and others have raised about these courts are inherent in the very enterprise of merging treatment and punishment. These concerns are further catalyzed by the heroic and empathic psychology that has resulted from the particular history of this movement and that attends the practice of its leaders. They may or may not be insurmountable, and they may or may not produce a crisis of legitimacy, as Casey predicts. What is clear, is that these characteristics call for a good deal of circumspection in order to determine whether a more limited field of application can safely be identified.

NOTES

1. Winick and Wexler, 2003.
2. Braithwaite, 2002. David Wexler, a founder of therapeutic jurisprudence has suggested that this theoretical perspective can be divided into "four overlapping areas of inquiry. These involve (1) the role of the law in producing psychological dysfunction, (2) therapeutic aspects of the law, (3) therapeutic aspects of the legal system, and (4) therapeutic aspects of judicial and legal roles." David Wexler, *Therapeutic Jurisprudence: The Law as a Therapeutic Agent* (1990). Problem-solving court advocates have focused both on the psychological dysfunction of the traditional criminal justice system, especially in the case of defendants with otherwise untreated substance use disorders, and on the positive therapeutic potential of the problem-solving court's use of treatment resources and on the positive therapeutic role played by the problem-solving court judge as leader of a treatment team.The meanings and definitions of restorative justice are more contested and less clearly defined. Nevertheless, a consistent theme among restorative justice theorists has been the importance of using legal processes "to repair the harm caused by criminal behavior," by "restoring" the victim to his or her pre-offense status, by "reintegrating the offender" into the community, and by "repairing the breach" between the offender and the victim and between the offender and the broader community. Richard Young and Carolyn Hoyle, "Restorative Justice and Punishment," in *The Use of Punishment* (S. McConville, ed., 2003).
3. Berman, 2000.
4. Robinson, 2005, p. 1539.

5. Fischer, 2003, p. 236.
6. Fischer, 2003, p. 236.
7. Gregoire and Burke, 2004.
8. Marlowe, 2002.
9. Hora, Schma, and Rosenthal, 1999, at 526.
10. Marlowe, 2003.
11. Winick and Wexler, 2002, p. 483.
12. Farabee, Predergast, and Anglin, 1998.
13. Kings County Bar Association Drug Policy Project, 2005, p. 32.
14. Bakht and Bentley, 2004.
15. Kings County Bar Association Drug Policy Project, 2005, p. 62.
16. Kings County Bar Association Drug Policy Project, 2005, p. 36.
17. Boldt, 1998.
18. LaPrairie, Gliksman, Erickson, Wall, and Newton-Taylor, 2002, p. 1539.
19. Miller, 2004.
20. Fischer, 2003, pp. 237–38.
21. Chiodo, 2002, p. 83.
22. Miller, 2004, p. 1553.
23. Thompson, 2002.
24. Thompson, 2002, p. 83.
25. Thompson, 2002, p. 82.
26. Thompson, 2002, pp. 90–91.
27. Malkin, 2003, p. 1590.
28. Goldkamp and Irons-Guynn, 2000, p. xv.
29. Tsai, 2000, p. 1314.
30. Fischer, 2003, p. 240.
31. American Friends Service Committee, 1971, p. 25.
32. Boldt, 1998, p. 1240.
33. Boldt and Singer, 2006, p. 87.
34. Miethe, Lu, and Reese, 2000.
35. Sanford and Arrigo, 2005.
36. Braithwaite, 1989.
37. Braithwaite, 1989.
38. Miethe, Lu, and Reese, 2000, pp. 537–38.
39. Bouffard and Taxman, 2004.
40. Marlowe, Festinger, Lee, Dugosh, and Benasutti, 2006.
41. Marlowe, DeMatteo, and Festinger, 2003, p. 4.
42. DeMatteo, Marlowe, and Festinger, 2006, p. 115.
43. Miller, 2004, p. 1560.
44. Boldt, 1998.
45. Kassebaum and Okamoto, 2001.
46. Lederman, 2000, p. 82.
47. Popovic, 2006, p. 66.
48. Lederman, 2000, p. 82.
49. Popovic, 2006, p. 63–65.
50. Thompson, 2002, p. 93.
51. Satel, 1998, pp. 54–55.
52. Kluger, 2000, p. 11.

53. McCoy, 2003, p. 1525.
54. Thompson, 2002.
55. Miller, 2004, p. 1563.
56. Ogletree, 1993, pp. 1243, 1268.
57. Miller, 2004, pp. 1564–65.
58. Miller, 2004, p. 1565.
59. Nolan, 2002, p. 33.
60. Nolan, 2002, p. 35.
61. Nolan, 2002, p. 34.
62. Miller, 2004, p. 1563.
63. Nolan, 2002, p. 32.
64. Nolan, 2003.
65. Nolan, 2002, p. 36.
66. Miller, 2004, p. 1565.
67. Beetham, 1991.
68. Casey, 2004, p. 1495.
69. Casey, 2004, pp. 1503–4.

REFERENCES

American Friends Service Committee. (1971). *Struggle for justice: A report on crime and punishment in America*. New York: Farrar, Straus and Giroux.

Bakht, N., & Bentley, P. (2004). *Problem solving courts as agents of change*. Canada: National Justice Institute.

Beetham, D. (1991). *The legitimation of power*. Highlands, NJ: Humanities Press International.

Berman, G. (2000). What is a traditional judge anyway?: Problem solving in the state courts. *Judicature, 84,* 78–80.

Boldt, R. C. (1998). Rehabilitative punishment and the drug treatment court movement. *Washington University Law Quarterly, 76,* 1205–1306.

Boldt, R., & Singer, J. (2006). Juristocracy in the trenches: Problem-solving judges and therapeutic jurisprudence in drug treatment courts and unified family courts. *Maryland Law Review, 65,* 82–99.

Bouffard, J., & Taxman, F. (2004). Looking inside the "black box" of drug court treatment services using direct observations. *Journal of Drug Issues, 34*(1), 195–218.

Braithwaite, J. (1989). *Crime, shame and reintegration*. Cambridge, UK: Cambridge University Press.

Braithwaite, J. (2002). Restorative justice and therapeutic jurisprudence. *Criminal Law Bulletin, 38,* 244–262.

Casey, T. (2004). When good intentions are not enough: Problem-solving courts and the impending crisis of legitimacy. *Southern Methodist University Law Review, 57,* 1459–1519.

Chiodo, A. (2002). Sentencing drug-addicted offenders and the Toronto drug court. *Criminal Law Quarterly, 45,* 53–100.

DeMatteo, D. S., Marlowe, D. B., & Festinger, D. S. (2006). Secondary prevention services for clients who are low risk in drug court: A conceptual model. *Crime & Delinquency, 52*(1), 114–134.

Farabee, D., Predergast, M., & Anglin, M. D. The effectiveness of coerced treatment for drug abusing offenders. *Federal Probation, 62,* 3.
Fischer, B. (2003). "Doing good with a vengeance": A critical assessment of the practices, effects and implications of drug treatment courts in North America. *Criminal Justice, 3*(3), 227–248.
Goldkamp, J., & Irons-Guynn, C. (2000). *Emerging judicial strategies for the mentally ill in the criminal caseload: Mental health courts in Fort Lauderdale, Seattle, San Bernardino, and Anchorage*. Washington, DC: Bureau of Justice Assistance, U.S. Department of Justice.
Gregoire, T. K., & Burke, A. C. (2004). The relationship of legal coercion to readiness to change among adults with alcohol and other drug problems. *Journal of Substance Abuse Treatment, 26,* 35–41.
Hora, P. F., Schma, W. G., & Rosenthal, J. T. A. Therapeutic jurisprudence and the drug treatment court movement: Revolutionizing the criminal justice system's response to drug abuse and crime in America. *Notre Dame Law Review, 74,* 439–537.
Hungerford, D. W. (2005). Interventions in trauma centers for substance use disorders: New insights on an old malady, *Trauma, 59,* S10–S17.
Kassebaum, G., & Okamoto, D. K. (2001). The drug court as a sentencing model. *Journal of Contemporary Criminal Justice, 17,* 89–104.
Kings County Bar Association Drug Policy Project. (2005). *Effective drug control: Toward a new legal framework: State-level regulation as a workable alternative to the "war on drugs."* Seattle, WA: Kings County Bar Association Drug Policy Project. Available at http://www.kcba.org/druglaw/pdf/EffectiveDrugControl.pdf
Kluger, J. H. (2000). Judicial roundtable: Reflections of problem-court justices. *New York State Bar Association Journal, 72*(5),11.
LaPrairie, C., Gliksman, L., Erickson, P., Wall, R., & Newton-Taylor, B. (2002). Drug treatment courts: A viable option for Canada? Sentencing issues and preliminary findings from the Toronto Drug Treatment Court. *Substance Use and Misuse, 37*(12–13), 1529–1566.
Lederman, C. (2000). What is a traditional judge anyway? Problem solving in state courts. *Judicature, 84*(2), 80–82.
Malkin, V. (2003). Community courts and the process of accountability: Consensus and conflict at the Red Hook Community Justice Center. *American Criminal Law Review, 40*(4), 1573–1593.
Marlowe, D. B. (2002). Effective strategies for intervening with drug abusing offenders. *Villanova Law Review, 47,* 989–1025.
Marlowe, D. B. (2003, August). Integrating substance abuse treatment and criminal justice supervision. *Science & Practice Perspectives,* 5–14.
Marlowe, D. B., DeMatteo, D. S., & Festinger, D. S. (2003). A sober assessment of drug courts. *Federal Sentencing Reporter, 16*(1), 1–5.
Marlowe, D. B., Festinger, D. S., Lee, P. A., Dugosh, K. L., & Benasutti, K. M. (2006). Matching judicial supervision to clients' risk status in drug court. *Crime & Delinquency, 52*(1), 52–76.
McCoy, C. (2003). The politics of problem-solving: An overview of the origins and development of therapeutic courts. *American Criminal Law Review, 40,* 1513–1534.
Miethe, T. D., Lu, H., & Reese, E. (2000). Reintegrative shaming and recidivism risks in drug court: Explanations for some unexpected findings. *Crime & Delinquency, 469* (4), 522–541.

Miller, E. J. (2004). Embracing addiction: Drug courts and the false promise of judicial interventionism. *Ohio State Law Review, 65,* 1479–1576.

Nolan, J. L., Jr. (2002, January/February). Therapeutic adjudication. *Society,* 29–38.

Nolan, J. L., Jr. (2003). Redefining criminal courts: Problem-solving and the meaning of justice. *American Criminal Law Review, 40,* 1541–1565.

Ogletree, C. J., Jr. (1993). Beyond justifications: Seeking motivations to sustain public defenders. *Harvard Law Review, 106,* 1239–1294.

Popovic, J. (2006). Court process and therapeutic jurisprudence: Have we thrown the baby out with the bathwater? *eLaw Journal,* Special Series 1, 60–77.

Robinson, L. O. (2005). Community court and community justice commentary. *American Criminal Law Review, 40,* 1535–1539.

Sanford, J. S., & Arrigo, B. A. (2005). Lifting the cover on drug courts: Evaluation findings and policy concerns. *International Journal of Offender Therapy and Comparative Criminology, 49*(3), 239–259.

Satel, S. (1998). Observational study of courtroom dynamics in selected drug courts. *National Drug Court Institute Review, 1,* 43–72.

Thompson, A. T. (2002). Courting disorder: Some thoughts on community courts. *Washington University Journal of Law and Policy, 10,* 63–99.

Tsai, B. (2000). The trend toward specialized domestic violence courts: Improvements on an effective innovation. *Fordham Law Review, 68,* 1285–1327.

Webster, J. M., Rosen, P. J., Krietemeyer, J., Mateyoke-Scrivner, A., Staton-Tindall, M., & Leukefeld, C. (2006). Gender, mental health, and treatment motivation in a drug court setting. *Journal of Psychoactive Drugs, 38*(4), 441–448.

Winick, B. J., & Wexler, D. B. (2002). Drug treatment court: Therapeutic jurisprudence applied. *Touro Law Review, 18,* 479–485.

Winick, B. J., & Wexler, D. B. (2003). *Judging in a therapeutic key: Therapeutic jurisprudence and the courts.* Durham, NC: Carolina Academic Press.

3

Adult Drug Courts: A Hope Realized?

MITCHELL B. MACKINEM and PAUL HIGGINS

Adult drug courts are court-supervised drug treatment programs. They are part of America's and other countries' struggles for more than 100 years to handle users of mood-altering chemicals. Drug courts have developed out of and reflect America's twin, but shifting, emphases on helping the sick drug abuser and punishing the drug-offending criminal. First established in Miami in 1989, they have developed rapidly throughout the United States and in countries throughout the world. Drug courts embody the hope that an alternative to the typical criminal justice approaches of incarcerating or putting on probation drug-using offenders will be more successful in helping problematic drug users to become law-abiding, productive citizens; families and communities to become healthier; and the criminal justice system to work more efficiently and effectively.

In what follows, we briefly discuss the history of America's adult drug courts that, as we will see, have developed out of America's ongoing response to problem drug use. They have spread rapidly throughout the United States in the past 20 years and have appeared in other countries. The portrayal of drug courts by professionals and the media helps drug courts garner political and community support. While drug courts vary throughout the country, all are staffed by a team of diverse professionals. Through a drug court process, the professionals work with drug-using offenders. Drug courts have been shown to be effective in reducing drug use and criminal behavior. Nevertheless, criticisms have been raised about drug courts. Whether drug courts have achieved or may achieve the hope on which they have been developed is uncertain.

AMERICA'S RESPONSE TO PROBLEM DRUG USE

America has responded to problem drug use through a changing and intertwined emphasis on treating the sick drug abuser and punishing the drug-offending criminal. Both approaches have existed throughout America's management of problem drug use. That tension in America's response to problem drug use rests on how America has identified problem drug users. Are problem drug users sick abusers morally deserving of help or are they dangerous criminals who happen to abuse drugs for whom punishment is appropriate?

Before the 1900s, Americans had easy access to a wide variety of mood-altering substances, including opium, cocaine, and marijuana. Many of these substances were ingredients in patent medicines. Opium was widely prescribed and often referred to as "God's Own Medicine." [1] During and immediately after the Civil War, 250,000 Americans were estimated to be addicted to drugs.[2]

Depending on the user's racial and cultural identity, the opium addict was regarded as a hapless victim of the drug or a sinister threat. The housewife who used a "tonic" to treat menstrual discomfort and the war veteran who treated his wounds with morphine were pitied and helped.[3] However, Chinese immigrants who smoked opium and ran "opium dens" were viewed as threats to America's way of life.[4] As the nineteenth century gave way to the twentieth century, drug use became a national crisis, no longer a matter for families, doctors, and local communities.

Since the early twentieth century, America has responded to its concern and fear of drug users through attempts to treat the worthy, but sick, user and punish the dangerous, unworthy criminal addict. As legislation criminalized drug use and severely punished those who used and/or sold illegal drugs, new treatments for helping the drug abuser were developed and additional resources were provided. At times the same legislation embodied both approaches.

America's punishment of the dangerous, unworthy criminal addict is seen in various responses throughout the past 100 years. The Harrison Narcotic Act of 1914, perhaps the most important law in the history of America's response to drugs, and subsequent court rulings made it illegal for doctors or pharmacists to prescribe narcotic drugs for nonmedical purposes.[5,6] One consequence of this act was the incarceration of many new drug users who now were law violators. In 1951, in part out of the fear that developed during the Cold War and the McCarthy era and in response to concern about the importation of drugs from Mexico, China, and Italy, Congress established minimum mandatory punishment for drug smuggling. By the 1980s, the fear of HIV/AIDS, the seeming flood of powder and crack cocaine into America, and the resurgence of highly potent marijuana underlay legislation, such as the Anti-Drug Abuse Act of 1986, that cracked down on illicit drug trafficking, sales, and use. Seventy percent of the $4 billion allocated by the 1986 legislation went toward interdiction efforts by law enforcement.

Accompanying America's punitive approach toward problem drug users were its efforts to treat the sick user. Often with the support of the federal government, more than 100 medical clinics provided safe, reliable sources of narcotics for the sick addict in the early decades of the twentieth century. Hospitals that treated addicts; antidrug clubs that aimed to help their members quit their drug use; "narcotic farms" that coerced federal drug offenders to receive treatment; the development of Alcoholics Anonymous and later Narcotics Anonymous; and the use of methadone, which limits the cravings for opiates without providing the euphoria of natural opiates, and Anatabuse, which produces strong negative side effects in the presence of alcohol, were important developments in the first half of the twentieth century for treating the sick addict. The second half of the twentieth century was marked by the development of residential treatment programs; Therapeutic Communities used in prison-based treatment; increased federal support for professional drug treatment; and the development of the precursor to drug courts, the federally supported Treatment Alternatives to Street Crime (TASC), which coerced alcohol- and drug-using defendants into treatment. Even the law enforcement-oriented Anti-Drug Abuse Act of 1986 put 30 percent of its $4 billion allocation toward treatment.

In the 1980s, cocaine from South America poured into Miami and other cities. At times, cocaine literally rained from the sky as drug traffickers in small prop planes dumped their load of cocaine over Dade County in order to avoid arrest by airborne agents of the Drug Enforcement Agency. Miami jails and courts became overwhelmed by the soaring drug arrests. Police officers commonly saw on Miami streets offenders they had arrested an hour earlier for possession of crack cocaine, a cheap, highly addictive drug. Something had to be done to stop this intolerable revolving door of justice. In the summer of 1989, Miami established the nation's first drug court.[7,8] Other drug courts soon arose in Oakland, California; Broward County, Florida; Portland, Oregon; Maricopa County, Arizona; and Las Vegas, Nevada, among other places.[9]

DRUG COURT: PREVALENCE AND PARTICIPATION

Drug courts have developed rapidly and widely in the United States since the first court in 1989 in Miami. The number of adult drug courts grew to 38 by 1994, to 353 by 1999, to 889 in 2004, and to 1,174 in 2007, covering all 50 states, Puerto Rico, Guam, and the Marina Islands. There are an additional 349 adult, juvenile, family, and tribal courts in the planning stages.[10,11,12,13] Similarly, federal funding for drug courts has increased markedly from an initial $6 million in 1993 to a proposed $40 million in 2008.[14] This funding to local jurisdictions for the development and operation of drug courts has been a major spur for their dramatic growth.[15]

More than 70,000 individuals presently participate in some form of drug court (adult, juvenile, family, or tribal) in the United States on any given day. Over 16,000 individuals nowadays graduate from drug courts in a given year.[16,17] As drug courts continue to become more common, the numbers of participants and graduates will increase. However, not all who participate graduate. According to the most recent comprehensive federal review, graduation rates vary widely across programs, ranging from 30 to 70 percent.[18]

As drug courts have proliferated, it has become more difficult to provide a comprehensive picture of drug court participants. A federal review of more than 100 published reports and evaluations of drug courts provides the best nationwide information on the participants in drug courts.[19] The participants in drug court programs have been "generally in their early 30s, predominately male and generally unemployed."[20] The racial composition of participants has varied across drug court programs. Most of the reviewed programs had a majority of White participants. However, many programs had a majority of African American or Hispanic participants. Previous criminal history has also varied among participants. Only 9 percent of drug court participants had no criminal record while 56 percent of participants had previously been incarcerated in prison, according to a nationwide review.[21]

PORTRAYING DRUG COURT

Being a relatively new component of the criminal justice system, drug court professionals and the media portray drug court to prospective applicants and their significant others, criminal justice officials not familiar with drug court, citizens, fellow professionals, and other audiences in order to educate about drug court. While the portrayals may vary by the targeted audiences, collectively they are composed of several elements. Drug courts are presented as being tough, as better than traditional approaches, as providing hope, even miraculously so, and as a new, even revolutionary, team approach that integrates legal and treatment staff and means for dealing with offenders who are drug users. The portrayals reflect the tension between punishing the offender and treating the addict that characterizes American policy toward problem drug users.[22]

Drug courts are tough. Brochures may emphasize the significant series of activities required of clients who remain "defendants" under the threat of prison or other punishment if they fail drug court. Drug courts are better than the traditional response to drug-using offenders because, among other reasons, drug courts move more quickly with less time between arrest and attention to the offender and they focus on nondangerous drug abusers, leaving the criminal courts to focus on the violent drug users and major traffickers.

Drug courts provide hope to those who have damaged their lives and the lives of their loved ones through their drug abuse. The media especially may present this human-interest angle with stories such as one about a young woman who was defiant when she entered drug court, telling others that she would never quit drugs. By the time the newspaper article appeared, the young woman had not only graduated from drug court and quit using drugs, but she had married, had a young child, and was taking evening courses at a local community college.[23] What seem like miracles may happen in drug court.

The National Association of Drug Court Professionals and federal drug control agencies present drug court as a revolution in the court system.[24,25] Drug courts are revolutionary because they offer a dynamic alternative to the failed punitive policies of traditional courts' responses to drug use. With therapeutic jurisprudence as a legal/philosophical underpinning, drug courts seek to change the goal of the court from punishment to changing lives. Being part of an innovative judicial model that holds offenders accountable for their actions and provides the tools needed by the offenders to turn their lives around, drug courts strive to enable the offenders to break their destructive patterns of drug abuse.[26] Drug courts also break from traditional courts in how they operate. They are touted for their cooperative team approach where legal and treatment professionals in a nonadversarial relation collaborate and draw upon community resources. Drug courts demand that participants change their lives.

TYPES OF AND VARIATIONS IN DRUG COURT

Three types of drug courts operate: pre-plea, post-adjudication deferred judgment, and post-adjudication condition of sentence. Since the development of drug court, the mix of these three types of programs has changed. The first generation of drug courts of the 1990s tended to be pre-plea programs. By the early 2000s post-adjudication programs dominated drug court. Over 60 percent of the existing drug courts had a post-adjudication component in 2001; by 2008 that had risen to 78 percent.[27]

In pre-plea programs defendants enter drug court with no finding of guilt or innocence. Defendants also make no admission of guilt. A distinct advantage to the defendants is that charges are dismissed should they complete the program. If they fail, the case follows the regular prosecution route. The disadvantage for the court is the challenge of prosecuting the case after the delay of drug court, which could be months or longer. Only 6 percent of the programs, nationally, follow this model exclusively.

In post-adjudication, deferred-judgment programs, defendants enter a guilty plea or statement. The court makes no finding of guilt and defers any punishment activity. If the defendants complete the program, the plea is withdrawn and the charge dismissed. Should the defendants fail the program, the court may impose punishment. The advantage lies in the quick prosecution of the case and certain outcome. The disadvantage for the defendants is the certain punishment of failure, although dismissal of the criminal charge is still a benefit.

Under the post-adjudication condition of sentence programs, the defendants' sentence is drug court. A judge may sentence a convicted defendant to drug court or order a convicted defendant who has failed probation to participate in drug court in lieu of incarceration. In a post-adjudication program, charges cannot be dismissed should defendants complete the program. However, should defendants fail drug court, they will likely have their probation revoked and be sent to prison. Post-adjudication drug court programs, which help prison-bound defendants avoid incarceration, will produce significant savings for local and state jurisdictions.

Many other variations may occur based upon local conditions. For example, if drug courts develop in response to local drug problems, the target problem will vary by the local definition of the drug problem. The court can target different levels and types of criminal offenses. These could range from first-time misdemeanors to multiple felony charges. Without taking into account these variations among drug courts, adequate evaluations of programs become difficult.[28]

DRUG COURT TEAM

The professionals who work in drug court typically understand themselves to be a team, not adversaries, working to help the drug-using offenders go straight and, thereby, helping the community to be safer. The drug court team is composed of professionals who have long been members of the criminal court system and of others who are more recent additions to the courts. Judges and defense and prosecuting attorneys are joined by program administrators, drug counselors, and other treatment providers.

While all share a common interest in helping drug-abusing offenders to become abstinent and law abiding, each may have somewhat different concerns, too. Typically having a large number of cases to handle and being pressured to move cases as quickly as possible through the court system, deputy prosecuting attorneys are interested in using drug court to help worthy offenders even if it means that those clients who are removed from drug court return to the prosecutors' caseload. Whether they are public defenders or private attorneys, defense attorneys typically understand drug court to be an opportunity for their clients who are guilty to receive needed treatment. They are disappointed when clients fail the program. The program administrator responds to somewhat competing demands, which reflect the historical tension between helping the deserving drug abuser and punishing the unworthy criminal who also abuses drugs. The administrator seeks to admit, retain, and graduate drug users who will benefit from the drug court program, to give the user who is presently viewed as worthy a chance. However, the administrator may also be concerned with efficiently using the limited resources provided to the drug court program and in protecting the support that drug court receives from the legal, political, and civic community. Clients may fail. However, clients who commit serious crimes while in the program may jeopardize the drug court's existence. Treatment staff focuses on helping drug users who are coerced into treatment, knowing that initial participation is primarily externally motivated but that with time and even with the coercion of the judge when clients fail to meet program requirements, the successful clients will become internally motivated to change their lives.

Drug court treatment counselors and program coordinators operate based on their professional beliefs about drug addiction, treatment, and testing. First, counselors typically understand drug addiction to be a compulsive behavior disorder, a disease, where addicts use drugs despite potentially significantly negative psychological, social, legal, and financial consequences. The compulsion is believed to be the result of biological, psychological, and social drives. Because of biological changes produced by the drugs and the users' psychological accommodations to their use, counselors believe that drug users cannot easily and effectively evaluate their condition. They often lie about or deny the significance of their behavior and condition. Treatment, as understood by the staff, attempts to enable the drug user to change biologically, psychologically, and socially. Treatment intensity lessens as the drug court client progresses. However, counselors are not surprised when during clients' movement toward abstinence, known as recovery, the clients use drugs or relapse. Counselors expect drug court clients to lie about their drug use, to make bad decisions, and to relapse. However, the counselors expect that after sufficient time in the program, the drug court clients should not relapse. Drug testing is understood by counselors and administrators as crucial for drug court. While staff may debate whether a drug test result is positive and whether a positive drug test is an indication of current use or even of illegal use, they do not doubt the validity of the tests.[29]

Drug court judges are the captains of the teams. They may have volunteered to sit on drug court in addition to their regular court duties or they may be full-time judges for drug court. They may become highly knowledgeable about drug addiction and treatment or become more experienced but still significantly dependent on drug court staff for evaluating the clients and deciding how they should be handled. Those who volunteer for drug court appear committed to using alternatives to managing problem drug users where standard incarceration or probation has not worked well. Drug court judges develop dramatically more extensive relations with the clients in drug court than defendants in criminal court. Drug court judges typically focus on helping clients turn around their lives, not on overseeing a legal contest as in criminal court. This shift from a focus on the legal proceedings against a defendant to a focus on coercively treating the abuser worries some observers of drug court, a worry that we address later in this chapter.

DRUG COURT PROCESS

Drug courts operate through a process of decisions and actions by the drug court team. Through admission, treatment and monitoring, and discharge, drug court professionals attempt to assist drug-using offenders to go straight. When drug court programs have discretion in who is admitted, the professionals attempt to admit those offenders for whom they have hope, a hope that the clients who are serious drug abusers will benefit from the treatment and monitoring of drug court. During admissions, drug court professionals evaluate the suitability of drug-using offenders for drug court, trying to determine who needs help and has the potential to do well in the program. As drug court clients participate in the program, the professionals provide or arrange for mandatory group and individual counseling, attendance at self-help meetings, and/or other treatment. The drug court professionals also monitor and evaluate the clients' participation and conformity to program regulations through drug testing, reviewing clients' participation with colleagues, and regular appearances before the judge at drug court sessions. As drug court clients' participation in drug court continues, the staff and the judge evaluate their performance, eventually deciding whether to remove the clients from the program or to arrange for them to graduate with whatever legal consequences removal or graduation bring.

Where drug courts have discretion as to whom they admit, staff may operate through an admission process similar to what occurred in three drug courts in the metropolitan area of a southeastern state that we observed. Once a drug court is firmly established, the program administrator may no longer need to recruit applicants for the program. Instead, through referrals from prosecuting and defense attorneys, administrators become notified of potential applicants. After notification, appointments to interview the defendants are set, criminal files are reviewed, interviews with the defendants are held, input from police and victims are requested and often, but not always, received, assessment of the applicants by drug counselors are conducted, deliberations are made, and finally the applicants are rejected or recommended by the administrator to the judge for acceptance into the program.

Once admitted to the program, drug court clients may begin by attending weekly two or three mandatory group and/or individual counseling sessions and a couple of self-help meetings of local chapters of Alcoholics Anonymous or Narcotics Anonymous, submitting to drug tests each week if not more often, paying participation fees, and regularly attending drug court sessions with the judge, perhaps every two weeks. As clients participate in treatment, the staff members monitor their behavior. Counselors evaluate the clients in counseling; program administrators and counselors regularly discuss clients' participation and, as warranted, their problems; and counselors, administrators, lawyers, and others discuss the clients' cases with the judge before the open drug court session. When clients violate program requirements, judges, using staff recommendations, may send the client to the local jail for 24 or 48 hours, require community service, and/or increase the frequency of counseling sessions and drug testing. As clients perform satisfactorily, staff will recommend to judges that clients be promoted through the phases of the program, attending counseling sessions and being drug tested less frequently. In the open drug court sessions, the judges talk to clients about their performance and punish or reward them for their behavior in front of their fellow clients. Staff members make their recommendations as they evaluate the participation of the clients and come to characterize them as worthy drug abusers who are trying to stop their drug use or as less worthy, even unworthy, criminals who happened to use drugs but have little intention of changing their behavior.

As clients participate in the drug court program, staff members evaluate the clients' performance. Staff members judge whether clients have succeeded in meeting the requirements of the program and deserve to graduate or whether they are performing so poorly that the judge should remove them. Staff recommends that drug-using offenders be admitted when the staff is hopeful that clients may benefit from the program. Staff members and judges know, however, that one never knows for certain which drug court clients will succeed and which will not. When staff members lose hope that clients will participate appropriately in drug court, meeting the requirements of the program, they move to remove the clients. Hope has been lost for these clients. Hope will arise again for new clients.

DRUG COURT EVALUATIONS

Studies of drug courts have evaluated their effectiveness and their potential cost savings and have examined who is most likely to succeed in drug court. The studies indicate that drug court reduces the recidivism of those who participate compared to those who do not, saves money compared to the traditional court system for handling drug-using offenders, helps clients more the longer they remain in the program even if they do not graduate from the program, and is most effective with clients who are socially integrated into conventional society compared to those who are less socially tied to conventional society.

The body of drug court research supports one fundamental conclusion: drug court reduces recidivism.[30,31,32,33,34,35] To examine this issue in greater detail we look at one outcome study of drug courts in New York State, described as a stringent evaluation by the National Drug Court Institute, and a recent examination of the cost savings of a mature drug court in Portland, Oregon.

The New York State study evaluated 11 different courts located throughout the state, including metropolitan, suburban, and rural settings. The researchers followed the subjects for three years beyond the program. At 6 of the 11 study sites, the graduates were compared to a matched comparison group for each court's population. When graduates are compared to a matched sample, the results from each court, individually, or all collectively, indicate that drug court graduates are less likely to be rearrested. The recidivism reduction averaged 32 percent. This finding is congruent with findings from 17 other drug court recidivism evaluations.[36]

A recent study of the Multnomah County Drug Court, the second oldest drug court in the United States, followed graduates and a matched comparison group for 10 years after program completion.[37] Located in Portland, Oregon, the court began in 1991 as a pre-plea diversion program. In 1995, the court became mixed with both pre-plea and post-adjudication participants. In 2000, the court became exclusively post-adjudicatory. Since its conception, the court has provided services to over 6,500 individuals. Researchers examined the cost of drug court for the 6,500 participants and compared this to the costs of "business as usual" for 4,600 subjects who were processed through the criminal justice system outside of drug court.[38] Researchers found that there was a significant reduction in rearrest rates for program graduates than for business-as-usual defendants. The 5-year rearrest rate for graduates was 4.2 percent compared to the sample's rearrest rates of 5.9 percent. The Portland, Oregon, drug court also saved $75 million for the 10 years of its operation compared to the traditional handling of drug offenders.

One key issue in the impact of drug courts upon recidivism rates is program retention. The amount of time clients spend in treatment is significantly related to recidivism.[39,40,41,42] The more time a client spends in treatment the greater the potential benefit, and it is here that drug courts excel. Even program failures may experience positive benefits from program participation if the program "dosage" was sufficient.

Studies have examined who is most likely to succeed in drug court. While the findings are diverse and occasionally contradictory, we believe the bulk of the research indicates that those who are most stable, have the most financial and social capital, and are successful members of the mainstream culture will do better than others. Generally, lower status clients do less well in the program than higher status clients.[43] The defendant's level of risk, in general criminal justice terms, is predictive of program failure and rearrest; the more risky a defendant, the less effective the program.[44] The number of previous arrests was the strongest predictor of rearrest in one study.[45] In another study, crack use, young age at first arrest, and diversity of charges were predictive of program failure.[46] Finally, drug court participants who were employed and married had the greatest likelihood of succeeding compared to those unemployed and/or not married in another evaluation.[47] Drug treatment court outcome is dependent upon the risk factors the defendants bring with them, as well as the changes and behavior while in the program.

While drug courts appear to be effective and cost efficient compared to traditional approaches for handling drug-using offenders, much still needs to be learned about what works and what does not work.[48] For example, it is unclear what components of drug court, such as the role of the judge, drug testing, or the use of intermediate sanctions, have the greatest impact on drug court outcomes.[49] Further, the importance of the motivation of clients on their performance in drug court has not been adequately assessed. The motivation of clients does affect how well they do in general drug treatment programs.[50,51,52] Does client motivation matter for drug court? Perhaps it does. Drug courts may be effective, in part, due to their admission process through which unmotivated drug-using offenders are rejected and motivated applicants are accepted.[53] Continuing to study drug courts is crucial for their improvement.

CRITICISM OF DRUG COURT

Scholars and criminal justice professionals, such as Richard Boldt in Chapter 2, have expressed serious concerns with the rise of problem-solving courts in general and drug courts in particular. Six categories of concerns have been raised: coercion, advocacy, structure, impartiality, paternalism, and separation of power.[54,55] Do defendants participate voluntarily in drug court or are they coerced? If drug courts are indeed coercive, are they any more coercive than standard state courts that resolve 95 percent of cases through the practice of plea bargaining?[56]

The remaining concerns center on the fairness of the judicial process as compared to traditional courts. For example, the departure from the traditional adversarial court system toward a treatment team concept may leave the defendant without an active defense.[57] All key criminal court personnel play diminished or significantly altered roles, which may greatly reduce the capacity of defense counsels to protect their clients from harsh, unjust court actions.[58,59,60] Inadequate attention may be given to clients' due-process rights in the nonad versarial, team approach of drug court. For example, in traditional criminal courts, urine testing can be done only if ordered by the court. A chain of custody of the specimen must be maintained so that no tampering can occur, and the defense is free to challenge the results. These due-process safeguards may not occur in drug court.

Traditional courts operate under a philosophy of "just desserts." This philosophy maintains that criminals are to be punished as a result of their criminal act and that the severity of the punishment should be commensurate with seriousness of the offense. In drug courts that operate within a therapeutic jurisprudence philosophy, punishment is used as a tool for compliance and thus is not related to severity of the crime. Therapeutic jurisprudence could lead to punishment that exceeds what offenders would receive in traditional court.

The changing role of the judge in drug court may contain specific dangers.[61] Judges have great power to punish but are only amateur therapists, opening the opportunity for naïve abuses of power. The judges are not independent but act in concert with others, including private therapy providers, who profit by the judge's decisions, such as to require drug court clients to receive more treatment from the providers.

While concerns have been raised about drug court, both participants and staff in one New York state drug court perceive drug court as more equitable and respectful than traditional court.[62] Participants felt they had a voice in the court; they could and did talk directly to the judge about their concerns and complaints. Treatment, not the court, was the source of most participant complaints. In another New York state drug court, women participants cited the staff's support as crucial to their success.[63]

In drug courts that we have studied, the concerns of critics did not significantly occur. Those admitted into the drug courts we studied were "dead bang guilty." Neither they nor their lawyers believed they were innocent. The offenders had committed the crime, were drug users, and needed help. The drug court clients voluntarily participated. While participating, some used drugs as indicated by their drug tests. They were not arrested, charged with a new offense, and removed from the program—at least not with their early use. Instead, they continued in the program and many graduated. Many graduates appreciated the opportunity drug court provided for them to become sober and to straighten out their lives.

Drug courts do rely on the good intentions and knowledge of professional staff to avoid legal abuse. Good intentions, however, may serve as justification for practices that are harsher than what the drug-using offenders would be subject to within criminal court. Misunderstandings may lead to legal consequences that should not have happened.

The good intentions and professional competence of drug court staff do not guarantee that mistakes will not be made and that the legal rights of offenders may not always be upheld. However, we should not overlook that mistakes and failure to uphold legal rights occur in criminal court, too. Perhaps more importantly, we should not forget that through dedication and competence and through working together within appropriate policies and procedures, drug court staffs throughout the country attempt tremendous good. They often help drug-using offenders make more law-abiding and satisfying lives for themselves. In doing so, drug court professionals help all of us.

CONCLUSION

Drug courts were founded on the hope that they would help the criminal justice system, and, more generally, help society handle more effectively offenders who are problem drug users. The drug court movement represents itself as a revolution to the punitive traditional courts. Instead of the traditional revolving door in an overloaded criminal justice system, drug courts would operate through a team approach to seriously, and coercively, change the drug abuse of offenders. Not only would drug court help a few select participants, but the whole approach to drug-involved criminals would be changed. Has the hope of drug court's founding been realized?

Drug courts can work more effectively and cost efficiently than traditional criminal courts in helping drug-using offenders to stop using drugs and committing crimes. Although effective, drug courts can be improved through further study and development. However, the number of drug offenders handled by drug courts in the United States is small compared to the number that could appropriately be managed. If admission criteria for drug courts were expanded, then an estimated 1.5 million defendants who are probably guilty of the crimes for which they are charged and are a high risk for drug abuse or dependence would be eligible to participate in drug court. The 55,000 drug-using offenders who were estimated to participate in drug courts in 2006 were less than 4 percent of these 1.5 million potentially eligible offenders. Even under existing admission criteria, almost 110,000 offenders could enter drug court.[64]

If drug courts do not expand, then perhaps the principles by which drug courts operate could become part of the traditional court system. If this were to happen, then each year drug courts could indirectly affect the lives of hundreds of thousands, even millions, of offenders, family members, potential victims, and others. However, at present this hoped-for change is not happening in the adult justice system and does not seem likely to happen in the near future.

Perhaps most importantly, since drug courts handle problem drug users after they have developed a serious drug problem and have become criminal offenders, they can never be the preferred solution to a society's drug problem. Developing a healthy society that produces fewer drug-abusing citizens should be the guiding aim. When that fails, however, drug court may give the offender and society renewed hope.

NOTES

1. Belenko, 2000.
2. Musto, 1999.
3. Belenko, 2000.
4. White, 1979.
5. Musto, 1999.
6. Inciardi, McBride, and Rivers, 1996.
7. The Miami Drug Court handled approximately 1,300 drug offenders its first year. Only 4 percent of clients were arrested for new drug crimes while participating in the program (Haigney, 1990).
8. Goldkamp, 1999.
9. Terry, 1999.
10. Drug courts have become an international movement. The International Drug Treatment Court Association has members throughout the world with its board representing nine different counties including Australia, Britain, Brazil, and Canada (Bentley, 2005).
11. Cooper, 2001.
12. Huddleston et al., 2005.
13. Justice Programs Office, 2007.
14. National Drug Court Institute, 2004.
15. Beyond this direct funding of drug courts by federal grants, designated block grant monies, administered by the state, are for drug court use. These local block grants include the Local Law Enforcement Block Grants and the Bryne Memorial Block grant. (Tauber et al., 2000).
16. Huddleston et al., 2005.
17. Roussell, 2005.
18. GAO, 2005.
19. GAO, 2005.

20. GAO, 2005, p. 41.
21. Cooper, 2001.
22. Mackinem and Higgins, 2008.
23. Ripton, 2000.
24. NADCP, 1999.
25. NIJ, 2006.
26. Freeman-Wilson, 1999.
27. Cooper, 2001.
28. Goldkamp, 1999.
29. Mackinem and Higgins, 2007.
30. Belenko, 2001.
31. Brewster, 2001.
32. Longshore et al., 2001.
33. Rempel et al., 2003.
34. Gottfredson and Exum, 2002.
35. Spohn et al., 2001.
36. BJA, 2004.
37. Finigan, Carey, and Cox, 2007.
38. Finigan, Carey, and Cox, 2007.
39. Peters, Hass, and Hunt, 2001.
40. Peters and Murrin, 2000.
41. Joe, Simpson, and Broome, 1999.
42. Young and Belenko, 2002.
43. Goldkamp and Weiland, 1993.
44. Goldkamp and Weiland, 1993.
45. Spohn et al., 2001.
46. Finigan, Carey, and Cox, 2007.
47. Miller and Shutt, 2001.
48. Peters, Haas, and Murrin, 1999.
49. GAO, 2001.
50. GAO, 2005.
51. Hiller et al., 2002.
52. Simpson and Joe, 1993.
53. Simpson, Joe, and Rowan-Szal, 1997.
54. Berman and Feinblatt, 2005, p. 78.
55. Mackinem and Higgins, 2008.
56. Berman and Feinblatt, 2005.
57. Berman and Feinblatt, 2005.
58. Spinak, 2003.
59. Nolan, 2003.
60. Boldt, 2002.
61. Quinn, 2000.
62. Hoffman, 2002.
63. Fischer, Geiger, and Highes, 2007.
64. Bhati, Roman, and Chafin, 2008.

REFERENCES

Belenko, S. (2001). Research on drug courts: A critical review, 2001 update. In *Research on Drug Courts*. New York: National Center on Addiction and Substance Abuse at Columbia University.

Belenko, S. R. (2000). *Drugs and drug policy in America: A documentary history, primary documents in American history and contemporary issues*. Westport, CT: Greenwood Press.

Bentley, P. (2005, Fall). An international take on drug treatment courts. *NADCP News*, 28.

Berman, G., & Feinblatt, J. (2001). Problem-solving courts: A brief primer. *Law and Policy*, *23*(2).

———. (2005). *Good courts: The case for problem-solving justice*. New York: The New Press.

Bhati, A., Roman, J. K., & Chafin, A. (2008). *To treat or not to treat: Evidence on the prospects of expanding treatment to drug-involved offenders*. Washington, DC: Justice Policy Center, Urban Institute.

Brewster, M. P. (2001). An evaluation of the Chester County (PA) Drug Court Program. *Journal of Drug Issues*, *31*(1), 177–206.

Bureau of Justice Assistance, Drug Court Clearinghouse Project (BJA). (2004). *Recidivism and other findings reported from selected evaluations of adult drug court programs published: 2000–present*. Washington, DC: School of Public Affairs, American University.

Cooper, C. (2003). *Drug court activities update: Summary information on all programs and detailed information on adult drug courts* [Internet]. Office of Justice Programs; Drug Court Clearinghouse and Technical Assistance Project 2001 [cited February 26, 2003]. Available from http://spa.american.edu/justice/docuements/1933.pdf (accessed January 29, 2008).

Deschenes, E., & Greenwood, P. (1994). Maricopa County's Drug Court: An innovative program for the first time drug offenders on probation. *Justice Systems Journal*, *17* (1), 99–115.

Finigan, M., Carey, S. M., & Cox, A. (2007). *Impact of a mature drug court over 10 years of operation: Recidivism and costs*. Washington, DC: National Institute of Justice, Office of Research and Evaluation.

Fisher, M., Geiger, B., & Highes, M. E. (2007). Female recidivist speak about their experience in drug court while engaging in appreciative inquiry. *International Journal of Offender Therapy and Comparative Criminology*, *51*(6): 703–722.

Freeman-Wilson, K. (2006). *DWI courts and DWI/drug courts: Reducing recidivism, saving lives* [Internet]. National Drug Court Institute 1999 [cited June 29, 2006]. Available from www.ndci.org/dui.pdf.

Goldkamp, J. (1999). Challenges for research and innovation: When is a drug court not a drug court? In W. C. Terry (Ed.), *The early drug courts: Case studies in judicial innovation*. Thousand Oaks, CA: Sage Publications.

Goldkamp, J., & Weiland, D. (1993). *Assessing the impact of Dade County's felony drug court*. Washington, DC: National Institute of Justice.

Goldkamp, J. S., White, M. D., & Robinson, J. B. (2001). Do drug courts work? Getting inside the drug court black box. *Journal of Drug Issues*, *31*(1), 27–72.

Gottfredson, D. C., & Exum, M. L. (2002). The Baltimore City Drug Treatment Court: One-year results from a randomized study. *Journal of Research in Crime and Delinquency*, *39*(3), 337–356.

Government Accountability Office (GAO). (2005). *Adult drug court: Evidence indicates recidivism reductions and mixed results for other outcomes*. Washington, DC: U.S. Government Accountability Office.

Haigney, L. (1990, June 19). First time drug offenders get second chance at clean slate. *Miami Herald*, 1-B.

Hiller, M., Knight, K., Leukefeld, C., & Simpson, D. (2002). Motivation as a predictor of therapeutic engagement in mandated residential substance abuse treatment. *Criminal Justice and Behavior, 29*(1), 56–75.

Hoffman, M. (2002). Therapeutic jurisprudence, neo-rehabilitationism, and judicial collectivism: The least dangerous branch becomes most dangerous. *Fordham Urban Law Journal, 29*(5), 2063–2098.

Huddleston, C. W., Wilson-Freeman, K., Marlowe, D. B., & Roussell, A. (2005). *Painting the picture: A national report card on drug courts and other problem solving court programs in the United States*. Alexandria, VA: National Drug Court Institute.

Inciardi, J. A., McBride, D. C., & Rivers, J. E. (1996). *Drug control and the courts: Drugs, health, and social policy series, 3*. Thousand Oaks, CA: Sage Publications.

Joe, G. W., Simpson, D. D., & Broome, K. M. (1999). Retention and patient engagement models for different treatment modalities in DATOS. *Drug and Alcohol Dependence, 57*(2), 113–125.

Longshore, D., Turner, S., Wenzel, S., Morral, A., Harrell, A., McBride, D., Deschenes, E., & Iguchi, M. (2001). Drug courts: A conceptual framework. *Journal of Drug Issues, 31* (1), 7–26.

Mackinem, M., & Higgins, P. (2007). Tell me about the test: The construction of truth and lies in drug court. *Journal of Contemporary Ethnography, 36*(3), 223–251.

Mackinem, M. B., & Higgins, P. C. (2008). *Drug court: Constructing the moral identity of drug offenders*. Springfield, IL: C. C. Thomas.

Miller, J. M., & Shutt, J. E. (2001). Considering the need for empirically grounded drug court screening mechanisms. *Journal of Drug Issues, 31*(1), 91–106.

Musto, D. F. (1999). *The American disease: Origins of narcotic control* (3rd ed.). New York: Oxford University Press.

National Association of Drug Court Professionals (NADCP). (1999). *National Drug Court Week: Field Kit*. Alexandria, VA: NADCP.

National Drug Court Institute (NDCI). (2004). *Drug courts today*. National Drug Court Association 2004 [cited May 4, 2004]. Available from http://www.ndci.org/courtfacts.htm.

National Institute of Justice (NIJ). (2006). *Drug courts: The second decade*. Washington, DC: Department of Justice, National Institute of Justice/NCJRS.

Nolan, J. (2003). Redefining criminal courts: Problem solving and the meaning of justice. *American Criminal Law Review, 40*(4), 1541–1565.

Peters, R. H., Haas, A. L., & Hunt, W. M. (2001). Treatment "dosage" effects in drug court programs. *Journal of Offender Rehabilitation, 33*(4), 63–72.

Peters, R. H., Haas, A. L., & Murrin, M. R. (1999). Predictors of retention and arrest in drug courts. *National Drug Court Institute Review, 2*(1), 33–60.

Peters, R. H., & Murrin, M. R. (2000). Effectiveness of treatment-based drug courts in reducing criminal recidivism. *Criminal Justice and Behavior, 27*(1), 72–96.

Peyrot, M. (1985). Coerced voluntarism: The micropolitics of drug treatment. *Urban Life, 13*(4), 343–365.

Quinn, M. C. (2000). Whose team am I on anyway? Musings of a public defender about drug treatment court practice. *N.Y.U. Review of Law and Social Change, 26*(37), 37–75.

Rempel, M., Kralstein-Fox, D., Cissner, A., Cohen, R., Labriola, M., Farole, D., Bader, A., & Magnani, M. (2003). *The New York State drug court evaluation.* New York: Center for Court Evaluation.

Ripton, K. (2000, March 10). A life changed: The anatomy of a drug court. *Chronicle-Independent,* 1.

Simpson, D. D., & Joe, G. W. (1993). Motivation as a predictor of early drop out from drug abuse treatment. *Psychotherapy, 30,* 357–368.

Simpson, D. D., Joe, G. W., & Rowan-Szal, G. A. (1997). Drug abuse treatment retention and process effects on follow-up and outcomes. *Drug and Alcohol Dependence, 47*(3), 227–235.

Spinak, J. M. (2003). Why defenders feel defensive: The defender's role in problem solving courts. *American Criminal Law Review, 40*(4), 1617–1622.

Spohn, C., Piper, R. K., Martin, T., & Frenzel, E. D. (2001). Drug courts and recidivism: The results of an evaluation using two comparison groups and multiple indicators of recidivism. *Journal of Drug Issues, 31*(1), 149–176.

Tauber, J., Weinstein, S. P., Allen, C., & Lieupo, K. (2000). *Resource and funding guide.* Alexandria, VA: National Association of Drug Court Professionals.

Terry, W. C. (1999). *The early drug courts: Case studies in judicial innovation: Drugs, health, and social policy series, 7.* Thousand Oaks, CA: Sage Publications.

White, W. L. (1979). *Themes in chemical prohibition.* Washington DC: National Institute of Drug Abuse.

Young, D., & Belenko, S. (2002). Program retention and perceived coercion in three models of mandatory drug treatment. *Journal of Drug Issues, 2*(1), 297–328.

4

Juvenile Drug Courts: More Difficult to Implement Than Originally Envisioned

CAROLINE S. COOPER

A juvenile drug court is a special docket that operates within a juvenile court system under the supervision of an assigned judge and is designed to provide immediate and ongoing intervention, case management, treatment, and an array of other services for juveniles charged with delinquent and/or status offenses who are also involved with chemical substances.[1,2] Juvenile drug courts were established with high hopes for having a significant impact on the burgeoning problems associated with the increasing numbers of drug users involved with the juvenile justice system. These hopes were based on both the recognition of the stated rehabilitative mission of the juvenile court system and the widely successful experience with implementing adult drug court programs. However, these hopes have, as yet, not been realized on any broad scale for a number of reasons, the most significant of which relate to the complexity of issues relevant to working with drug-using youth in a justice system context for which many practitioners have been unprepared. As a result, the level of support for implementing juvenile drug courts appears to have not kept pace with that for adult drug courts. This waning support has also made it more difficult to further develop and evaluate the juvenile drug court approach on any national level.

This chapter provides an overview of the goals and operational characteristics of juvenile drug court programs, includes a summary of the outcomes that have been reported to date and implementation issues that have emerged, and concludes with a discussion of lessons learned and the challenges that need to be addressed in order to sustain juvenile drug courts in the future.

The first juvenile drug courts opened in 1995 with great anticipation that their impact would be even more significant than that of their adult drug court counterparts that had begun in 1989 and that their implementation would be easier. Many practitioners considered that the stated rehabilitative mission of the juvenile court system, coupled with the established infrastructure of service providers and provision for judicial discretion, could provide a strong foundation for implementing the juvenile drug court concept and promoting widespread application of the model to address the special needs of substance-using youth. Within three years, over 60 juvenile drug courts had been implemented in 23 states and the District of Columbia.[3]

Although there was little concrete information readily available that could provide a baseline for subsequently assessing the impact of these juvenile drug court programs statistically, the practitioners involved shared a common sense of the challenges the conventional juvenile court was facing that made adoption of the juvenile drug court model an urgent and promising priority: the increasing complexity of delinquency and dependency dockets, entailing more serious and violent criminal activity coupled with escalating degrees of substance involvement. Juvenile justice system practitioners were also recognizing that the situations bringing many juveniles—and their parents—under the court's jurisdiction were frequently closely linked with widespread drug use, often multigenerational, in the environment in which the juvenile lived, and complicated by other family and personal problems. Many practitioners also recognized that, insofar as substance abuse was an issue, the "juvenile," "family," and "criminal" dockets were increasingly handling the same types of situations, and often the same litigants. They were also finding that, although the juvenile court has traditionally been considered an institution specifically geared to addressing a youth's needs holistically, the juvenile court's conventional approach to case disposition was frequently ineffective when applied to the problems of juvenile substance-abusing offenders. They therefore began to look at the experiences of the adult drug courts to rethink how juvenile courts might adapt the drug court concept to more effectively deal with the increasing population of substance-abusing juveniles.

GOALS AND OPERATIONAL CHARACTERISTICS

Overview

The goals for juvenile drug court programs have been to provide participating youth with the following: (1) immediate *intervention* to address their drug use and promote their development of the skills and competencies to enable them to become and remain drug-free; and (2) *structure* and accountability through the ongoing, active oversight and involvement of the juvenile drug court judge. These goals have been achieved generally by providing participating youth with the following: (1) an opportunity to become drug-free through a combination of adolescent-appropriate treatment services and other skill-building and self-esteem–building activities; (2) constructive support to promote their successful performance in school and the development of positive relationships in the community; and (3) skills to effectively deal with personal, family, and peer situations to increase the likelihood they can lead productive, substance-free, and crime-free lives.[4]

Juvenile drug courts have used a variety of strategies to achieve these goals, primarily through developing systems of triage applied at intake to better screen, assess, and identify the underlying needs of youth entering the juvenile justice system. Through these processes, they have worked to better utilize community services to respond to these needs and to also recognize and respond to the cultural diversity of children involved in court proceedings and the environments in which they live. The overall premise of juvenile drug courts has been that the needs of these children and their families should be treated individually and holistically. Most programs have therefore tried to overcome the dichotomy (for management purposes) between *juvenile delinquency* and *family/dependency* matters so as to provide substance abuse treatment that addresses family issues regardless of whether the case arose on the "juvenile" or "family/dependency" docket. Through these efforts, practitioners have attempted to establish a framework for providing intensive judicial intervention and supervision of youth that has not otherwise been available in many juvenile courts, in part because of high caseloads and in part as a result of the lack of comprehensive treatment and other services, making the traditional juvenile court more a forum for determining guilt than a place for focusing on the court's original mission of rehabilitation.

The juvenile drug court has therefore been designed to fill this gap by providing immediate and continuous court intervention that includes requiring both the child and the family to participate in treatment; submit to frequent drug testing; appear at regular and frequent court status hearings; and comply with other court conditions geared to promoting accountability, long-term sobriety, and development of pro-social skills; as well as, of course, requiring the cessation of criminal activity and drug use. Enhancements introduced by the juvenile drug court to the traditional court process for handling these types of cases have included: (1) immediate intervention (as soon as possible after initial detention) by the court and continuous supervision of the progress of the juvenile and his/her family by the judge, including frequent (often weekly) status hearings of participants before the drug court judge; (2) development of an individualized program of treatment, counseling, social services, skill building, academic support, and other services that addresses the *family*'s needs as well as the child's; (3) judicial oversight and coordination of the treatment and other support services provided to promote accountability and reduce duplication of effort; (4) immediate response by the court to the ongoing as well as emergency needs of the child and his/her family and to noncompliance by either the child or the family with the court's program conditions; and (5) judicial leadership to bring together the schools, treatment resources, public health services, social services, and other community agencies to work together to achieve the drug court's goals.[5]

STRUCTURE, PROCESS, AND SERVICES

The Judge

The judge is central to the juvenile drug court program. The judge not only oversees the child's performance and progress and that of his/her family but has also been critical in bringing together all parts of the program—those within the criminal justice system as well as those associated with community, educational, public health, mental health, and other resources needed to support the child and his/her family's progress. In many instances, these component parts had never previously worked constructively together.

Juvenile Drug Court "Team"

The representatives of the multidisciplinary services upon which the juvenile drug court relies comprise the drug court "team." The judge is the key leader of the juvenile drug court team, overseeing not only the juvenile's performance and that of his/her family but also the coordination and delivery of treatment and other core services managed by the various team members. These services include those within the juvenile justice system and those associated with community, educational, vocational, public health, mental health, and other prosocial resources needed to help the participating youth develop the skills and competencies needed to lead productive, drug-free, and crime-free lives. While the judge is the key leader for the juvenile drug court program and retains ultimate decision-making authority, the team members work together collegially, drawing on the perspectives and expertise of the members: the judge, prosecutor, defense attorney, treatment provider, case manager, family therapist, probation official, law enforcement official, school representative, and others involved in the provision of treatment and other support services to the juvenile and his/her family. Most juvenile drug courts conduct "staffings" prior to each drug court hearing at which the team members meet to discuss issues that have arisen in each participant's case to agree on appropriate responses by the Court to both progress and problems. The team recommendations discussed at these staffings are then generally followed by the judge at the court status hearing with the participant, consistent with the requirements of due process.[6]

ADJUDICATION PROCESS

The key elements introduced by juvenile drug courts to the traditional juvenile case process are the following: (1) gathering of comprehensive information at intake relating to the youth's situation, including information relating to the youth's family situation, drug use, school situation, personal goals, skills, medical and psychological history, and related information versus simply focusing on the nature of the offense charged; (2) use of information gathered at intake to develop an individualized plan for service delivery, which is updated periodically as the needs of the youth and his/her situation change versus simply using intake information for disposition purposes; (3) gathering of intake information by professional staff skilled in assessing adolescent needs versus by clerical staff recording the information provided; (4) frequent court hearings for six or more months to assess the youth's progress and make adjustments in his/her plan for treatment and other services, as needed, versus one or two court hearings to determine involvement and case disposition.

Most juvenile drug courts have been post-adjudication programs that operate after the youth has been determined "involved" (e.g., "guilty"). The frequency of the post-adjudication, rather than pretrial diversion, model for juvenile drug courts reflects the recognition early on that the post-adjudication model provided the court with more extensive authority and options if the child failed to comply with program conditions. The case disposition process, however, has been generally designed to promote suspending a sentence of commitment, deferring sentencing, and/or striking the finding of "involved" and dismissing the charge altogether, if the juvenile successfully completed the program.

ELIGIBILITY REQUIREMENTS AND TARGET POPULATION

For each jurisdiction, the process for determining the juvenile drug court's target population has centered upon deciding how best to apply limited resources to the youth who will be most effectively able to utilize them. As with adult drug courts, there has been concern that the populations targeted for participation not be dictated by desires to achieve high "success" rates, and that programs focus, rather, on children with more serious problems who can benefit from the intensive services and supervision the program provides. Given this concern, most juvenile drug courts, at least initially, focused on juveniles charged with nonviolent offenses who displayed moderate to heavy substance use, who demonstrated the absence of "protective factors" that might promote pro-social development without the court's intervention, and who did not pose a danger to the community.[7] The first two criteria could be addressed through the use of appropriate screening instruments. However, the third criteria—determining a youth's potential danger to the community—has frequently presented a greater challenge to juvenile drug courts than to their adult counterparts because little historical information regarding a youth's propensity for violence is generally available for many of the youth brought before the juvenile court who might otherwise be eligible for program participation. Determining a youth's propensity for violence has been further complicated by confidentiality requirements that inhibit the exchange of information regarding a youth's prior activities, including acts of violence. Many programs have therefore appeared to err on the side of caution, focusing primarily on those youth who *appear* to pose no danger to the community by whatever criteria they deem appropriate.

TREATMENT, CASE MANAGEMENT, AND OTHER CORE SERVICES

Juvenile drug courts are designed to provide a wide range of treatment and other services that are specially tailored to the developmental needs of the participating youth. All actions taken by juvenile drug court—judges, treatment staff, and others—are designed to have therapeutic value: those services or activities that promote competency development (e.g., writing, computer literacy, artistic skills, etc.), sanctions imposed for noncompliance, and the ongoing interaction between treatment and court processes. Among the special attributes of juvenile drug court treatment services include: (1) early and ongoing assessment of the juvenile and his/her family situation to develop an individualized plan for treatment and other services; (2) special attention to ensure the provision of developmentally based, gender-specific, and culturally appropriate treatment and other core services; (3) significant focus on family therapy and other services to assist and improve the capacity of the family and juvenile to work together to achieve program goals; (4) sustained attention to each juvenile participant's school performance, peer relationships, and development of competencies and self-esteem; and (5) ongoing case management to ensure that the program services meet each participant's current and evolving needs.[8] In many instances, treatment or other services and support for juvenile drug court participants may be necessary beyond the period of the court's jurisdiction, so the availability of aftercare services is vital.

Monitoring and Supervision

The hallmark of juvenile drug courts is the intensive, continuous judicial monitoring and supervision of participants that provides both accountability and structure for all involved. Each member of the juvenile drug court team works closely with the juvenile and monitors his or her progress in meeting the court-imposed conditions of participation and goals established for participating youth (e.g., treatment program participation, school attendance, drug testing, community service, court appearances, etc.). The judge's frequent involvement and continual supervision is considered to play a paramount role in promoting improvement in the functioning of a participating youth and his/her family. Noncompliance by a participant as well as failure to provide services by a service provider is immediately detected and brought to the court's attention for prompt action.

STRATEGIES FOR MOTIVATING PARTICIPATING YOUTH: INCENTIVES AND SANCTIONS

As noted earlier, sanctions in the juvenile drug court are designed to be therapeutic to the extent possible and to promote each youth's ability to take responsibility, be accountable for his or her actions, and, where possible, promote skill development and, ultimately, the self-esteem and self-confidence to be able to develop into a responsible adult member of the community. Most drug court professionals agree that the hallmarks of any sanctioning and motivational scheme need to be consistency, predictability, and, when working with juveniles in particular, immediacy. Among the responses commonly used by juvenile drug courts to noncompliance with program conditions include: (1) imposition of or increase in curfew conditions; (2) requirement of additional community service hours; (3) assignment of an essay on a particular topic relevant to the youth's situation; and/or (4) increase in the frequency of court and/or treatment contacts and/or urinalysis. Positive rewards and incentives for compliance with program conditions are considered as important as sanctions for noncompliance. Examples of positive incentives that juvenile drug courts frequently use to recognize participant progress include: (1) promotion to a subsequent program phase with generally associated reductions in reporting or other requirements; (2) award of a gift voucher or ticket to a local sports or other event contributed by local merchants; and/or (3) presentation of a certificate or other token acknowledging the participant's accomplishments. The praise of the judge is, as always, also of immeasurable motivational value.

WHO ARE THE JUVENILE DRUG COURTS SERVING? AND HOW SUCCESSFUL ARE THEY?

Demographic Information and Reported Drug Use

During the first several years of juvenile drug court development, the Office of Justice Programs, U.S. Department of Justice's Drug Court Clearinghouse at American University, compiled information from operating programs regarding the volume and demographics of participating youth. The latest comprehensive information available, published in June 2001,[9] indicated that the majority of juvenile drug court participants were 15–17 years of age,[10] were male, and had completed grade 9 or 10 at the time of program enrollment. Slightly more than half had been enrolled in a mainstream school at the time of program entry; the rest were enrolled in an alternative school, studying for their GED, or expelled.

In terms of drug use characteristics, at the time of program entry, the majority of participants had been using drugs for two or more years and were between 11 and 13 years old when they first used drugs. Their first drug used was most frequently alcohol and/or marijuana, although most participants were also using a wide array of other drugs by the time of program entry.[11] Over 80 percent of reporting programs noted that at least some participants were taking prescription drugs for behavioral problems at the time of program entry. Over 60 percent of the reporting programs also indicated that most juvenile drug court participants smoked cigarettes.[12]

PRIOR CONTACTS WITH THE JUSTICE SYSTEM AND TREATMENT SERVICES: PARTICIPATING YOUTH AND THEIR FAMILIES

Most juvenile drug court participants have had at least one prior contact with the juvenile justice system prior to entering the juvenile drug court, with approximately one-third having had three or more prior contacts. In terms of prior treatment, however, almost 70 percent of the juvenile drug court participants had never received any treatment for substance use and many, if not all, were never previously screened for substance use. Although many drug court practitioners have observed that it was common for juvenile drug court participants to come from families with other members also involved in the justice system, only a small portion of the juvenile drug courts were able to produce data to indicate the justice system involvement of other family members. For those programs that could produce such data, the most frequent involvement was noted for siblings of the participants (32 percent) and fathers (26 percent) in criminal, including drug, matters.

Special Needs Presented

One of the most significant—and, perhaps, unanticipated—findings to emerge from the early years of juvenile drug court experience has been the significant mental health, emotional, and behavioral needs presented by the participants. These findings have been mirrored by other recent studies of adolescent mental health and substance usage.[13] Among the most serious special needs presented by juvenile drug court participants reported as of 2001, the last year in which any systematic reporting on the topic was conducted, the following were highlighted: (1) unhealthy peer relationships; (2) low sense of personal identify/self-esteem; (3) problems in family/living situation that needed to be addressed; (4) academic underachievement; (5) lack of meaningful community ties; and (6) depression or other mental health condition.[14] It has also been common for a juvenile drug court participant to become a parent during the course of program participation.

These underlying needs have made it apparent that, to be effective, the juvenile drug court must marshal and coordinate the provision of a wide array of services, and that the mix and intensity of these services will vary depending on the individual participant and his/her situation at any given time. The need for flexibility—within a structure of consistency—has therefore been critical.

Outcomes Reported

Like their adult counterparts, most juvenile drug courts have attempted to measure their impact primarily through evaluative information relating to drug use, rearrests, and, to a lesser degree, school performance.[15,16,17] In regard to recidivism, most programs have noted a marked reduction in recidivism for juvenile drug court participants while participating in the program compared, primarily, with various control groups studied. Most have also noted a marked reduction in drug use and extended drug-free periods for participants.

Practitioners, however, have struggled with determining the most significant indicia of program effectiveness and "success" over the longer term. Even measures of recidivism are of limited value since the period for program participation in most juvenile drug courts is a maximum of one year, with the active period for participating considerably less for most programs. Most participants then leave the jurisdiction of the juvenile justice system shortly thereafter, making possible subsequent criminal activity in the adult system difficult to readily trace.[18,19] It is therefore difficult to determine the longer term impact of juvenile drug courts on criminal activity once the participant is no longer subject to the juvenile justice system process.[20]

Among the "pro-social" indicia many juvenile drug court program officials reported informally in 2001 that suggest longer term impact were the following: (1) participants had improved relationships with their family; (2) provision of treatment for mental health or emotional problems was made; (3) participants were developing plans for the future; (4) participants had improved academic performance and/or involvement in school activities; and (5) participants had improved their nutritional habits.

OPERATIONAL AND PROGRAMMATIC ISSUES THAT HAVE EMERGED

Current Activity

As of June 2008, the bulk of the approximately 475 existing juvenile drug courts had been operating for at least several years, with relatively few (less than 10 percent) new programs having been implemented during the past two years. An additional 100 programs had reportedly suspended operations or planning efforts. The maximum participation level has generally not exceeded 20 at any one time, with most program enrollments substantially lower. While there has been no comprehensive compilation of information compiled on juvenile drug court activity since 2001,[21] anecdotally, enrollments appear to be dropping in many programs, resulting purportedly from a decline in referrals from prosecutors or other potential referral sources for no overt reasons.

Taking into account the development of juvenile drug courts since their inception in 1995, it appears that the growth and evolution of these programs occurred primarily during the early years of their implementation, spurred significantly by the comprehensive training and technical assistance provided through the Drug Courts Program Office (DCPO) of the Office of Justice Programs, U.S. Department of Justice. With the closing of the DCPO in 2002 and transfer of its responsibilities for juvenile drug courts to the Office of Juvenile Justice and Delinquency Prevention, these specialized training programs and comprehensive technical assistance services were substantially curtailed. Most current juvenile drug courts, with a few exceptions, are now operating at less than their former capacity and substantially modeled after the adult drug court model with few of the adolescent-specific innovations that marked their early years—holistic, therapeutic approaches using an array of treatment, experiential, skill-building, and other services geared specifically to address the range of emotional, mental health, drug use, academic, and other needs presented by the adolescent participants. This situation is likely the result of a number of factors, including the decline of the specialized training programs and comprehensive technical assistance services that had been made available during the early years that highlighted the special issues presented by adolescent substance users; frequent turnover among both judges and staff working with these programs; and the vicissitudes resulting from the unstable funding situation that has been a perennial problem even in the best of times.

What Have We Learned?

Without a doubt, the initial experience of juvenile drug courts has reinforced the perceptions of judicial system leaders who developed these programs regarding the complexity of factors that surround adolescent substance abuse and the urgent need for the juvenile justice system to devise a more holistic and intensive approach to address them. It has also brought to light a number of special issues that need to be addressed in order to fully realize the potential of the juvenile drug court concept and were not readily apparent at the start.

In terms of the premises upon which juvenile drug courts have been grounded —for example, the need for more coordinated, continuous, and holistic management of cases involving adolescent substance abuse—most juvenile drug court practitioners agree that the juvenile drug court model is clearly more effective in addressing the needs of substance-involved adolescents than the traditional juvenile justice process. It has proved significantly more capable of the following: (1) identifying and comprehensively responding to the individual needs of each juvenile participant; (2) promoting much greater access to and coordination of available social, medical, mental health, substance abuse, and other community services; (3) providing far greater supervision of juveniles in the community who are under the court's jurisdiction; and (4) building upon the "strengths" of the participating youth and their families—as well as taking into account their shortcomings—in the development of a support structure to promote their capacity to lead drug-free and crime-free lives. Like its adult counterpart, the juvenile drug court also offers the judge an effective and potentially satisfying role in the management of cases, often involving complex and long-standing family dysfunction, that have traditionally lingered or been recycled on the court dockets for months, and often for years.

Most jurisdictions that have implemented juvenile drug courts have previously established adult drug court programs. While officials involved with the implementation of the juvenile drug courts were aware that the juvenile drug court could not simply be modeled after its adult counterpart, a *true* understanding of the reality of what is entailed in developing an effective juvenile drug court program emerged for most programs only out of experience and experimentation.

This experience has underscored the critical importance of the following program elements.

(1) The entire program design and services must be geared to adolescents.

The juveniles in these programs are not "little adults." Cognitively, teenagers think differently from adults. Actual biochemical distinctions exist between the adolescent and the adult brain that prompt teenagers to take more risks than adults, including the risks involved in securing and using chemical substances. At a minimum, effective adolescent treatment services must, as follows: (a) be educationally appropriate to the reading level, educational level, and experience of the participant, who will frequently present deficiencies in academic achievement; (b) focus on the concerns of the participating youth, which are varied and may include many topics not related to their substance abuse; (c) address health issues presented by the participating youth, including those relating to physical and mental health issues and sexually transmitted diseases; (d) incorporate restorative justice[22] or community-based concepts, which view the youth as part of the community and promote the youth's sense of accountability to the community as well as to his/her family; (e) raise the participant's awareness of why he/she is in the drug court and why he/she is struggling to overcome drug use; and (f) provide a strong support structure to sustain the youth during—and after—the period of program participation.

Most juvenile drug courts have also found that, while the 12-step model is extremely effective in providing a support system for *adult* substance users, it has not had similar success with juveniles. Most adolescents do not see themselves as "addicts" and, with their minute-to-minute thinking, do not focus on the longer term consequences of their drug use upon which successful 12-step participation is premised. Juvenile drug court programs have therefore needed to find substitute "curriculum"[23] and community support networks for participants that can function for youth much as AA/NA programs do for adults.[24]

(2) Assessments of participants must be comprehensive and ongoing.

Assessments of participants must be comprehensive and ongoing in order to identify the range of substance abuse, physical health, mental health, family, and personal needs of each juvenile at the time of program entry and/or subsequently emerge during the course of program participation. Youth entering juvenile drug courts have presented a wide range of complex needs and problems, many of which are not readily apparent at the time of program entry. Assessments must therefore be comprehensive and continually updated. Programs report, for example, a significant frequency of children who have been physically or emotionally abused; who are taking prescribed medications for behavioral problems; who have below-level literacy skills and academic achievement; and/or whose immediate family members are involved with substances and with the criminal justice system. Many juvenile drug court participants are also dually diagnosed—for example, have co-occurring mental disorders in addition to their substance use. Often the nature and extent of their mental health problems does not become apparent until participants have been in the program for some time and/or have ceased their use of drugs. The life of an adolescent can also change significantly over a few months time in terms of his/her developmental, emotional, psychological, physical, and/or family situation. And, as noted earlier, it is not uncommon for a youth to enter the drug court as a *child,* only to also become a *parent* during the period of program participation.

(3) Programs need to provide incentives that motivate youth to change their outlooks and consequent behavior—even when these "incentives" are imposed as sanctions.

Recognizing that most youth who participate in a juvenile drug court program enter the program with very low self-esteem and little, if any, vision for the future, juvenile drug court judges and others involved with these programs are discovering the importance of capitalizing on opportunities to provide *incentives* to motivate youth to change. Even when sanctions for noncompliant behavior are imposed, it is important that these sanctions be structured, to the extent possible, as strategies for *motivating* the participant to comply with program requirements and reinforcing constructive behavior rather than simply *punishing* for noncompliance. Participating youth need to recognize that positive developments are or will be occurring in their lives *because* they are not using drugs. Tokens of accomplishment, praise from the drug court judge, or temporary relaxation of a program requirement, such as a curfew or status hearing attendance, take on a very special meaning to a youth who, despite his/her outward demeanor, may not see much worth to his/her life.

(4) Strengthening the family support structure is critical.

While working with families of substance abusers is important in almost every situation, it is particularly critical for juveniles. Most programs have come to recognize that, despite the best efforts of service providers to assist a juvenile in becoming drug-free, their work will likely be futile unless the family—the environment, however structured, in which the youth must function daily—is meaningfully involved with and actively participating in the program. This realization is generated, in large part, from the recognition that juvenile drug abuse and delinquent behavior are often symptomatic of a youth's personal, family, social, and peer problems that must ultimately be addressed if the youth is to be able to cease his/her drug use.

Practitioners recognize that dealing with families of substance-abusing youth presents complex issues, particularly in regard to the frequency with which the substance abuse of an adolescent is indicative of a multigenerational pattern of substance abuse within his/her family and the varying degrees of psychosocial impacts that this substance abuse has had. Although the court may have authority to compel parental participation in the program through statutory and/or contempt powers, the consensus of most juvenile drug court practitioners is that *persuasion* is the preferred means for constructively involving parents and/or other family members in this process.

(5) Programs need to provide participants with opportunities for skill-building and competency development, not simply drug treatment.

Many youth involved with substance use are found to have very low self-confidence and little self-esteem—factors frequently related to their substance use. During the course of program participation, many have also exhibited special talents in a variety of areas—art, music, creative writing, athletics, computers, for example—which they have never themselves recognized or developed. Activities aimed at promoting skill-building and competency development and that also capitalize on and promote development of the *strengths* of each youth are important to give him/her a reason to be drug-free and to sustain him/her as an adult. Most juvenile drug court programs therefore have developed an extensive array of experiential activities, such as art therapy, creative writing, athletic programs, computer training, modified "outward bound" programs, as well as vocational and job-readiness training and placement, that can both tap the talents of participating youth and provide them with a foundation for drug-free living once their program participation is ended.

(6) Ongoing training, retraining, and cross-training is critical for all involved in the program and at all levels.

Despite the degree of academic training and prior experience of those involved with juvenile drug courts, these programs represent a radical departure from traditional practice of the disciplines involved. The need for ongoing *practical* training and cross-training of practitioners working with the juvenile drug court at all levels cannot be overstressed. Training topics need to include addiction; pharmacology; recovery (as it applies to youth, compared with adults); adolescent development and the impact of adolescent developmental concepts on program design and communication; and cross-training on the roles and disciplines represented among the agencies comprising the drug court team. The absence of this training on any broad-scale basis during the past several years has been a major detriment to not only the growth of juvenile drug courts but the capacity to sustain the programs and services that had been developed early on.

CONTINUING CHALLENGES

The insights garnered during the early years of juvenile drug court experience have offered perspective as to what appears to work and what does not, providing a useful framework for further experimentation for those interested in further developing—and reinvigorating—the model. The following are but a few of the significant issues that still need to be addressed.

(1) Developing meaningful program goals and measures of program "success."

Despite the wide range of impacts achieved, adult drug courts have had a fairly focused primary purpose: reduce drug use and recidivism. If the adult program achieves these goals, the program is considered successful. However, because the youth participating in juvenile drug courts are at such a vulnerable developmental stage, most agree that juvenile drug courts must seek additional goals beyond those of reducing drug use and recidivism if they are to effectively break the cycle of addiction and criminal activity. Unless the youth become involved in activities that hold long-term promise of sustaining their efforts to be drug-free, many practitioners are concerned that their effort to stop using drugs while in the drug court program will not be sustained in the long run. What measures should a juvenile drug court program realistically seek to achieve in terms of behavioral change in participants in addition to cessation of drug use[25] and criminal activity? The following are those most commonly suggested: (a) improved academic performance, including graduation, attainment of a GED, enrollment in college, and/or enrollment in vocational training; (b) obtaining/retaining a job; (c) developing indicia of a healthy "lifestyle"; (d) association with a peer group whose activities and interests appear to reduce the likelihood of further drug and criminal justice system involvement; (e) meaningful participation in a school activity, hobby, or other constructive activity; (f) development of skills and competencies; (g) improved capability to manage stress; and (h) improved relationships with family members.

(2) Determining how to reach the youth who need the services of a juvenile drug court.

There has always been a great sense that juvenile drug courts are only touching "the tip of the iceberg." In part, the limitations of existing programs are due to resource shortages, both for general treatment and support services and for addressing the diversity of special needs presented by youth who are otherwise eligible for program participation. In part, they also call into question the eligibility and screening procedures that programs are using and the cultural relevancy of the services that are being provided. Juvenile drug courts need to analyze the demographic and other characteristics of the youth who are entering their justice systems and compare these characteristics with those of the participants who are entering and remaining in the juvenile drug court. To the extent significant differences emerge in any one category, these differences should trigger reexamination of program policies, procedures, and services.

(3) Getting the "family" involved.

As noted earlier, the experience of juvenile drug court programs has highlighted the need to focus on the family and environment of the juvenile.

Regardless of skill and training of service providers, it has become increasingly apparent that the programs cannot effectively deal with a youth's substance use and other behavioral problems without focusing on the family environment in which the youth functions. Almost all programs, however, have experienced frustration in getting families involved, even with the recognition that "family" must be defined liberally. The direction in which many programs have moved at one time or another has been to provide family services in the home—for example, "family focused" services.

The underlying philosophy of family focused services is to empower the family to address the needs of the juvenile as well as resolve the family's own problems related to those needs. Recognizing that families may be defensive, resentful, and distrustful of the court and the justice system, the court has needed to stress to the family that these services are designed to *support* the family and that the court and family are working together to help the child. Requirements need to be simple and expectations attainable.

The goals of most family intervention services being developed by juvenile drug courts to date have been the following: (a) to obtain an accurate picture of the family dynamics that may bear on a youth's behavior and that might not surface in a group setting or in court; (b) to identify the strengths of the family and the youth that can provide a foundation and framework for developing a support structure for the youth; and (c) to develop a strategy to empower the family to deal supportively with the youth during the period of the court's involvement and afterward. Although the family services components developed by juvenile drug courts have differed, they have shared common elements: (a) provision of a family caseworker, or therapist, to work with the entire family in the home several times each week for several months to help establish the changes in relationships and support necessary for the juvenile to meet the goals of the juvenile drug court program; and (b) efforts by the caseworker to identify—through *conversation,* rather than interrogation—the strengths and values within the juvenile's family and environment that can be built upon to support the youth's participation in the juvenile drug court program. Who are the influential members in the youth's life? What are the youth's interests? aspirations? What factors in the child's history need to be taken into account in dealing with his/her current needs? What "resiliency factors" are present in the youth and the family that can be capitalized on?

Practitioners will recognize that there will always be problems with which many families will be unable to deal and that, regardless of the effectiveness of the family support system, the program must also help the juvenile develop his/her own coping skills to sustain him/her in the long run. Nevertheless, it has become increasingly apparent that the family must be considered a primary resource for the juvenile drug court program because the family and the dynamics within the family frame the environment in which the youth must function.

(4) Determining how to motivate youth.

Regardless of the nature of services provided and incentives offered, the bottom line for most programs has been, how to motivate youth to want to change their behavior? To look beyond the moment to where they might be in six months or a year, let alone a lifetime? To get beyond the values of their current peers for whom the goals of the drug court may likely be in total opposition to their present lifestyle? There have been no easy answers. Most programs have experimented with a variety of strategies, some formal and some informal, many of which have already been discussed. In the long run, creating a stable environment that promotes trust, credibility, and respect, together with the confluence of intangible factors that comprise optimum *timing*, has been considered key.

(5) Developing agreement on what constitutes appropriate and effective treatment.

Juvenile drug court judges, in particular, have expressed the need to become informed consumers of treatment services for juveniles and families. What are the critical elements of programs and services they should look for? What are the "deliverables" these services should provide? While the characteristics listed earlier provide a framework for reviewing treatment services, what practical examples have been developed that illustrate their effective application? To date there has been little published for the juvenile drug court practitioner that can guide the development of sound juvenile drug court programs, drawing on "promising practices" or sound adolescent development theory.[26]

(6) Adapting drug testing protocols to juvenile drug court participants.

Drug testing is the cornerstone of drug court programs. Adult drug testing has been practiced for several decades in a number of settings. Drug testing of juveniles, however, is relatively new and must address a number of special issues relating to both their adolescent developmental and legal status. Most adolescents have a highly developed sense of privacy and perception of their bodily image. Many juvenile drug court participants have also been sexually or physically abused. Juvenile drug testing protocols and staff have therefore needed to take these factors into account. Most programs have recognized that, like any medical procedure, the testing process also needs to be explained to the participants at the outset.

(7) Dealing with dually diagnosed participants.

As has been the adult drug court experience, juvenile drug courts are finding that a significant percentage of participants have co-occurring mental health problems. As noted earlier, since the first juvenile drug courts were implemented, a considerable body of research has been published highlighting the widespread and serious mental health problems affecting adolescents, with adolescent depression common and adolescent suicide a leading cause of death. Adequately addressing the needs of these youth presents special challenges for juvenile drug courts. What type of services are needed and who will provide them?

(8) Addressing the role of gang involvement in program eligibility criteria.

Since their inception, juvenile drug courts have not developed consistent policies regarding the role a participant's gang involvement should play in determining program eligibility. This situation continues. During the early period of juvenile drug courts, many programs looked toward the *nature* of the gang involvement rather than simply making a decision based on whether or not a potential participant had gang ties. With the increasing participant selectivity that now appears to characterize juvenile drug courts, it is likely that youth with gang affiliations are not considered eligible for most programs. If this situation is, in fact, the case, it is extremely unfortunate since at least some of these youth may be prime candidates to benefit from the drug court and the opportunity to turn their lives around.

(9) Determining how to address peer pressures.

Peer ties for an adolescent are extremely strong—in many ways much stronger than for the adult drug court participant. Simply telling an adolescent that he or she must find new friends who do not use drugs and who share the goals of the drug court has very limited effect. Nurturing the youth's involvement in constructive activities and with individuals who can reinforce positive values requires substantial efforts on the part of drug court practitioners, continuous reinforcement—and patience.

(10) Determining the optimum length for program participation.

The adult drug court model has generally required 12–15 months or more of participation. Many juvenile drug courts started out with that required time frame as well. But is that too long a period in a youth's life? Should the required period of participation be, for example, half that period? Should program services be structured in terms of dealing with acute issues and then following up with less intensive aftercare services? Most juvenile drug courts have now significantly reduced the period for intensive participation, to often six months or less. This may be adequate for adolescents, as long as follow-up services are available, as needed.

(11) Promoting cultural competency throughout all program components.

Recognizing the importance of defining "culture" in terms that include, but also go beyond, race and ethnicity, what are the earmarks of a *culturally competent* program? What indicia might suggest the need for improvements in this area? Are special issues presented for drug courts in rural areas versus urban in terms of the exposure of youth to street violence? economic and/or social isolation? What training do those involved with these programs need? Are juvenile drug courts attracting and engaging African American and Hispanic youth, particularly males who currently comprise such a significant proportion of the population under criminal justice supervision? Are changes in policies, procedures, services, and staff training, for example, needed in this regard?

(12) Interdisciplinary team building and dealing with the practical implications of "collaboration."

Juvenile drug court programs entail the working together of a myriad of legal, justice system, social service, educational, substance abuse, public health, and other agencies. Coordination of these various services and service delivery processes is particularly critical to prevent both fractured and/or redundant service provision. Despite the best efforts at collaboration, frequently territorial issues are also encountered. Who, then, sets priorities in terms of services that need to be delivered, particularly when the services needed for juvenile drug court participants and their families may be competing with the service needs of other clients in these agencies' caseloads?

As in the adult drug court model, there is also the continuing need for team building—sustaining the commitment of those who have already been involved with the program and getting buy-in from new individuals who come on line.

(13) Institutionalizing the juvenile drug court and dealing with changing local political situations.

Like their adult counterparts, juvenile drug courts have been addressing "institutionalization" issues from a variety of perspectives: developing acceptance from the court as a whole; obtaining funding sources to sustain them; developing the interagency collaborations to support them; and developing management information to provide evaluative reporting. Changes in local political situations, whether within the justice system or beyond, as well as turnover among judges, staff, and providers have frequently made these programs vulnerable.

THE FUTURE

As has already been noted, the vast majority of juvenile drug courts currently operating were implemented a number of years ago, with relatively few recently implemented or planned for the near future. Even those existing programs, while still operating, have suffered a marked decrease in the number of participants and many have lost the special adolescent focus, which is critical for any significant impact. Regrettably, the growth period for juvenile drug courts may have passed, or at least be in hiatus. The situation may, however, not be without its bright side.

The almost 15 years of experience with juvenile drug court program implementation has provided a sound foundation for validating the critical importance of providing youth involved with the justice system the holistic, therapeutic services and structure that have been the hallmark of the early juvenile drug court programs as well as for determining and documenting "best practices" and promising approaches. While national enthusiasm for juvenile drug courts currently appears to need a "jump start," with proper education and training, there should be receptivity not only for reinvigorating the "movement" but for expanding its strategies to the "young adult" populations of many adult criminal justice systems where these defendants display many of the cognitive, developmental, and other needs of adolescents still within the juvenile court's jurisdiction. These 18- to 25-year-olds (or younger if the state's adult jurisdiction applies at an earlier age)[27]—many of whom enter the justice system as a result of marijuana use—may otherwise fall through the cracks until their criminal justice system involvement becomes severe enough to attract the court's attention. This population would be a logical target for extending and reinvigorating the juvenile drug court model.

The present quandary, however, is how to effect this jump start. Perhaps our best hope is for judges to step forward across the country—as they did in the early 1990s at the start of the juvenile drug court "movement"—and take the lead in developing support for reinvigorating the juvenile drug court model and for broadening its expanse. If this occurs, there is great potential that the juvenile drug court can build on "lessons learned" and have a significant impact the second time around.

NOTES

1. Juvenile drug court participants have exhibited a range of substance use, including illegal drugs and alcohol as well as abuse of inhalants and other commonly available chemicals. A relatively high percentage of juvenile drug court participants have also reported the use of prescribed medications for mental health or behavioral reasons. See *Juvenile Drug Court Activity Update:* June 2001. OJP Drug Court Clearinghouse. American University.

2. Bureau of Justice Assistance, 2001.

3. In order of implementation: Florida, Nevada, Utah, Delaware, California, Illinois, Montana, Oklahoma, Missouri, Arizona, Kentucky, Washington, Ohio, Tennessee, South Carolina, New Mexico, Michigan, New Jersey, Iowa, Maryland, the District of Columbia, North Carolina, Virginia, and Louisiana.

4. Bureau of Justice Assistance, 2003.

5. Ibid.

6. While the juvenile drug court incorporates treatment and other services and conditions, it operates within the juvenile court process and must comply with constitutional and statutory requirements applicable to court proceedings.

7. Assessment of "protective factors" has focused on five areas: social bonding in school; social bonding within the family; self-confidence/self-concept; self-control; and evidence of a positive outlook on life.

8. Tribal Law and Policy Institute, 2002.

9. *Juvenile Drug Court Activity Update*. June 15, 2001. Office of Justice Programs (OJP) Drug Court Clearinghouse and Technical Assistance Project. American University. In June 2002, the Drug Courts Program Office of the Office of Justice Programs at the U.S. Department of Justice was closed, with responsibility for juvenile drug courts transferred to the Office of Juvenile Justice and Delinquency Prevention. Since that time, there have been no comprehensive compilations of programmatic or other information on juvenile

drug court operations and, for the most part, whatever information has been published regarding juvenile drug courts has been either published anecdotally on specific programs or in individual program evaluations, or as part of the follow-up information compiled on DOJ drug court grantees by the BJA Drug Court Clearinghouse at American University.

10. This statistic is derived from programs operating in the 38 states that have jurisdiction over juveniles until age 18. Three additional states relinquish jurisdiction over juveniles at age 16, and 10 additional states relinquish juvenile jurisdiction at age 17.

11. See *Juvenile Drug Court Activity Update*. June 2001. OJP Drug Court Clearinghouse and Technical Assistance Project. American University. At that time, the most common drugs used by juvenile drug court participants were reportedly alcohol, cocaine, and marijuana, with some programs also reporting methamphetamine use and prescription drug abuse. Since that time, a number of programs have anecdotally reported continued increases in the frequency of methamphetamine use and prescription drug abuse, along with that of other controlled substances and alcohol.

12. Bureau of Justice Assistance, 2001.

13. See, for example, *The Formative Years: Pathways to Substance Abuse Among Girls and Young Women Ages 8–22*. National Center on Addiction and Substance Abuse, Columbia University, February 2003; Monitoring the Future. *National Results on Adolescent Drug Use, Overview of Key Findings*. National Institute for Drug Abuse. 2005.

14. National Center on Addiction and Substance Abuse, Columbia University, 2003.

15. See *Recidivism and Other Findings Reported in Selective Evaluation Reports of Juvenile Drug Court Programs: 2000–Present*. BJA Drug Court Clearinghouse. American University. Last update: August 22, 2008. As referenced in that report, the juvenile drug courts in North Dakota are among the few that have systematically compiled a range of "impact" information on participants relating to subsequent school performance, family relationships, and other pro-social indicators.

16. Bureau of Justice Assistance Drug Court Clearinghouse, 2008.

17. Kevin M. Thompson, 2001; 2002.

18. One of the few evaluation efforts tracing juvenile drug court participants in the adult system was published in 2004 by Kevin Thompson of the University of North Dakota, focusing on North Dakota's juvenile drug courts.

19. Kevin M. Thompson, 2004.

20. In most states, the identifiers that can trace the criminal history of an individual through both the juvenile and adult justice systems are different. To determine longer term recidivism patterns across systems would therefore require special data runs and programming to match juvenile identifier information with adult information, which would be costly and therefore not conducted by most programs on any large scale basis.

21. See note 4 above.

22. "Restorative justice" is a concept that entails the use of dispositional strategies for criminal offenses that promote repair of the harm done to the community and/or individual victim by the offender.

23. Several programs reported positive experience using "The Seven Challenges" Curriculum, developed by Dr. Robert Schwebel, and geared to common situations and decisions adolescents encounter.

24. R. Schwebel, "The Seven Challenges."

25. A number of programs also preclude tobacco use.

26. One of the most valuable tools that has been published to date for juvenile drug court practitioners, particularly in terms of treatment strategies, is *Tribal Healing to Wellness Courts: Treatment Guidelines for Adults and Juveniles,* published by the Tribal Law and Policy Institute under a cooperative agreement with the Drug Courts Program Office, Office of Justice Programs, U.S. Department of Justice in 2002.

27. See note 6 above.

REFERENCES

Bureau of Justice Assistance. (2003). *Juvenile Drug Courts: Strategies in Practice.* Washington, DC: Office of Justice Programs, U.S. Department of Justice (NCJ 197866).

Bureau of Justice Assistance Drug Court Clearinghouse. (2001). *Juvenile Drug Court Activity: Update.* Washington DC: American University, from http://www.american.edu/justice.

Bureau of Justice Assistance Drug Court Clearinghouse. (2001, June). *Juvenile Drug Court Activity: Update.* Washington, DC: American University, from http://www.american.edu/justice.

Bureau of Justice Assistance Drug Court Clearinghouse. (2008). *Recidivism and Other Findings Reported in Selective Evaluation Reports of Juvenile Drug Court Programs: 2000–Present.* Last Update: August 22, 2008, from http://www.american.edu/justice.

National Center on Addiction and Substance Abuse. (2003). *The Formative Years: Pathways to Substance Abuse Among Girls and Young Women Ages 8–22.* New York: Columbia University.

National Institute for Drug Abuse. (2005). *Monitoring the Future. National Results on Adolescent Drug Use, Overview of Key Findings.* Ann Arbor, MI: University of Michigan.

Schwebel, R. (2008 last update). *The "Seven Challenges" Curriculum,* from http://www.sevenchallenges.com/About.aspx.

Thompson, K. M. (2001). *A Preliminary Outcome Evaluation of North Dakota's Juvenile Drug Court. Department of Sociology. North Dakota State University. Fargo, ND 58105.*

Thompson, K. M. (2002). *The Impact of North Dakota's Juvenile Drug Court on School Achievement. Department of Sociology. North Dakota State University. Fargo, ND 58105.*

Thompson, K. M. (2004). *An Adult Recidivism Outcome Evaluation of North Dakota's Juvenile Drug Court. Department of Sociology. North Dakota State University. Fargo, ND 58105.*

Tribal Law and Policy Institute. (2002). *Tribal Healing to Wellness Courts: Treatment Guidelines for Adults and Juveniles,* published by the Tribal Law and Policy Institute under a cooperative agreement with the Drug Courts Program Office, Office of Justice Programs, U.S. Department of Justice in 2002.

5

DWI Courts: Effectively Addressing Drunk Driving

DAVID J. HANSON

The development of specialized courts for dealing with offenders convicted of driving while intoxicated (DWI) or driving under the influence (DUI), sometimes known by other names such as sobriety, accountability, and wellness courts, arose after the efficacy of drug and other problem-solving courts had been clearly demonstrated.

The proportion of alcohol-related traffic fatalities has fallen from over 60 percent in the mid-1970s to about 40 percent in recent years. When calculated in terms of the number of vehicles on the road, vehicle miles traveled, or number of licensed drivers, the proportion has been cut in about half since the early 1980s. Nevertheless, over 15,000 people are still killed each year in alcohol-related crashes, several thousand of which involve intoxicated drivers.[1,2]

The first DWI court in the United States was established in New Mexico's Dona Ana County in 1995. The number has been growing rapidly and there were about 396 such courts operating in 2008.[3]

The need for DWI or DUI (hereafter referred to as DWI) courts is obvious. Every single injury and death caused by drunken driving is totally preventable. Unfortunately, in spite of great progress, alcohol-impaired driving remains a serious national problem that requires continuing efforts.

Most drivers who have had something to drink have low blood alcohol content or concentration (BAC) and relatively few are involved in fatal crashes. On the other hand, while only a few drivers have BACs higher than 0.15, a much higher proportion of those drivers have fatal crashes.[4]

- The average BAC among fatally injured drivers is 0.16.[5] That is, it is twice the maximum legal BAC limit for driving.
- The relative risk of death for drivers in single-vehicle crashes with a high BAC is 385 times that of a zero-BAC driver and for male drivers the risk is 707 times that of a sober driver, according to estimates by the Insurance Institute for Highway Safety.[6]
- High BAC drivers are disproportionately male, aged 25–35, and have a history of DWI convictions and polydrug use.[7]

DWI offenders tend to fall into two categories. Some have made a poor decision and driven after having had too much alcohol to drink. These drivers tend to have relatively low BACs. They are usually dissuaded from committing the crime in the future by punishment. The second category is offenders addicted to alcohol (alcoholics) who are hard-core repeat offenders. These drivers tend to offend with very high and dangerous BACs. They are very resistant to changing their drunken driving behavior.[8]

DWI courts apply the successful drug court model to alcohol-impaired drivers. They reflect the experience that society cannot rely solely on punishment to solve a serious social problem rooted largely in a medical problem—addiction to alcohol. The traditional approach of relying on punishment without treatment and accountability has proven to be largely ineffective with repeat offenders. As one judge observed, we cannot "jail our way out of the problem." These courts address the problem by holding offenders to a high level of accountability, providing long-term, intensive treatment, and carefully monitoring offender behavior for compliance.[9]

DWI courts can play an important role in reducing traffic crashes, fatalities, and deaths. As another judge said, "When a hardcore drunk driving offender comes before the judiciary system and is found guilty of DWI, it may be one of the only opportunities for the system to address the reasons for the offender's recidivism."[10]

Ten basic principles guide DWI courts. These courts, as we will see, are both similar to and different from drug courts. DWI courts rely on coercive treatment, a complex issue. Several promising or effective DWI court practices have been identified. Comprehensive sentencing is an important component of these courts. While DWI courts have been shown to be more effective than traditional criminal justice ways of handling drunk drivers, evaluations of DWI and other problem-solving courts need to be done carefully in order to be useful. Educating the public about DWI courts may lead to these courts having greater future support.

BASIC PRINCIPLES FOR DWI COURTS

The National Drug Court Institute has identified ten guiding principles for DWI courts.

First Principle: Identify Target Population.[11] The first principle is to carefully identify the target population to be included in the court program. It is important that the target population be clearly identified with specific criteria that are listed. The overall goal is to identify those individuals who constitute a threat to the community by having significant violation and substance dependency/abuse histories and to change those behaviors.

Because DWI courts are a new, innovative, and major departure from traditional criminal courts, it is essential to gain community support through outreach to stakeholders including law enforcement agencies, prosecutors, elected officials, activist and victim advocate groups such as Mothers Against Drunk Driving (MADD), substance abuse treatment groups, and others. Although it may be virtually impossible to achieve consensus with such a large group, the process increases broad community support for the new court. The result of such outreach is often the formation of a steering or policy advisory committee from the community in connection with the DWI court.

Loeffler and Wanamaker assert that

> One overriding concern is paramount in the selection of a target population: *community impact.* Taking this one concern into account means accepting those offenders into the DWI court program who are having the most negative impact on the community, and who are seen as wanting to alter their impaired driving behavior to achieve more positive results. Accordingly, DWI Courts should target primarily repeat offenders with serious alcohol/drug dependences or addictions.[12]

Although a few DWI courts focus on first-time offenders, there are several problems associated with this approach. One is that most first-time offenders who are apprehended are dissuaded from further violations as a result of their unpleasant experience. Therefore, using a DWI court to deal with them may not be a wise deployment of scarce financial and human resources.

Another problem is that by focusing on first-time offenders, a DWI court reduces its positive impact on improving community road safety. This is because it is the hard-core repeat offender who causes a large and disproportionate share of vehicular crashes and other problems associated with alcohol abuse.

Finally, most first-time offenders will not be addicted to alcohol, which is the problem for which DWI courts are best suited to deal. On the other hand, some communities may decide that there are hard-core recidivists whose crimes have been so numerous and led to such serious injury or death that they need to be incarcerated in order to protect society. In that case, it may be wise for the DWI court to exclude by its criteria these most serious criminal offenders.

Eligibility criteria can refer to either characteristics of the offender or characteristics of the offense. Offender characteristics would be personal factors such as age, education, employment history, and status as an alcoholic. Offense characteristics would be the nature and number of specific offenses that have brought the offender into the criminal justice system.

DWI courts need to decide what combination of offender and offense characteristics describes those they believe would most protect the community and with whom they can be most effective in rehabilitating. It is important that courts not attempt to deal with more clients than their resources permit.

Second Principle: Perform a Clinical Assessment.[13] Determining eligibility is only the first step in accepting offenders into a DWI court's program. It is next necessary to conduct a clinical assessment of the individual, including alcohol abuse severity, any drug abuse or illegal drug involvement, medical health, mental/psychiatric health, employment history, financial status, family and social status, alcohol triggers and beliefs, motivation for change, self-efficacy or confidence in the ability to abstain from alcohol and, if necessary, drugs, and level of treatment needed.

All of this is important for developing a clinically sound treatment plan. Conducting an adequate clinical assessment is essential because it helps identify an appropriate treatment care plan that focuses resources where they are likely to be the most effective both in changing behavior and in doing so efficiently and cost effectively.

Third Principle: Develop the Treatment Plan.[14] The third guiding principle is that "DWI courts must carefully select and implement treatment practices demonstrated through research to be effective with the hard-core impaired."[15]

Research suggests that there is no single approach that is best for all individuals, that treatment plans should be created from a diversity of approaches that have been proven effective, and that treatment plans should be tailored to meet specific clinical needs that have been identified.

Ideally, DWI courts would be able to provide motivational enhancement therapies, cognitive behavioral therapies, behavioral contracting, social skills training, community reinforcement, and marital therapy as needed. Research suggests that motivational approaches, cognitive-behavioral therapy, and aftercare are very important if not crucial for achieving desired long-term behavioral change.

Cognitive-behavioral therapies are based on the assumption that feelings and behaviors are based on cognitions, including thoughts and beliefs, rather than on externalities such as people, events, or situations.[16] The goal of motivational enhancement therapies is to help clients see the discrepancies between their current behaviors and personal goals that are important to them.[17]

Research evidence also suggests that the most important factor contributing to success is an environment in which participants remain in treatment for adequate periods of time. DWI court programs should be designed to provide such an environment through adequate structure. Well-chosen treatment interventions with high retention rates can dramatically improve positive behavioral outcomes.

Fourth Principle: Supervise the Offender.[18] Repeat DWI offenders are a major threat to public safety. Therefore, close supervision and monitoring by the DWI court is essential as part of a coordinated program to reduce recidivism and to protect the public from harm. Court personnel must closely monitor the behaviors of DWI offenders and that monitoring must extend into the community, including offenders' homes and work environments. Monitoring can also involve the use of risk screeners and assessments to evaluate the effectiveness of treatment as well as through technological methods such as alcohol breath testing, drug testing, and ignition interlocks.

It is essential that offenders clearly and unambiguously understand what is required of them to follow the orders of the court as well as the specific consequences of noncompliance. Requiring offenders to appear before the court on a weekly basis maintains pressure on them to follow the orders of the court and to behave in a positive manner. Both positive and negative reinforcements of specific behaviors as quickly as possible after they occur have been found important in promoting personal accountability among offenders.

Fifth Principle: Forge Agency, Organization, and Community Partnerships.[19] Establishing broad-based community partnerships is essential for DWI courts. They educate the public, increase cooperation and involvement of stakeholders, reduce opposition, enhance credibility, increase visibility, and help build political and economic support. They should be viewed as the foundation upon which DWI courts are built.

Obvious partners are law enforcement organizations, judges, prosecutors, defense attorneys, and alcohol addiction treatment providers. However, they might also include elected officials, victim advocate and anti-drunken driving groups such as Mothers Against Drunk Driving and Students Against Driving Drunk, hospitals and medical groups, 12-step programs (especially Alcoholics Anonymous), military bases, insurance companies, alcohol beverage trade groups, treatment groups, chambers of commerce, alcohol licensing agencies, departments of motor vehicles, highway traffic safety agencies and organizations, colleges and universities, schools, and educators.

Partnerships can usually be categorized as falling into one of the following models:

- The *Endorsement Model* consists of a list of endorsers who lend credibility and a base of support to the effort;
- The *Associate Model* is made up of groups or individuals who take a more active role, but one person or organization is responsible for making decisions, with occasional meetings to inform members; and
- The *Partner Model* shares power and active participation by partners including various groups and volunteers working closely together. (It is this model, with a horizontal decision making process, that best suits the DWI court setting.)[20]

Clearly identifying roles and responsibilities from the beginning of partnerships can reduce misunderstandings. Signing detailed memoranda of understanding or agreements with partners can avoid possible disagreements. Good communication will facilitate cooperation and commitment essential to delivering effective treatment and protecting the public.

Sixth Principle: Select a Strong Judicial Leader.[21] The judge obviously plays a central and vital role in the success of a DWI court. Therefore, the careful selection of the person to assume this leadership position is of utmost importance. Ideally, the judge selected would be one with extensive experience handling DWI cases, who has knowledge of substance addiction and associated problems, who enjoys an excellent reputation in the community, who has demonstrated skills as a strong leader and team builder, who is willing to work to obtain and increase funding and effectively work with community partners, and who is deeply committed to making the DWI court program successful.

In selecting the judge, it is important to remember that this person will be the keystone or lynchpin of the entire program. No other decision will be more important.

Seventh Principle: Develop Case Management Strategies.[22] Case management is the framework around which the DWI court program is built. Successful DWI courts need strong teamwork and collaboration among all components of both the criminal justice and addiction treatment components of the program.

> Case management is the series of inter-related functions that provides for this co-ordination and seamless collaboration and ensures that: (1) clients are linked to and guided through relevant and effective services; (2) all service efforts are monitored, connected, and in synchrony; and (3) pertinent information gathered during assessment and monitoring is provided to the entire drug court team in real-time.[23]

The task of the primary case manager is to ensure that all five core functions of case management are adequately performed. Those functions are assessing offenders, planning the treatment program, linking all parts of the criminal justice and treatment, monitoring offender progress or lack thereof, and advocating for both the offender and public safety. DWI court case management must be prepared to deal with the unique problems posed by the highly variable demographic, economic, age, and cultural characteristics of the offenders with whom it works. It must also be flexible and increase, decrease, or modify the nature of treatment interventions to support the progress being made and to reflect the offender's changing needs.

Eighth Principle: Address Transportation Issues.[24] Because virtually all states suspend or revoke the driving license of anyone convicted of DWI, and many states do the same based on alcohol breath machine results or refusal to submit to a breath or blood test at the time of arrest, every offender in the DWI court program will experience transportation problems. Although the program may be able to provide some very limited assistance under some circumstances, such as transporting them while they are still being incarcerated, it must emphasize to offenders that it is their responsibility to solve their own transportation problems and to do so legally. They must also realize that solving them by driving without having a valid license is strictly prohibited, will be monitored, and can lead to rearrest and other serious consequences. It is the DWI court's responsibility to address the transportation issue, but not to solve it.

Ninth Principle: Evaluate the Program.[25] It is important to evaluate the effectiveness of the DWI court program. Doing so can provide accountability, help increase public support, assist in obtaining or maintaining financial support, convince stakeholders and potential stakeholders of the value of partnering with the court, sustain the morale of program personnel, and provide data necessary to make improvements in the program.

Too often the need for evaluation is not recognized or is addressed only as the need becomes apparent. However, evaluation capability should be built into the program from the onset of its development. A credible evaluation program requires the involvement of a competent evaluator and a commitment from the program team members to conform to all requirements of the evaluation design.

Evaluation should identify the characteristics of offenders who had the best outcomes, those interventions that were most predictive of improved outcomes, and which offenders had better outcomes when exposed to which interventions. It should also distinguish between short-term and long-term outcomes of the program. Ideally, the evaluation design should randomly assign offenders either to the DWI court (experimental condition) or to a comparison (control condition) such as probation or adjudication as usual.

By taking into consideration the factors controlled by the program (for example, the characteristics of offenders treated and the types of intervention provided) and those not controlled by the program (for example, legal constraints and level of funding), the resulting evaluation will be more credible. Team members should view any negative findings as providing the opportunity to modify the program to improve its effectiveness. As a practical matter, it is also important to understand the concerns and types of data of interest to those who are able to affect the future of the program and to plan the collection of data and reporting of results accordingly.

Tenth Principle: Create a Sustainable Program.[26] A sustainable program is one that demonstrates that it is effective and efficient in reducing the problem of DWI in the community and that it should remain an integral part of continuing to reduce that problem and improve public safety. It will then have strong public support and the continuing cooperation of numerous stakeholders.

Developing a sustainable program requires careful planning. This includes identifying human, organizational, and financial resources; determining the appropriate structure and size of the program; selecting effective leadership; creating sustainable collaborative partnerships with stakeholders; setting administrative standards; establishing assessment and treatment protocols; and developing an evaluation design. Planning for sustainability may mean progressing slowly while reducing resistance from within the community, especially from potential partners and other components of the criminal justice system.

Once established, the program should continue involving partners and sharing credit for successes with them, widely disseminating evidence of success and publicizing the findings from program evaluations, and maintaining the morale and motivation of DWI court team members.

DWI COURTS, DRUG COURTS, AND DWI/DRUG COURTS

DWI Courts, hybrid DWI/Drug Courts, and Drug Courts all operate on the same general organizational, treatment, and philosophical model. Although they all typically require that offenders plead guilty to the legal charges against them before acceptance into the treatment program, DWI and DWI/Drug Courts limit their target population to those arrested for impaired driving and a history of impaired driving arrests. Among the differences between Drug Courts and DWI Courts are the following:[27]

- Drug Courts frequently have diversion programs, whereas DWI Courts rarely do because of the desire to prevent DWI offenders from reoffending and threatening public safety. It is also important not to let DWI offenders avoid having the crime on their record.
- Drug Courts are nonadversarial, whereas DWI Courts maintain an adversarial and coercive component because of mandatory sentencing laws and public pressure for severe punishments.
- Drug Courts tend to be incentive-oriented, whereas DWI Courts tend to be more punishment-oriented.

Although there is often considerable overlap between drug and DWI offenders, there are good reasons for operating separate DWI Courts.[28] Such courts generally:

- exist to reduce the DWI problem rather than divert offenders out of the judicial system,
- concentrate on impaired driving and its consequences,
- provide a specialized treatment focus,
- coordinate the activities of resources available to address DWI including DWI victims as victim advocates in the treatment process,
- unify in one locus the accountability of DWI offenders,
- serve as visible evidence of community commitment to deal seriously with the crime of DWI,
- protect public safety by effectively preventing DWI offenders from driving and committing additional DWI offenses,
- coerce alcohol-addicted DWI offenders into effective long-term treatment and rehabilitation, and
- are in a stronger position to provide comprehensive sentencing.

COERCIVE TREATMENT

Coercive treatment is often contrasted to noncoercive or voluntary treatment. However, coercion and voluntary treatment do not exist as dichotomies but as points on a continuum.

National survey data on individuals who entered treatment for alcohol problems found that few did so without pressure from family or friends.[29] In addition to marital and social pressures, there are also economic, career, health, and legal contingencies that can operate, often in varying combinations of importance to the individual. Employee Assistance Programs (EAPs) are usually seen as voluntary programs although a suggestion from a supervisor to participate may not be seen as entirely voluntary by the employee in question. Seeking treatment because of a serious health problem resulting from alcohol abuse may similarly be seen as voluntary, although a client or patient may not view it as such.

Surprisingly little is known about the relationship between coerced versus noncoerced treatment for alcohol abusers. This largely results from methodological problems. For example, studies of DWI offenders that may compare the outcomes of different treatments do not provide evidence of the outcomes of coerced compared to noncoerced offenders.

A study finding that an EAP program yields better outcomes compared to a court-mandated DWI treatment program provides virtually no evidence concerning coerced versus noncoerced treatment. Not only is the degree of coercion different but so are the desired outcomes. The EAP program may seek improved job performance or perhaps reduced alcohol consumption (frequency, quantity, etc.). On the other hand, the court-mandated program may seek a lower recidivism rate and may or may not be concerned about alcohol consumption *per se*. In addition, there may be many other differences such as the treatment strategies used, the demographics of those being treated, and their motivations for participating.

It is not at all surprising that research on the subject of coercion and outcomes yields conflicting findings. The methodological problems in the research studies are so serious that it is difficult to draw conclusions with confidence. Alcoholics Anonymous (AA) is a commonly used component of DWI court programs. However, the role of this self-help group in coercive treatment is controversial.

It is the belief of AA that for it to be effective, attendees or members must have "hit bottom" (reached a point of despair and helplessness with their addiction and its effects on their lives) and have a sincere desire for change. Many repeat DWI offenders will not have hit bottom, will insist that they are not alcoholic, and will resent being coerced into attending AA meetings. AA members tend not to be sympathetic to such offenders, whose hostility sometimes results in their being disruptive at the 12-step meetings.[30] There is evidence that mandated AA participation does not reduce DWI recidivism, and there is research evidence that "forced AA attendance may be worse than no treatment."[31] AA has officially recognized some of these issues and issued guidelines for cooperating with the criminal justice system including evidence of offender attendance at meetings.[32]

SPECIFIC PRACTICES

Court Monitoring

DWI courts typically encourage community residents and activist organizations such as Remove Intoxicated Drivers and MADD to participate in the adjudication process and monitor the actions of the courts. There is some evidence that court monitoring leads to higher conviction rates and more severe punishments.[33]

Court monitoring may also increase the consistency of sentencing. Many DWI offenders avoid the intended consequence of the law by plea bargaining. However, inconsistency of sentencing can occur for many reasons. Some judges may believe that the prescribed sentence is too harsh, jails may be full, or charges may be dropped because the BAC recorded is not significantly above the maximum legal limit. Of course, consistency in sentencing must always be tempered by the desirability of tailoring sanctions and treatment programs to meet both the needs of the community and the rehabilitation of the individual offender.

To promote court monitoring, some organizations have developed guides or handbooks to help volunteers become effective monitors. For example, the DWI Resource Center in New Mexico publishes and distributes a free *Court Monitoring Handbook* for residents. Included are guidelines for court decorum, a description of the state court system, an explanation of the criminal process, a discussion of sentencing, and generalizations about effective sanctions and treatment.[34]

Staggered Sentencing

Staggered sentencing is an innovative technique that has been found very effective in reducing recidivism. It has four key components:[35]

1. *A staggered incarceration period.* Under this program, the court places the offender on probation for several years and orders the executed period of incarceration to be served in two or more installments during that period.

   Those installments are spaced several months to one year apart, and the offender is given specific dates to report for incarceration. The first incarceration period begins immediately.

2. *Active participation by the offender.* If the offender can remain abstinent and is involved in a sobriety group (such as Alcoholics Anonymous), the offender can file a motion about one month before the next scheduled jail date to request forgiveness of all (or a portion) of the next period of incarceration (can also request to have a segment of the alcohol monitoring period forgiven or reduced).

   An offender who does not file a motion must serve the next incarceration segment as scheduled. A failure to appear to serve an incarceration segment would be a probation violation and could result in additional sanctions being imposed.

3. *Remote electronic monitoring* is ordered at the initial sentencing, usually in segments of 30 days per year, with frequency and timing determined by the specific circumstances of the offender. The monitoring results are weighed heavily in subsequent hearings.

4. *Clearly articulated consequences for specific violations* are laid out at the initial sentencing. For example, usually an offender is informed that any arrest for a new DWI violation will result in the revocation of the person's probation and immediate incarceration for the entire period of stayed sentence remaining.

Dedicated Detention Facilities

Dedicated DWI offender detention facilities combine incarceration in combination with supervised alcohol abuse treatment. Such dedicated detention facilities typically provide incarceration for periods ranging from 14 to 90 days. Some DWI jails are similar to residential treatment programs, whereas others are primarily traditional jails with a strong emphasis on treatment.[36]

Plea Bargaining

Plea bargaining agreements are a common practice in the judicial system and reduce the time and expense that would otherwise be devoted to trials. However, plea bargains that reduce the charges against a DWI defendant to that of a non-alcohol-related offense such as reckless driving are common but undesirable. They permit a defendant to escape proper identification as a DWI offender, and a subsequent arrest for DWI may mistakenly be considered a first such offense. Thus, the offender avoids appropriate punishment along with any potential deterrent benefit as well as any appropriate treatment for alcohol addiction.

Restrictions should be placed on plea bargaining to prevent such undesirable outcomes that compromise traffic safety. As one DWI Court judge observed, "You can't effectively treat people without knowing what they're bringing to the bench in terms of prior offenses and BAC levels."[37]

COMPREHENSIVE SENTENCING

Comprehensive sentencing is figuratively "building around the offender a box of combined sanctions, the only way out of which is changed conduct." To accomplish this, "a judge must approach sentencing by sizing up the offender correctly and building the right size and type of box, using the tools allowed by law."[38]

The National Association of State Judicial Educators urges judges to "build an effective sentencing box" by the following:

- strictly limiting plea bargaining,
- avoiding the use of diversion programs,
- implementing intensive pretrial supervision,
- requiring alcohol assessment and evaluation for all hard-core drunken drivers,
- utilizing presentence evaluation,
- avoiding lighter punishments,
- imposing significant fines,
- implementing measures to reduce failure-to-appear,
- utilizing vehicle sanctions,
- requiring the installation of ignition interlock devices paid for by offenders,
- utilizing "home arrest" with electronic monitoring and sobriety testing, and
- mandating aftercare.[39]

There are a number of actions that can facilitate the construction of "sentencing boxes." One such action is the expansion of blood alcohol education. Nationwide survey research has found that 70 percent of those questioned did not know the maximum legal BAC for driving.

Blood alcohol education should include information on the alcohol equivalence of standard drinks. Research has also found that most people do not know that standard drinks of beer (12 ounces), wine (5 ounces), and distilled spirits (1.5 ounces) all contain equivalent amounts of alcohol, specifically, 0.6 ounces. They do not understand that, to an alcohol breath estimating machine, they are the same. The importance of eating while drinking, of pacing drinks, and of other relevant information should also be included.

Laws specifying the period of time over which prior convictions for DWI can be considered for sentencing should extend them for a minimum of ten years and, preferably, abolish any time limit. The resulting information would be very useful in evaluation and assessment for both sentencing and treatment.

Essential for valid information about an offender's DWI conviction history is accurate statewide and interstate record keeping. This works to the advantage of the courts and traffic safety by preventing offenders from "slipping through the cracks."

More serious sanctions for refusing to submit to BAC testing would strengthen the ability of prosecutors to obtain convictions for DWI offenses in other states. Lawyers in some states advise drivers with prior DWI offenses to invoke their right not to take an alcohol test. That is because drivers are better able to defend themselves against drunken driving charges if there is no evidence of their BAC and the severe consequences of being convicted as a hard-core drunken driver outweigh the penalties for refusing. Increasing sanctions for test refusal would close this loophole.

Passing administrative license revocation laws would help protect the public from DWI until defendants come to trial. However, many offenders will drive without a valid license so mandatory alcohol ignition interlocks can be useful and are currently underutilized.

EVALUATION

There is substantial empirical evidence that drug courts are effective in reducing recidivism. DWI courts share many characteristics with drug courts and they might reasonably be expected to be effective as well. Although few DWI outcome evaluations have yet been conducted, those that have demonstrate effectiveness in reducing recidivism.

For example, 24 months after graduation from Georgia's DUI courts, participants were found to be almost four times less likely to receive a new DUI arrest than nonparticipants.[40] Similarly, an evaluation of DWI courts in three Michigan counties found that DUI court participants were significantly less likely than comparable offenders sentenced to probation to be arrested for a new DUI offense within two years. Participants in the DUI courts also averaged fewer numbers of reoffenses and remained arrest-free for significantly longer periods of time after leaving the programs.[41]

An evaluation of New Mexico's Bernalillo County Metropolitan DWI/Drug Court found that recidivism rates of court graduates were significantly lower than those who successfully completed probation.[42] Those violators who completed Idaho's Kootenai County DUI Court had a significantly lower recidivism rate than did those who failed to complete it; the program retention rate was 70 percent.[43]

Evaluation of DWI courts is essential both for accountability and for the facilitation of improvements. However, the quality of the evaluation research on DWI courts to date has been highly variable. This necessarily compromises the credibility of the findings. Therefore, it is important that all studies evaluating the effectiveness of DWI courts be of the highest quality possible given the available resources.

The gold standard of evaluation research is the experimental design, in which defendants are randomly assigned to an experimental condition (the DWI court) or to a control condition (a traditional court). Any differences in recidivism are analyzed statistically to determine if they are greater than would be expected by chance if the program had no impact at all. That is, it determines if any differences are statistically significant.

Quasi-experimental designs fall short of this standard of evidence and their conclusions command less confidence in their validity. A stronger quasi-experimental design might compare defendants in DWI courts to defendants in traditional courts whose characteristics are carefully matched. Weaker designs might match subjects but not to such a high degree of precision. Much less credible are the results of studies that simply compare defendants in DWI courts to those in traditional courts, including those who refuse to participate in a DWI court.

Randomization of subjects is important because it greatly reduces the possibility that alternative explanations are responsible for any differences between groups that are detected. For example, if there are socioeconomic, racial, ethnic, gender, personality, or other differences between groups being compared, those factors, instead of program differences, may be the reason for any differences observed.

Unfortunately, most programs in the field of criminal justice are either not evaluated at all or are evaluated with weak research designs that make drawing conclusions about program effectiveness very difficult.

THE FUTURE

The effectiveness of DWI courts is, in itself, not sufficient to ensure their continued expansion and growth. Although a national survey of trial court judges in 2008 did not specifically address DWI courts, it found that 75 percent approved of and reported being willing to use problem-solving techniques in their courtroom.[44] This finding is promising, but it also suggests the need for additional judicial education to reduce the resistance that remains.

The greater problem appears to be the lack of public information about DWI and other problem-solving courts. David Rottman of the National Center for State Courts has said,

> I don't think people know what a problem-solving court is—there's not much awareness of them among the general public. But when you describe the key elements of a problem-solving court, the public is overwhelmingly supportive.[45]

Taxpayers are the major source of financial support for DWI courts. Therefore, educating the public about the nature and effectiveness of DWI courts is essential for their long-term success. This is especially the case in times of general economic difficulties when budgets are strained. It is essential that DWI courts not be seen as "soft on crime."

A major need is for DWI courts to build evaluation processes into their ongoing activities. This makes evaluations easier and more economical to conduct.

Establishing a system of accreditation for DWI courts might be a way for effective courts to demonstrate their accountability to taxpayers and to garner greater support. This would give new meaning to the term "accountability court."

CONCLUSION

Hard-core repeat DWI offenders constitute a serious threat to public health and safety. Traditional efforts to reduce violations among this group have not demonstrated their effectiveness. However, the proven effectiveness of drug courts led to the development of DWI courts designed to apply the successful drug court model to alcohol-impaired drivers.

DWI courts reflect the recognition that society cannot rely solely on punishment to solve a serious social problem mainly rooted in the addiction to alcohol. They intervene to break the revolving door pattern of continual arrest and reviolations.

"Best practices" guidelines are now available to assist those who wish to establish DWI courts and to increase the effectiveness of court interventions. Although controversial, coercive treatment appears to contribute to the success of treatment. Planners might wish to consider promoting court monitoring, implementing staggered sentencing, instituting comprehensive sentencing, promoting the establishment of dedicated detention facilities, and promoting the elimination of plea bargaining.

Evaluating DWI court programs and their components is important both for accountability and for the improvement of outcomes. This is to the benefit of both court participants and the public.

NOTES

1. National Highway Traffic Safety Administration, 2008, p. 35.
2. Centers for Disease Control and Prevention, 2008.
3. Wallace, 2008.
4. Hanson, 2008.
5. National Highway Traffic Safety Administration, 2008, p. 35.
6. Lund, McCartt, and Farmer, 2007, p. 4.
7. Hedlund and Fell, 2007, p. 2.
8. Hanson, 2008.
9. National Drug Court Institute, 2008, p. 3.
10. National Association of State Judicial Educators, 2009, p. 10.
11. Loeffler and Wanamaker, 2006, pp. 2–5.
12. Loeffler and Wanamaker, 2006, pp. 2–3.
13. Devine, Huddleston III, and Marlowe, 2006, pp. 6–9.
14. Bell and Robinson, 2006, pp. 10–14.
15. Bell and Robinson, n.d., p. 10.
16. National Association of Cognitive Behavioral Therapists, 2008.
17. Miller, 2003.
18. Harberts and Waters, 2006, pp. 15–19.
19. Pfeifer, 2006, pp. 20–25.
20. Pfeifer, 2006, p. 23.
21. Kavanaugh, Howerton, Lawrence, and Wanamaker, 2006, pp. 26–29.
22. Monchick, 2006, pp. 30–32.
23. Monchick, 2006, p. 30.
24. Pickle and Wanamaker, 2006, pp. 33–36.
25. Marlowe and Monchick, 2006, pp. 37–41.
26. Jaeger and Reilly, 2006, pp. 42–47.
27. Tauber and Huddleston, 1999, pp. 6–7.
28. National Drug Court Institute, 2008.
29. Room, 2000.
30. Philips, 1998, p. 59.
31. Dill and Wells-Parker, 2006, 43–44.
32. Alcoholics Anonymous World Services, Inc., 1987.
33. Shinar, 1992.
34. DWI Resource Center, 2006.
35. National Association of State Judicial Educators, 2004, pp. 35–36.
36. National Association of State Judicial Educators, 2004, p. 29.
37. National Association of State Judicial Educators, 2004, p. 24.
38. National Association of State Judicial Educators, 2004, p. 11.
39. National Association of State Judicial Educators, 2004, pp. 21–30.
40. Judicial Council of Georgia, n.d.
41. NPC Research, 2008.
42. Guerin and Pitts, 2002; Stokes, 2005.
43. Crancer, 2003.
44. Yeung, 2008, p. 64.
45. Yeung, 2008, p. 64.

REFERENCES

Alcoholics Anonymous World Services, Inc. (1987). *AA guidelines: Cooperating with court, A.S.A.P., and similar programs.* New York: Alcoholics Anonymous World Services, Inc.

Bell, C., & Robinson, K. (2006). Guiding principle #3. Develop the treatment plan. In *The ten guiding principles of DWI courts* (pp. 10–14). Alexandria, VA: National Drug Court Institute. Available at http://www.ndci.org/pdf/Guiding_Principles_of_DWI_Court.pdf.

Crancer, A. (2003). *An analysis of Idaho's Kootenai County DUI Court.* Boise, ID: National Highway Traffic Safety Administration Region X. Available at http://www.ndci.org/pdf/Kootenai_County_DUI_Evaluation.pdf.

Devine, M., Huddleston, III, C., & Marlowe, D. (2006). Guiding principle #2. Perform a clinical assessment. In *The ten guiding principles of DWI courts* (pp. 6–9). National Drug Court Institute. Available at http://www.ndci.org/pdf/Guiding_Principles_of_DWI_Court.pdf.

Dill, P., & Wells-Parker, E. (2006). Court-mandated treatment for convicted drinking drivers. *Alcohol Research and Health, 29,* 41–48, 43–44.

DWI Resource Center. (2006). *Court monitoring handbook.* Albuquerque, NM: DWI Resource Center. Available at http://www.dwiresourcecenter.org/downloads/naap/CourtHandbook.pdf

Guerin, P., & W. Pitts. (2002). *Evaluation of the Bernalillo County Metropolitan DWI/Drug Court: Final report.* Albuquerque, NM: University of New Mexico, Institute for Social Research.

Hanson, D. (2008). DWI courts are effective in reducing DWI/DUI. *Alcohol: Problems and solutions.* Available at http://www.alcoholinformation.org.

Harberts, H., & Waters, K. (2006). Guiding principle #4. Supervise the offender. In *The ten guiding principles of DWI courts* (pp. 15–19). National Drug Court Institute. Available at http://www.ndci.org/pdf/Guiding_Principles_of_DWI_Court.pdf.

Hedlund, J., & Fell, J. (2007). *Repeat offenders and persistent drinking drivers in the U.S.* Washington, DC: National Highway Traffic Safety Administration.

Jaeger, N., & Reilly, D. (2006). Guiding principle #10. Ensure a sustainable program. In *The ten guiding principles of DWI courts* (pp. 42–47). National Drug Court Institute. Available at http://www.ndci.org/pdf/Guiding_Principles_of_DWI_Court.pdf.

Judicial Council of Georgia. (n.d.). *Research results: Georgia's DUI courts work.* Available at http://www.georgiacourts.org/courts/accountability/DUICourtRecidivism.pdf.

Kavanaugh, J., Howerton, P., Lawrence, K., & Wanamaker, J. (2006). Guiding principle #6. Take a judicial leadership role. In *The ten guiding principles of DWI courts* (pp. 26–29). National Drug Court Institute. Available at http://www.ndci.org/pdf/Guiding_Principles_of_DWI_Court.pdf. For consistency, "Take a Judicial Leadership Role" was changed to "Select a Strong Judicial Leader."

Kramer, A. (1983). The drunk driver: Where is he heading? The courts need a new sentencing policy to get the alcoholic offender on the right road to recovery. *The Judges' Journal, 36*(4), 8–11, 63–64.

Loeffler, M., & Wanamaker, J. (2006). Guiding principle #1. Determine the population. In *The ten guiding principles of DWI courts* (pp. 2–5). National Drug Court Institute. Available at http://www.ndci.org/pdf/Guiding_Principles_of_DWI_Court.pdf.

Lund, A., McCartt, A. T., & Farmer, C. M. (2007, August 26–30). Contributions of Alcohol-Impaired Driving to Motor Vehicle Crash Deaths in 2005. Arlington, VA:

Insurance Institute for Highway Safety. Presented at the joint annual meetings of the International Council on Alcohol, Drugs; and Traffic Safety and the International Association of Forensic Toxicologists. Seattle, WA.

Marlowe, D. (2007). *Recent studies of drug courts and DWI courts: Crime reduction and cost savings*. Arlington, VA: National Association of Drug Court Professionals. Available at http://www.isc.idaho.gov/dcourt/DC_Research_Update408.pdf.

Marlowe, D., & Monchick, R. (2006). Guiding principle #9. Evaluate the program. In *The ten guiding principles of DWI courts* (pp. 37–41). National Drug Court Institute. Available at http://www.ndci.org/pdf/Guiding_Principles_of_DWI_Court.pdf.

Miller, W. R. (2003). *Motivational enhancement therapy: Description of counseling approach*. Washington, DC: National Drug Institute. Available at www.drugabuse.gov/ADAC/ADAC9.html.

Monchick, R. (2006). Guiding principle #7. Develop case management strategies. In *The ten guiding principles of DWI courts* (pp. 30–32). National Drug Court Institute. Available at http://www.ndci.org/pdf/Guiding_Principles_of_DWI_Court.pdf.

National Association of Cognitive Behavioral Therapists. (2008). *What is cognitive behavioral therapy?* Available at www.nacbt.org/whatiscbt.htm.

National Association of State Judicial Educators. (2004). *Hardcore drunk driving judicial guide* (pp. 35–36). Williamsburg, VA: National Association of State Judicial Educators and the Century Council. Available at http://nasje.org/resources/HCDrunk/HCDrunkJudicialGuide.pdf

National Drug Court Institute. (2008). *DWI courts and DWI/drug courts: Reducing recidivism, saving lives*. Available at http://www.ndci.org/dwi_drug_court.htm.

National Highway Traffic Safety Administration. (2008). Performance measures. *NHTSA FY 2009 Budget Overview*. Washington, DC: National Highway Traffic Safety Administration.

NPC Research. (2008). *Michigan DUI courts outcomes evaluation final report*. Portland, OR: NPC Research. Available at http://www.npcresearch.com/Files/MI_DUI_Outcome_Evaluation_FINAL_REPORT_Re-Release_March_2008.pdf.

Pfeifer, J. (2006). Guiding principle #5. Forge agency, organization and community partnerships. In *The ten guiding principles of DWI courts* (pp. 20–25). National Drug Court Institute. Available at http://www.ndci.org/pdf/Guiding_Principles_of_DWI_Court.pdf.

Phillips, M. (1989). *The American criminal justice system and mandates to alcohol treatment: The role of Alcoholics Anonymous*. Berkeley, CA: Alcohol Research Group. Cited by Weisner, C. M. (2000). Coercion in Alcohol Treatment. Appendix D. In Institute of Medicine, *Broadening the base of treatment for alcohol problems* (pp. 579–609). Washington, DC: National Academy Press.

Pickle, M., & Wanamaker, J. (2006). Guiding principle #8. Address transportation issues. In *The ten guiding principles of DWI courts* (pp. 33–36). National Drug Court Institute. Available at http://www.ndci.org/pdf/Guiding_Principles_of_DWI_Court.pdf.

Room, R. (2000). The U.S. general population's experience with response to alcohol problems. Paper presented at the Alcohol Epidemiology Section of the International Congress on Alcohol and Addictions. Aix-en-Provence, France, June 7–June 12. Cited by Weisner, C. Coercion in Alcohol Treatment. Appendix D. In Institute of Medicine, *Broadening the base of treatment for alcohol problems* (pp. 579–609). Washington, DC: National Academy Press.

Shinar, D. (1992). Impact of court monitoring on the adjudication of driving while intoxicated (DWI). *Accident Analysis and Prevention, 24,* 167–179.

Stokes, J. (2005). *Traffic safety bureau supplemental follow-up report.* Albuquerque, NM: Bernalillo County Metropolitan Court. Available at http://www.ndci.org/dwi_drug_court.htm.

Tauber, J., & Huddleston, C. (1999). *DWI/drug courts: Defining a national strategy.* Alexandria, VA: National Drug Court Institute. Reprinted 2004.

Wallace, D. (2008, July 30). Personal communication. Alexandria, VA: National DWI Court Institute.

Yeung, B. (2008, August). Succor. Succor in the court. *Miller-McCune* (pp. 61–69).

6

Mental Health Courts: Cautious Optimism

PATRICIA A. GRIFFIN and DAVID DEMATTEO

Today, the interface between the mental health and criminal justice systems is the new frontier for innovative services and research in the community mental health field. The challenges of diverting hundreds of thousands of mentally ill persons from jail. . . .[1]

In recent years, there has been a dramatic proliferation of problem-solving courts across the United States. Rather than simply punishing criminal offenders, which contributes to an ongoing cycle of arrest, incarceration, release, and rearrest, these special jurisdiction courts emphasize dispositions such as mental health treatment, drug abuse treatment, the provision of social services, and ongoing judicial monitoring of offenders' progress. Moreover, many problem-solving courts provide for the dismissal of criminal charges and expungement of the offender's arrest record upon successful completion of the treatment program, which allows offenders to have a fresh start without the stigma of an arrest record. The theory underlying problem-solving courts is that criminal recidivism can be reduced if the problems presumed to underlie or fuel criminal behavior, such as drug abuse and mental illness, are treated with a wide range of services under the watchful eye of a court.

Often modeled after drug courts, which have been shown to be successful,[2,3,4,5,6] mental health courts emerged in the late 1990s to address the significant numbers of offenders with mental illness entering the criminal justice system. Although mental health courts tend to operate somewhat idiosyncratically, they share some common features.[7,8,9] Mental health courts facilitate access to community-based mental health treatment services for criminal offenders with mental health problems while providing judicial monitoring "to enhance offender accountability." [10] The underlying belief is that treating an offender's mental health problems through the provision of community-based services improves clinical functioning and reduces criminal recidivism. The first mental health courts in the United States were established in 1997 in Indianapolis and Broward County (Florida).[11] The most recent numbers from the National GAINS Center, funded by the federal Center for Mental Health Services to collect and disseminate information about effective services for people with severe mental illness and often co-occurring disorders involved in the justice system, indicate there are at least 182 mental health courts currently in existence.[12]

Given the recent proliferation of problem-solving courts, including mental health courts, it is important to have a clear understanding of the historical development of mental health courts, the attendant goals and philosophies of these courts, how mental health courts are organized and operated, and how these courts differ from traditional approaches used with criminal offenders with mental illness. Although mental health courts have been well received by many in the criminal justice and mental health fields, they are not without their critics. Several studies examining the effectiveness of mental health courts have yielded promising results, yet more thorough and better-conducted evaluations are needed. Specific areas are ripe for future research.

MENTAL HEALTH COURTS: DEVELOPMENT, GOALS, AND OPERATION

Adult Mental Health Courts

The most comprehensive and rigorous picture of the prevalence of mental health disorders in jail settings comes from the research of Linda Teplin and her colleagues examining individuals as they were admitted to Chicago's jail.[13,14,15,16] They found that 6.4 percent of males and 12.2 percent of females being admitted to jail met diagnostic criteria for the severe mental health disorders of schizophrenia, mania, and major depressive disorder. For both males and females with severe mental disorder, the rate of co-occurring substance use disorders was 72 percent. At mid-year 2005, which is the most recent year for which there are reliable statistics, 56 percent of state prison inmates, 45 percent of federal prison inmates, and 64 percent of jail inmates reported a recent history (i.e., within the previous 12 months) of mental health symptoms or problems.[17] As with many offenders, those with mental health disorders have often experienced a revolving door characterized by arrest, incarceration, release, and rearrest.[18,19] As this cycle gained increasing visibility over the past 10 years, the lack of adequate treatment and management for offenders with mental health needs within the criminal justice system became much more apparent.

One response of the criminal justice system to this bleak situation was the development of mental health courts. The first mental health courts were established in 1997 in Marion County (Indiana), Indianapolis, and Broward County (Florida).[20] At the beginning of 2005, 90 operational adult mental health courts were found in the United States.[21] Thirty-four states had mental health courts with Ohio having the largest number of courts. At the time 7,560 persons were under mental health court supervision. The number of active clients for each court ranged from 3 to 852, with an average of 36 per court. Forty-nine percent of the courts served primarily misdemeanors while 14 percent served primarily felony cases. In the past three years, the number of mental health courts has doubled to 182,[22] with more in the advanced planning and development stages.[23,24] Following in the well-paved footsteps of drug courts, a number of juvenile mental health courts have been developed in recent years.[25,26] Other countries have also adopted the mental health court model, including Canada, Australia, and the United Kingdom.

Most mental health courts do not begin in a vacuum. The majority of communities with a mental health court have preexisting drug courts. Many have other mental health diversion programs, such as the Crisis Intervention Team model for law enforcement.[27,28]

As will be discussed in this chapter, the body of research regarding mental health courts is growing, and there is some reason to be optimistic regarding the effectiveness of these interventions.[29]

As previously noted, most mental health courts borrowed their underlying philosophy from their prevalent and successful predecessors, drug treatment courts. The philosophy underlying both of these problem-solving courts is "therapeutic jurisprudence," which is the concept that the criminal justice system can act as an effective form of treatment for offenders while simultaneously ensuring public safety.[30,31,32] Mental health courts follow the principle of therapeutic jurisprudence by providing comprehensive and judicially supervised behavioral health treatment services to criminal offenders with mental health disorders.

Although mental health courts often differ quite considerably from one jurisdiction to another,[33] mental health courts typically share the same underlying purpose. Broadly stated, the purpose of mental health courts is to divert criminal offenders with mental health needs away from traditional criminal justice processing and into judicially supervised community-based mental health treatment.[34,35] The belief underlying mental health courts is that providing treatment to criminal offenders with mental illness will decrease the behaviors associated with mental illness that lead to involvement in the criminal justice system, thereby reducing the revolving door of arrest, incarceration, release, and rearrest. Other goals of mental health courts typically include reducing the inappropriate incarceration of offenders with mental health needs, relieving the burden on jails posed by inmates with mental health disorders, and reducing the psychiatric hospitalization of offenders with mental health disorders.[36] Additionally, many mental health courts often hope to save valuable criminal justice and mental health system resources.

Mental health courts typically follow one of three basic operational models,[37] which are similar to the models underlying drug courts. In the pre-adjudication model, the prosecution of the offender is deferred and, in return, the offender agrees to participate in a mental health treatment program. In the post-plea-based model, the disposition of the offender's criminal case is deferred while the offender participates in the treatment program. Finally, in the probation-based model, the offender is convicted and sentenced to probation, and participating in the treatment program is imposed by the court as a condition of the probation. To our knowledge, researchers have not yet examined whether these different operational models lead to differences in outcomes among mental health court clients.

Clients in mental health court programs are required to participate in mental health treatment, often provided by existing, community-based treatment providers that enter into a formal agreement with the courts and sometimes provided by treatment programs dedicated to serving the mental health court's population. Treatment often consists of individual and group counseling, the provision of appropriate psychotropic medications, and intensive case management with a social worker. Importantly, the client's progress in the treatment program is monitored on a regular basis by the presiding mental health court judge, and a series of escalating sanctions and rewards are used to punish the clients for program infractions and reward the clients for compliance with program requirements. Rewards commonly offered in mental health courts include verbal praise, reductions in treatment requirements, required attendance at fewer judicial status hearings, or gift certificates. Sanctions may include verbal reprimands from the judge, required attendance at more frequent status hearings, community service, brief periods of incarceration, or, in extreme circumstances, termination from the program.[38,39] Early studies found that the sanctions of brief incarceration and termination from the program were used infrequently in mental health court programs.[40] More recent research found that 92 percent of courts surveyed were "willing to use jail for non-adherence," although a third reported putting people in jail less than 5 percent of the time.[41] Courts with more frequent judicial hearings used incarceration as a sanction more frequently.

Mental health courts, as follows, typically: (1) consist of separate criminal court dockets for offenders with mental health needs; (2) employ a problem-solving approach designed to divert offenders with mental health needs from incarceration into community-based mental health treatment; (3) mandate and monitor the community mental health treatment; (4) provide continuing supervision through judicial status hearings and direct supervision in the community; (5) use a contingency management system in which escalating rewards and sanctions are provided for accomplishments and infractions; (6) require participation in the mental health court program to be voluntary; and (7) define specific criteria for when a participant has successfully completed the program.[42,43,44] Most mental health courts are established for the same primary reasons, which typically include a desire to provide alternatives to incarceration, increase public safety, facilitate the provision of mental health treatment in the community, improve the quality of life for offenders with mental health needs, and make more efficient use of criminal justice and mental health treatment resources.[45]

Other research regarding the common features of mental health courts suggests that mental health courts typically include a nonadversarial team approach that includes dedicated defense attorneys and prosecution attorneys, a designated judge that oversees all cases in the court, and the promise of dismissed charges upon an offender's successful completion of the program.[46,47]

A recent report on behalf of the Council of State Governments Justice Center[48] identified ten essential elements important to the design and implementation of mental health courts. This report was modeled after a similar report published in 1997 by the National Association of Drug Court Professionals that identified the ten key components of drug courts. Identified through interviews with former Bureau of Justice Assistance Mental Health Courts Program grantees, site visits to several mental health courts, and a review of the relevant literature, the essential elements to be considered in planning for mental health courts were the following:

- Planning and administration of the court should be guided by stakeholders representing various systems, including the criminal justice, mental health, and substance use treatment systems;
- Eligibility criteria for the mental health court should take into account public safety, the community's treatment capacity, and the availability of alternatives to pretrial detention for offenders with mental health problems;
- Potential participants should be identified, referred, and accepted into mental health courts, and subsequently linked to community-based mental health treatment providers in a timely manner;
- Terms of participation should be clear, promote public safety, facilitate the offender's engagement in treatment, be individualized to correspond to the offender's level of risk, and provide for positive legal outcomes for those who successfully complete the program;
- Potential participants must fully understand the program requirements before agreeing to participate;
- Mental health courts should connect participants to comprehensive and individualized community-based treatment;
- Efforts should be made to protect the confidentiality of participants' health and legal information;
- Criminal justice and mental health staff and service/treatment providers receive specialized and ongoing training;
- Criminal justice and mental health staff should collaboratively monitor participants' adherence to the requirements of the program, provide graduated incentives and sanctions for program accomplishments and infractions, and modify the treatment plan as needed to protect public safety and promote participants' recovery; and

- The effect of the mental health court should be evaluated periodically through the collection and analysis of data.

Despite similarities in general structure, describing a typical mental health court is not a straightforward task. Whereas drug courts tend to be quite similar across jurisdictions, both in terms of operation and structure, mental health courts exhibit greater variability.[49,50,51,52] For example, the methods used to ensure that offenders are appropriate candidates for participating in mental health courts differ considerably by jurisdiction. Although some courts require that offenders meet criteria for a specific mental health diagnosis prior to entry, other courts simply confirm a previous mental health diagnosis.[53,54] Some courts require clients to attend status hearings in court several times per week, while other courts require less frequent court appearances (either weekly or monthly). The available sanctions for noncompliance with program requirements also differ among courts. While some mental health courts simply ratchet up the treatment requirements in response to infractions, other courts resort to brief incarceration and/or termination from the program.[55,56] Finally, after successful completion of the program's requirements, some mental health courts dismiss the criminal charges, while other courts place the offenders on probation or impose a suspended sentence.[57,58]

The National Center for State Courts identified several variations among mental health courts, including the varying mental health and criminal offense criteria for program eligibility, the requirement of entering a plea before entering the program, terms of supervision, the use of sanctions in response to program infractions, and the methods used to dispose of a case (e.g., adjudication is withheld without entering a conviction, guilty plea is entered with credit for time served, conviction is entered and the sentence is suspended, deferred dispositions lead to dismissal of the criminal charges).[59] It is possible that differences in these criteria can have substantial effects in the operation and effectiveness of mental health courts, and future research should examine the effects of these differences on client outcomes.

Researchers examined case processing of seven mental health courts to better understand who gets referred to mental health courts and who ultimately is accepted.[60] There was wide variability in how cases were processed with time from referral to acceptance into the court taking from 1 to 47 days. Fourteen percent were accepted on the same day. For everyone else, acceptance averaged 32 days. Fifty-two percent of referrals were accepted. The main reasons for rejection from the court were lack of a mental health disorder meeting the court's eligibility criteria (30 percent), current or past criminal history (19 percent), rejection by the prosecutor (18 percent), and incompetent/unstable defendant (7 percent). Consistent with the research on other jail diversion programs,[61] persons accepted into the court were more likely to be older, White, and women than the general criminal justice population. Interestingly enough, this tendency occurred at referral rather than courts' acceptance.

Juvenile Mental Health Courts

A number of mental health courts specifically designed for juvenile offenders with mental health disorders have also been developed in recent years.[62] Recent statistics indicate that approximately 130,000 juveniles reside in juvenile detention facilities and correctional facilities throughout the United States.[63] Studies suggest that 65 percent to 70 percent of these juveniles have a diagnosable mental health disorder.[64,65] As such, adult and juvenile mental health courts share a similar impetus, and the emergence of mental health courts targeted at juvenile offenders is gaining momentum in the United States.

The first mental health court for juveniles was opened in February 2001 in Santa Clara County (California).[66] Since that time, approximately one dozen juvenile mental health courts have opened in other jurisdictions across the United States[67] and more than 20 additional jurisdictions are either currently considering or actively planning a juvenile mental health court.[68] Given the relatively recent development of juvenile mental health courts, the relevant literature is quite small. As such, the focus of the current chapter will be on research examining adult mental health courts.

There are some notable similarities in operation and structure between adult and juvenile mental health courts.[69] Much like adult mental health courts, juvenile mental health courts operate as a separate court docket from the standard juvenile court proceedings, and the mental health court cases are usually overseen by one judge. Juvenile mental health courts are typically administered by the juvenile court, although several juvenile mental health courts are administered by the probation department. In most juvenile mental health courts, the juvenile is referred to the court after adjudication, but prior to disposition. There is, however, some variability regarding the point of referral, with some courts following the preadjudication model and other courts functioning as an aftercare program for juveniles who are leaving residential treatment facilities following the disposition of their cases.[70]

As with adult mental health courts, juvenile mental health courts typically utilize a multidisciplinary team approach that often includes an assistant district attorney, public defender, treatment providers, case managers, and probation officers. Importantly, the judge is also viewed as part of the treatment team. The length of involvement in these programs ranges from 3 to 6 months on the low end to two years on the high end, with an average length of involvement of 10 to 18 months.[71] There is also variability in the size of the mental health court dockets, with some courts handling small caseloads of less than 10 juveniles and other courts handling larger caseloads of 75 or more juveniles. The size of the caseload is typically determined by the availability of necessary resources, including community-based treatment providers.

As with adult mental health courts, juvenile mental health courts accept misdemeanor and felony offenders, although some courts refuse to accept juveniles who are charged with violent offenses. In terms of mental health disorders, some courts limit involvement to juveniles with serious mental health disorders, while other courts accept juveniles with any identifiable mental health concern. Like their adult counterparts, these courts often utilize escalating sanctions and rewards to modify behavior. Roughly one-half of the juvenile mental health courts either expunge the juvenile's record or drop all of the charges upon successful completion of the program. Courts may recognize program accomplishments through reduced attendance requirements at status hearings, reduced treatment obligations, and formal graduation ceremonies. Sanctions can include electronic monitoring, brief placement in detention, and increased treatment and status hearing requirements. Finally, most juvenile mental health courts have formal linkages with community-based mental heath treatment providers.

Criticisms of Mental Health Courts

Mental health courts are not without their critics. Much of the criticism has focused on legal rather than clinical issues. A number of critics have voiced concerns about the blurring of traditional criminal justice roles moving from a focus on the protection of rights to the "best interests" of the defendants.[72] Others have questioned some of the procedural aspects of mental health courts. One of the most commonly voiced concerns relates to the voluntary nature of participating in these courts.[73,74,75] As previously noted, it is commonly agreed that participation in mental health courts must be voluntary. Some commentators[76] have correctly noted that *requiring* participation in a mental health court would, in effect, result in the singling out of offenders with mental illness for separate and different treatment, which would likely run afoul of the Equal Protection Clause of the Fourteenth Amendment to the U.S. Constitution. As such, it is important that mental health courts make known the voluntary nature of the program before clients make a decision to enter the court.

Unfortunately, little research has examined how or whether the issue of voluntariness is addressed within mental health courts. In one study of the Broward County Mental Health Court[77] that addressed the issue of voluntariness, only 16 percent of mental health court transcripts contained explicit discussions of the voluntary nature of the court. Forty-six percent of the clients reported that they were not aware that participation in the mental health court was voluntary, and another 29 percent reported that they were not told participation was voluntary until after they agreed to enter the court.

Hypothesizing that perceptions of coercion can potentially influence satisfaction and outcomes among mental health court clients, further research of the Broward County Mental Health Court examined whether awareness of the voluntary nature of the court was associated with perceived coercion to enter the court.[78] Clients who reported being unaware of the voluntary nature of the program reported significantly higher levels of coercion. Importantly, it is reasonable to believe that perceptions of coercion can potentially influence satisfaction and outcomes among mental health clients, and this is a question that should be addressed in future research.

Another issue related to voluntariness is whether mental health court clients have a right to withdraw from the court and be placed back in traditional criminal court. Several mental health courts do not permit clients to withdraw from the court.[79] The question of whether clients can withdraw from a problem-solving court has been addressed in the context of drug courts. In 2005, a Florida appellate court[80] held that a defendant could not be required to remain in a drug court program against his or her will. The court ruled that the voluntary design of the drug court treatment program permitted a defendant to opt out of the program and face the criminal charges at trial. Although this ruling is not binding on other jurisdictions, it is likely that courts will continue to recognize a client's right to withdraw from drug courts and other problem-solving courts.

It is also important that clients make informed decisions regarding whether to participate in the mental health court or proceed with standard criminal justice processing. There are little data regarding whether clients have the cognitive and, therefore, legal capacity to consent to participating in these courts. A study of the first three years of the Akron (Ohio) Mental Health Court examined 80 misdemeanor defendants referred by the mental health court for evaluation of competency to stand trial.[81] Seventy-eight percent were later adjudicated incompetent to stand trial, significantly more than the 50 percent hypothesized by the researchers. In another study, almost half of those rejected from Brooklyn's mental health court were "considered incompetent or too unstable at that time to make the decision to enroll and to participate in the court's proceedings."[82]

Some have questioned how mental health courts are being developed and implemented,[83] raising concerns about the stigma of a court specifically for defendants with mental illness. One court responded to this concern by titling itself a "Community Resource Court" rather than a mental health court. In a related concern, others have raised the issue of using a segregated court to respond to the challenges defendants with mental illness find in the criminal justice system noting, "I support diversion programs for people with mental health problems from the criminal court system, but I do not support creating a separate court system for people already excluded and stigmatized by society."[84] The potential for mental health courts to actually expand criminalization[85] of people with mental illness rather than decrease criminalization has also been raised citing examples of some mental health courts using a longer length of jurisdiction for their defendants with mental illness than traditional courts would use for defendants with the same criminal charges but without mental illness. A more specific example is courts that extend the length of their jurisdiction when a defendant relapses and requires hospitalization.

Some commentators have taken issue with the whole mental health court model itself.[86,87] One writer noted, "having a criminal court administer a social service system . . . strikes me as imprudent, a violation of the separation of powers, and an avoidance of the problem of inadequate community mental health services."[88] Another writer argues, "Mental health courts can help a few consumers obtain access to services, and perhaps they can divert some people out of jail or prison if they are carefully designed and implemented with that as their purpose. They may also draw public attention to the need for more and better mental health services. But mental health courts will not fix the mental health system; in fact, their efficacy will be limited and undermined by the deficits of the mental health system. We must understand the limits of 'tidy' solutions like mental health courts; to *end* criminalization, we will need to fight for a real mental health system."[89]

Finally, as noted by the previous commentator, the challenge of meeting the needs of the substantial numbers of people with mental illness involved in the criminal justice system is daunting. Mental health courts, like other specialty courts, started out as experiments in single jurisdictions with comparatively small caseloads. Reaching scale[90] or full implementation of mental health courts across all jurisdictions and sufficient to meet the need requires significant resources and infrastructure.

RESEARCH FINDINGS

Although the research literature on mental health courts has grown in recent years, it still lags well behind the relatively large and well-developed body of literature regarding drug courts. Whereas a sizable portion of the drug court literature consists of outcome and dismantling studies, with some researchers using randomized controlled designs, most of the literature regarding mental health courts consists of basic descriptive studies, process evaluations, or nonempirical policy/theoretical papers. Single-site studies of mental health courts have focused primarily on five courts: Broward County (Florida), Santa Barbara (California), Clark County (Washington), San Francisco (California), and a county in the southeastern United States. Several studies on various aspects of the Broward County Mental Health Court have been published. One study compares two mental health courts, Seattle and King County (Washington). Several multisite studies have examined multiple courts to understand what happens in mental health courts and how they compare to one another. When compared to drug courts, we know considerably less about the operations and effectiveness of mental health courts. Moreover, mental health courts often present unique challenges, including the nature of the population (i.e., offenders with mental health disorders) and variations among courts, which make it difficult for researchers to examine the effectiveness of these interventions in an empirically defensible manner.[91]

In the following sections, we will summarize the existing research on mental health courts. We will focus primarily on quantitative studies that address either or both of the two major outcomes of mental health courts—i.e., reductions in clinical symptoms (including increased access to and utilization of treatment services) and reductions in criminal recidivism. By reviewing the existing research in these important areas, we hope to clearly define areas in which more research is needed.

Access to Services and Clinical Improvement

A key component of mental health courts is the provision of community mental health treatment services to offenders with mental health needs. As such, an important question is whether the existence of mental health courts effectively increases the access and provision of behavioral health services. In an early study addressing this issue, researchers compared 121 offenders from the mental health court in Broward County (Florida) and 101 offenders from a traditional misdemeanor court in another county in Florida to determine whether the mental health court impacted the offenders' access to behavioral health services.[92] The percentage of offenders from the mental health court who received behavioral health services significantly increased from 36 percent during the eight months prior to their initial court appearance to 53 percent during the eight months after their initial court appearance. For the offenders in the traditional criminal court, the likelihood of receiving behavioral health services remained virtually unchanged during the same time periods (29 percent vs. 28 percent). As such, the researchers concluded that the Broward County Mental Health Court was effective in increasing access to treatment services.

A study of 368 misdemeanor offenders enrolled in the Clark County (Washington) Mental Health Court from April 2000 through April 2003[93] examined whether mental health court participation increased access to and utilization of treatment services among their clients by comparing one year prior to court enrollment to one year following enrollment. Mental health court clients received more hours of case management, medication management, and outpatient services in the one year following enrollment in the court. Furthermore, clients received fewer hours of crisis services and fewer days of inpatient treatment.

Despite some research suggesting that mental health court clients have greater access to behavioral health services than their counterparts in traditional criminal courts, few researchers have examined whether the provision of these treatment services leads to significant clinical improvement. One early study of the Santa Barbara Mental Health Court[94] examined whether participating in a mental health court with accompanying Assertive Community Treatment led to improved clinical outcomes as compared to a traditional criminal court. The researchers randomly assigned 235 offenders either to a mental health court with Assertive Community Treatment (described as frequent contact with a case manager within an intensive care team and the provision of needed resources, including transportation, housing vouchers, horticultural vocational training, group skills training in community reentry, and substance abuse management maintenance) or to a traditional criminal court with treatment as usual (i.e., adversarial criminal processing and less intensive case management services). Participants in both groups demonstrated improvements over 24 months in several areas, including life satisfaction, psychological distress, independent functioning, and substance use. However, participants in the mental health court showed greater gains in reducing psychological distress and their use of illicit substances along with reporting improvements in their quality of life.

As part of the large body of research on the Broward County Mental Health Court, researchers examined whether the provision of mental health services resulted in identifiable clinical improvement among clients.[95] Ninety-seven mental health court clients were compared with 77 defendants in a traditional magistrate criminal court in another Florida county. All defendants were assessed at one, four, and eight months after their initial court appearances using the Brief Psychiatric Rating Scale. There were no significant changes in defendants' clinical conditions related to the receipt of treatment services or participation in the mental health court. In fact, all defendants showed greater severity of mental health symptoms over time. Given these unexpected results, the researchers hypothesized that the failure to observe reductions in clinical symptoms among the mental health court clients was related to the lack of control that mental health courts exercise over the type and quality of treatment services provided to participants, as opposed to a general failure of the mental health court model. The researchers also suggested that a larger follow-up period (i.e., more than eight months) might be necessary to demonstrate clinical improvement. Others[96] have suggested that the low rate of defendants returning to the mental health court for monitoring (36 percent) may also be a factor to be considered.

A look at the employment status of participants in a southwestern U.S. mental health court[97] found employment status to be unchanged after one year in the program although written information was provided about vocational services. Seventy-five percent were unemployed, 13 percent employed full-time, and 7 percent employed part-time. The authors suggested referrals to vocational services in addition to providing written information about vocational services might result in increased rates of employment.

Criminal Recidivism

Do mental health courts reduce criminal recidivism by treating mental disorders that are believed to underlie or contribute to some types of criminal behavior? The evidence is mixed. One of the earliest studies to address this issue compared misdemeanants with mental health disorders who participated in Seattle's two mental health courts to similar offenders who chose not to participate in mental health court.[98] Offenders who participated in mental health court had significantly fewer arrests over an average follow-up period of nine months after entry into the court than they did in a comparable amount of time before their entry into the court. Offenders who participated in mental health court had significantly fewer arrests than those who chose not to participate in the mental health court. Although this study suggests that participation in a mental health court is associated with decreased rates of criminal recidivism, the nonexperimental nature of the study design prohibits the researchers from making any causal inferences regarding the effects of the mental health court on recidivism rates.

In another study of the Broward County Mental Health Court, researchers examined criminal recidivism outcomes for mental health court clients.[99] The number of arrests for clients in the mental health court significantly decreased from one-year pre-entry to one-year post-entry into the court. However, they also found that the mean number of arrests, felony arrests, proportion arrested, and average time to arrest were not significantly different from comparable defendants who did not participate in the mental health court. As such, the results of the study called into question the effectiveness of mental health courts vis-à-vis traditional criminal courts.

In a study of the mental health court in Santa Barbara (California) described in the previous section, researchers used an experimental research design to randomly assign 235 offenders with misdemeanor or felony charges for 18 months either to mental health court with Assertive Community Treatment ($n = 137$) or to "Treatment as Usual" traditional criminal court that offered less intensive case management services ($n = 98$).[100,101] One-year post-entry, participants in the mental health court had significantly fewer convictions for new offenses, and their criminal charges were typically related to probation technical violations rather than the commission of a new criminal offense. By contrast, criminal charges for the participants randomly assigned to the traditional criminal court were typically for new criminal offenses.[102] Despite these positive findings, the outcomes at two years proved to be less impressive. All study participants, regardless of whether they were in the mental health court or traditional criminal court, showed increased arrests and no change in either the number of convictions or days in jail.[103] A closer look found that a small group of mental health court participants accounted for 54 percent of all post–mental health court jail days. The researchers noted, "The program was not able to hold or help all participants; for some offenders, continued criminal activity resulted in prison or levels of jail time higher than had been the case before entering the program."[104] Once the group of frequent offenders and those sent to prison were removed from the analysis (approximately 20 percent of the original participants), the rest of the participants showed a decrease in jail days, with the mental health court participants showing the greatest decrease. The seriousness of substance abuse problems at intake distinguished the successful participants from those who were not successful in reducing their criminal activity.

One study examined rearrest rates for 368 misdemeanor offenders participating in the Clark County (Washington) Mental Health Court during a three-year period.[105] The researchers compared rearrest rates in the one year pre- and post-enrollment in the court. Clients showed significant reductions in criminal arrests post-enrollment, with the average number of arrests being significantly reduced from 1.99 pre-enrollment to 0.48 post-enrollment. Moreover, the overall crime rate was reduced by 400 percent post-enrollment. Further, 54 percent of the clients had no arrests in the one year following enrollment, and probation violations were reduced by 62 percent in that same time period. The most significant factor in determining the success of the mental health court clients was whether they graduated from the program. Graduates were almost four times less likely to reoffend compared to nongraduates. Of the 368 clients, 69 or 19 percent successfully graduated. Another 222 or 60 percent were terminated without graduation due to noncompliance with court requirements, opting out of the court, transfer to another specialty court, or leaving the court's jurisdiction. Seventy-seven were still enrolled in the mental health court at the end of the study. A closer look at a smaller group of mental health court clients "suggested that relationships developed between the MHC coordinator, the judge, and the consumer were critical to the client's success."[106] Increased intensity of mental health services and prior felony charge were not significant factors in reducing rearrest.

In a study of a mental health court in a southeastern state, researchers compared 82 offenders in mental health court with 183 similar offenders whose cases were processed in a traditional criminal court in the same county before the mental health court was established.[107] The mental health court participants had significantly fewer new arrests and less severe criminal offenses during the one-year follow-up period compared to the participants in the traditional criminal court. Participants who completed the mental health court requirements of six months of court-ordered treatment, court appearances, and no new arrests had a rearrest rate that was roughly one-fourth the rearrest rate of the participants who went through the traditional criminal court. The rearrest rates for participants who *did not* complete the mental health court program did not significantly differ from the rearrest rates for participants who went through traditional criminal court. It was the "full dose of mental health court, rather than a partial dose, which made the difference in reducing arrests."[108]

Other research has also found mental health courts to be effective in reducing criminal recidivism. In a recent study of San Francisco's Behavioral Health Court,[109] a retrospective observational design was used to compare the occurrence of new criminal charges for 170 participants who entered the mental health court after arrest and 8,067 individuals with mental health disorders who were booked into the county jail after arrest during the same time period. Two-thirds of the participants had felony charges. Eighteen months after enrollment, participation in the mental health court was associated with longer time without new criminal charges (26 percent reduction) or new charges for violent crimes (55 percent reduction). As with previous studies,[110,111] graduating from the mental health court program was found to be an important correlate of reduced criminal recidivism. Successful completion of the mental health court program was associated with maintenance of reductions in criminal recidivism (39 percent) and violence (54 percent) after the graduates were no longer under the supervision of the mental health court. Twenty-six percent of those enrolled in mental health court were removed by the time of follow-up: 11 voluntarily opted out, 5 were arrested for new charges, 11 were removed for noncompliance, and 17 left for other reasons.

Summary of the Research

The results of the existing research present a mixed picture with respect to clinical improvement and reductions in criminal recidivism among mental health court clients. On the one hand, some research suggests that mental health courts are effective in increasing access to and utilization of behavioral health services. However, on the other hand, the existing research is mixed in terms of whether the provision of treatment services leads to measurable reductions in clinical symptoms. The picture is also mixed with respect to reductions in criminal recidivism. Although some research supports the proposition that mental health courts reduce recidivism, other research has found few differences in recidivism rates between offenders in mental health courts and offenders in traditional criminal courts. Moreover, one study that included a longer follow-up period appears to suggest that the beneficial effects of mental health courts decline the longer clients are out of the court after graduation.

However, taken as a whole, there is reason to be cautiously optimistic about the effects of mental health courts. Despite some mixed empirical findings, the weight of the evidence appears to suggest that mental health courts can lead to increased provision of behavioral health treatment services, improvements in clinical functioning, and reductions in criminal recidivism. As such, mental health courts appear to be fulfilling their basic objectives.

The biggest limitation in drawing conclusions about the operations and effectiveness of mental health courts is the relatively small body of existing research. As previously noted, the body of research on mental health courts is considerably smaller than the body of research on similar interventions, including drug courts. Although this may not be surprising given that drug courts were developed almost a decade before mental health courts, the reality is that much more research is needed on mental health courts before we can draw firm and empirically defensible conclusions about the effectiveness of these interventions. Most of the existing literature on mental health courts consists of basic descriptive studies (such as pre- or post-observational designs), process evaluations, program evaluations focusing on one court, and nonempirical theory papers. Moreover, many of the evaluations conducted on mental health courts are "in-house" products that do not get published in scientific journals.

Future Directions for Research

One of the biggest limitations of the existing research on mental health courts is the absence of true experimental studies. From a methodological standpoint, the only reliable way to draw causal inferences about the effects of an intervention is by using an experimental design, which involves randomly assigning participants to treatment and control/comparison groups. The use of randomized controlled designs would permit researchers to make causal inferences about the effects of mental health courts, in terms of both clinical improvement and recidivism reduction. Several drug court studies have used experimental designs to examine the effects of these courts. Conducting experimental studies to examine the effects of mental health courts should be considered a necessary next step in the continuing evaluation of these interventions.

One model for examining the effects of an intervention involves following a two-step approach. The first step involves conducting outcome research to support the effectiveness of the intervention as a whole. Once the effectiveness of the intervention has been firmly established through randomized controlled studies, the second step involves conducting a series of dismantling studies to identify the active ingredients of the intervention. In other words, the first step is establishing *whether* the intervention works, and the second step involves studying *how* the intervention works.

Studying the active ingredients in drug courts was facilitated by the publication of *Defining Drug Courts: The Key Components*, by the National Association of Drug Court Professionals (NADCP) in January 1997.[112] This report identified the ten "key components" of drug courts and, by doing so, identified key areas for future research. Among other elements, the NADCP report identified regularly scheduled judicial status hearings as being one of the defining elements of drug courts, and researchers soon began to examine the effects of status hearings on client outcomes. For example, researchers examined the effects of judicial status hearings on client outcomes in a series of randomized controlled trials in misdemeanor and felony drug courts in Delaware.[113] They found that high-risk drug court clients (i.e., met *Diagnostic and Statistical Manual of Mental Disorders-IV* criteria for Antisocial Personality Disorder or had a history of drug treatment) achieved greater rates of drug abstinence and higher rates of graduation when they attended more frequent status hearings (i.e., bi-monthly), whereas the low-risk clients (i.e., no Antisocial Personality Disorder or prior drug treatment) performed equivalently or better when they attended status hearings only in response to serious or repeated program infractions.[114,115,116] Recently, researchers confirmed these findings in a prospective study in which drug court clients were matched to an optimal level of status hearings based on their risk level, and then compared to clients randomly assigned to a standard hearing schedule.[117]

One suggestion would be for mental health court researchers to follow the two-step approach previously outlined. Specifically, once it is established that mental health courts are effective in terms of improving clinical functioning and reducing recidivism, which should be accomplished through randomized controlled studies followed by replication, the next step would involve examining the active ingredients or defining elements of mental health courts. Because drug courts and mental health courts share many features, an examination of the key elements of drug courts may be instructive for mental health court researchers.

For example, it would be valuable for researchers to examine different dosages of status hearings, the use of sanctions and rewards, and the use of interventions that are specifically tailored to offenders' clinical needs and risk levels. These are aspects of drug courts that have received a good deal of attention from researchers in recent years, and these topics are ripe for being researched in mental health courts. Although commentators have addressed the unique aspects of mental health courts, including the role of defense counsel[118] and the presiding judge,[119] systematic dismantling studies are lacking. With that said, the first step in the process of studying an intervention is firmly establishing its effectiveness, and the current state of the literature suggests that more research is needed before we can make firm conclusions regarding the effectiveness of mental health courts.

CONCLUSION

The advent of mental health courts more than a decade ago has given the criminal justice system a promising approach for handling the high numbers of criminal offenders with mental health disorders. Although some research appears to support the effectiveness of these novel interventions, the body of empirical literature is still rather small, particularly when compared to drug courts. Nevertheless, as we have discussed, there is reason to be optimistic about the merits of mental health courts. As the proliferation of mental health courts continues, it will become increasingly more important to establish the effectiveness of these courts using methodologically sound research designs that permit inferences of causality. In this chapter, we emphasized the importance of using rigorous empirical methods to establish the overall effectiveness of mental health courts, and we highlighted several specific aspects of mental health courts that would then be ripe for study. We hope that researchers view this as a call to arms, and we look forward to the next generation of mental health court research.

NOTES

1. Morrissey, Meyer, & Cuddleback, 2007, p. 540.
2. Belenko, 2001.
3. Belenko, 2002.
4. Belenko, DeMatteo, & Patapis, 2007.
5. Government Accountability Office, 2005.
6. Marlowe, DeMatteo, & Festinger, 2003.
7. Griffin, Steadman, & Petrila, 2002.
8. Redlich, Steadman, Monahan, Petrila, & Griffin, 2005.
9. Steadman, Davidson, & Brown, 2001.
10. Farole, 2006, p. 1.
11. Redlich, Steadman, Monahan, Petrila, & Griffin, 2005.
12. Brian Case, National GAINS Center, personal communication, 8-4-2008.
13. Teplin, 1990.
14. Abram & Teplin, 1991.

15. Teplin, 1994.
16. National GAINS Center for People with Co-Occurring Disorders in the Justice System, 2004.
17. James & Glaze, 2006.
18. Steadman, Cocozza, & Veysey, 1999.
19. Trupin & Richards, 2003.
20. Redlich, Steadman, Monahan, Robbins, & Petrila, 2006.
21. Redlich, Steadman, Monahan, Robbins, & Petrila, 2006.
22. Brian Case, National GAINS Center, personal communication, 8-4-2008.
23. Thompson, Osher, & Tomasini-Joshi, 2007.
24. Erickson, Campbell, & Lamberti, 2006.
25. Cocozza & Shufelt, 2006.
26. Thompson, Osher, & Tomasini-Joshi, 2007.
27. Council of State Governments, 2005.
28. Redlich, Steadman, Monahan, Robbins, & Petrila, 2006.
29. Kuehn, 2007.
30. Odegaard, 2007.
31. Rottman & Casey, 1999.
32. Wexler, 2001.
33. Erickson, Campbell, & Lamberti, 2006.
34. Boothroyd, Poythress, McGaha, & Petrila, 2003.
35. Moore & Hiday, 2006.
36. Casey & Rottman, 2003.
37. Griffin, Steadman, & Petrila, 2002.
38. Goldkamp & Irons-Guynn, 2000.
39. Griffin, Steadman, & Petrila, 2002.
40. Griffin, Steadman, & Petrila, 2002.
41. Redlich, Steadman, Monahan, Robbins, & Petrila, 2006, p. 358.
42. Redlich, 2005
43. Redlich, Steadman, Monahan, Robbins, & Petrila, 2006.
44. Thompson, Osher, & Tomasini-Joshi, 2007.
45. Thompson, Osher, & Tomasini-Joshi, 2007.
46. Redlich, Steadman, Monahan, Robbins, & Petrila, 2006.
47. Watson, Hanrahan, Luchins, & Lurigio, 2001.
48. Thompson, Osher, & Tomasini-Joshi, 2007.
49. Bernstein & Seltzer, 2003.
50. Casey & Rottman, 2003.
51. Erickson, Campbell, & Lamberti, 2006.
52. Redlich, Steadman, Monahan, Robbins, & Petrila, 2006.
53. Erickson, Campbell, & Lamberti, 2006.
54. Griffin, Steadman, & Petrila, 2002.
55. Erickson, Campbell, & Lamberti, 2006.
56. Redlich, Steadman, Monahan, Robbins, & Petrila, 2006.
57. Erickson, Campbell, & Lamberti, 2006.
58. Griffin, Steadman, & Petrila, 2002.
59. Casey & Rottman, 2003.
60. Steadman, Redlich, Griffin, Petrila, & Monahan, 2005.
61. Naples & Steadman, 2003.

62. Cocozza & Shufelt, 2006.
63. Sickmund, 2004.
64. Teplin, Abram, McClelland, Dulcan, & Mericle, 2002.
65. Wasserman, Ko, & McReynolds, 2004.
66. Arrendondo, Kumli, Soto, Colin, Ornellas, Davilla, Edwards, & Hyman, 2001.
67. National Center for Mental Health and Juvenile Justice, 2005.
68. Cocozza & Shufelt, 2006.
69. Cocozza & Shufelt, 2006.
70. Cocozza & Shufelt, 2006.
71. Cocozza & Shufelt, 2006.
72. Stefan & Winick, 2005.
73. Casey & Rottman, 2003.
74. Redlich, 2005.
75. Seltzer, 2005.
76. Seltzer, 2005.
77. Boothroyd, Poythress, McGaha, & Petrila, 2003.
78. Poythress, Petrila, McGaha, & Boothroyd, 2002.
79. Seltzer, 2005.
80. Mullin v. Jenne, 2005.
81. Stafford & Wygant, 2005.
82. Steadman, Redlich, Griffin, Petrila, & Monahan, 2005, p. 222.
83. Acquaviva, 2006.
84. Stefan & Winick, 2005, p. 254.
85. Barr, 2001.
86. Bernstein & Seltzer, 2003.
87. Seltzer, 2005.
88. Stefan & Winick, 2005, p. 513.
89. Barr, 2001, p. 3.
90. Farole, 2006.
91. Wolff & Pogorzelski, 2005.
92. Boothroyd, Poythress, McGaha, & Petrila, 2003.
93. Herinckx, Swart, Ama, Dolezal, & King, 2005.
94. Cosden, Ellens, Schnell, Yamini-Diouf, & Wolfe, 2003.
95. Boothroyd, Mercado, Poythress, Christy, & Petrila, 2005.
96. Moore & Hiday, 2006.
97. Sneed, Koch, Estes, & Quinn, 2006.
98. Trupin & Richards, 2003.
99. Christy, Poythress, Boothroyd, Petrila, & Mehra, 2005.
100. Cosden, Ellens, Schnell, Yamini-Diouf, & Wolfe, 2003.
101. Cosden, Ellens, Schnell, & Yamini-Diouf, 2005.
102. Cosden, Ellens, Schnell, Yamini-Diouf, & Wolfe, 2003.
103. Cosden, Ellens, Schnell, & Yamini-Diouf, 2005.
104. Cosden, Ellens, Schnell, & Yamini-Diouf, 2005, p. 206–207.
105. Herinckx, Swart, Ama, Dolezai, & King, 2005.
106. Herinckx, Swart, Ama, Dolezai, & King, 2005, p. 856.
107. Moore & Hiday, 2006.
108. Moore & Hiday, 2006, p. 670.
109. McNiel & Binder, 2007.

110. Herinckx, Swart, Ama, Dolezai, & King, 2005.
111. Moore & Hiday, 2006.
112. National Association of Drug Court Professionals, 1997.
113. Festinger, Marlowe, Lee, Kirby, Bovasso, & McLellan, 2002.
114. Marlowe, Festinger, Dugosh, & Lee, 2005.
115. Marlowe, Festinger, & Lee, 2003.
116. Marlowe, Festinger, & Lee, 2004.
117. Marlowe, Festinger, Lee, Dugosh, & Benasutti, 2006.
118. Keele, 2002.
119. Talesh, 2007.

REFERENCES

Abram, K. M., & Teplin, L. (1991). Co-occurring disorders among mentally ill jail detainees. *American Psychologist, 46,* 1036–1045.

Acquaviva, G. L. (2006). Mental health courts: No longer experimental. *Seton Hall Law Review, 36,* 971–1013.

Arrendondo, D., Kumli, J., Soto, L., Colin, E., Ornellas, J., Davilla, R., Edwards, L., & Hyman, E. (2001). Juvenile mental health court: Rationale and protocols. *Juvenile and Family Court Journal, 52*(4), 1–19.

Barr, H. (2001). *Mental health courts: An advocate's perspective.* Available from the Urban Justice Center at http://www.urbanjustice.org/pdf/publications/mentalhealth/MentalHealthCourts.pdf.

Belenko, S. (1998). Research on drug courts: A critical review. *National Drug Court Institute Review, 1,* 1–42.

Belenko, S. (1999). Research on drug courts: A critical review: 1999 update. *National Drug Court Institute Review, 2*(2), 1–58.

Belenko, S. (2001). *Research on drug courts: A critical review: 2001 update.* New York: National Center on Addiction and Substance Abuse at Columbia University.

Belenko, S. (2002). Drug courts. In C. G. Leukefeld, F. Tims, & D. Farabee (Eds.), *Treatment of drug offenders: Policies and issues* (pp. 301–318). New York: Springer.

Belenko, S., DeMatteo, D., & Patapis, N. (2007). Drug courts. In D. W. Springer & A. R. Roberts (Eds.), *Handbook of forensic mental health with victims and offenders: Assessment, treatment, and research* (pp. 385–423). New York: Springer Publishing Co.

Bernstein, R., & Seltzer, T. (2003). The role of mental health courts in system reform. *University of the District of Columbia Law Review, 7,* 143–162.

Boothroyd, R. A., Mercado, C. C., Poythress, N. G., Christy, A., & Petrila, J. (2005). Clinical outcomes of defendants in mental health court. *Psychiatric Services, 56,* 829–834.

Boothroyd, R. A., Poythress, N. G., McGaha, A., & Petrila, J. (2003). The Broward mental health court: Process, outcomes, and service utilization. *International Journal of Law and Psychiatry, 26,* 55–71.

Casey, P. M., & Rottman, D. B. (2003). *Problem-solving courts: Models and trends.* Williamsburg, VA: National Center for State Courts.

Casey, P. M., Rottman, D. B., & Bromage, C. G. (2007). Problem-solving justice toolkit. Available from the National Center for State Courts at http://www.ncsconline.org/d_research/Documents/ProbSolvJustTool.pdf.

Christy, A., Poythress, N. G., Boothroyd, R. A., Petrila, J., & Mehra, S. (2005). Evaluating the efficiency and community safety goals of the Broward County mental health court. *Behavioral Sciences and the Law, 23,* 1–17.

Cocozza, J. J., & Shufelt, J. L. (2006, June). *Juvenile mental health courts: An emerging strategy.* Available from the National Center for Mental Health and Juvenile Justice at http://www.ncmhjj.com/pdfs/publications/JuvenileMentalHealthCourts.pdf.

Cosden, M., Ellens, J., Schnell, J., & Yamini-Diouf, Y. (2005). Efficacy of a mental health treatment court with assertive community treatment. *Behavioral Sciences and the Law, 23,* 199–214.

Cosden, M., Ellens, J., Schnell, J., Yamini-Diouf, Y., & Wolfe, M. (2003). Evaluation of a mental health court with assertive community treatment. *Behavioral Sciences and the Law, 21,* 415–427.

Council of State Governments. (2005). *Mental health courts: A national snapshot.* Available at http://consensusproject.org/mhcp/national-snapshot.pdf.

Ditton, P. M. (1999). *Mental health and treatment of inmates and probationers.* Washington, DC: U.S. Department of Justice, Office of Justice Programs, Bureau of Justice Assistance.

Erickson, S. T., Campbell, A., & Lamberti, J. S. (2006). Variations in mental health courts: Challenges, opportunities, and a call for caution. *Community Mental Health Journal, 42,* 335–344.

Farole, D. J. (2006). The challenges of going to scale: Lessons from other disciplines for problem-solving courts. Available from the Center for Court-Innovation at http://www.courtinnovation.org/_uploads/documents/Lessons.pdf.

Festinger, D. S., Marlowe, D. B., Lee, P. A., Kirby, K. C., Bovasso, G., & McLellan, A. T. (2002). Status hearings in drug court: When more is less and less is more. *Drug and Alcohol Dependence, 68,* 151–157.

Goldkamp, J. S., & Irons-Guynn, C. (2000). *Emerging judicial strategies for the mentally ill in the criminal caseload: Mental health courts in Fort Lauderdale, Seattle, San Bernardino, and Anchorage.* Washington, DC: U.S. Bureau of Justice Assistance.

Government Accountability Office. (2005). *Adult drug courts: Evidence indicates recidivism reductions and mixed results for other outcomes.* Washington, DC: Author.

Griffin, P. A., Steadman, H. J., & Petrila, J. (2002). The use of criminal charges and sanctions in mental health courts. *Psychiatric Services, 53,* 1285–1289.

Haimowitz, S. (2002). Can mental health courts end the criminalization of persons with mental illness? *Psychiatric Services, 53,* 1226–1228.

Herinckx, H. A., Swart, S. C., Ama, S. M., Dolezal, C. S., & King, S. (2005). Rearrest and linkage to mental health services among clients of the Clark County Mental Health Court Program. *Psychiatric Services, 56,* 853–857.

James, D. J., & Glaze, L. E. (2006). *Mental health problems of prison and jail inmates.* Washington, DC: U.S. Department of Justice, Office of Justice Programs, Bureau of Justice Statistics.

Keele, C. E. (2002). Criminalization of the mentally ill: The challenging role of the defense attorney in the mental health court system. *University of Missouri at Kansas City Law Review, 71,* 193–210.

Kuehn, B. M. (2007). Mental health courts show promise. *Journal of the American Medical Association, 297,* 1641–1643.

Marlowe, D. B., DeMatteo, D. S., & Festinger, D. S. (2003). A sober assessment of drug courts. *Federal Sentencing Reporter, 16,* 113–128.

Marlowe, D. B., Festinger, D. S., Dugosh, K. L., & Lee, P. A. (2005). Are judicial status hearings a "key component" of drug court? Six and twelve months outcomes. *Drug and Alcohol Dependence, 79,* 145–155.

Marlowe, D. B., Festinger, D. S., & Lee, P. A. (2003). The role of judicial status hearings in drug court. *Offender Substance Abuse Report, 3,* 33–46.

Marlowe, D. B., Festinger, D. S., & Lee, P. A. (2004). The judge is a key component of drug court. *Drug Court Review, 4*(2), 1–34.

Marlowe, D. B., Festinger, D. S., Lee, P. A., Dugosh, K. L., & Benasutti, K. M. (2006). Matching judicial supervision to clients' risk status in drug court. *Crime and Delinquency, 52,* 52–76.

McNiel, D. E., & Binder, R. L. (2007). Effectiveness of a mental health court in reducing criminal recidivism and violence. *American Journal of Psychiatry, 164,* 1395–1403.

Moore, M. E., & Hiday, V. A. (2006). Mental health court outcomes: A comparison of re-arrest and re-arrest severity between mental health court and traditional court participants. *Law and Human Behavior, 30,* 659–674.

Morissey, J., Meyer, P., & Cuddeback, G. (2007). Extending assertive community treatment to criminal justice settings: Origins, current evidence, and future directions. *Community Mental Health, 43,* 527–544.

Mullin v. Jenne, 890 So.2d 543 (Fla. Ct. App. 2005).

Naples, M. & Steadman, H. J. (2003). Can persons with co-occurring disorder and violent charges be successfully diverted? *International Journal of Forensic Mental Health, 2,* 137–143.

National Association of Drug Court Professionals. (1997). *Defining drug courts: The key components.* Washington, DC: Office of Justice Programs, U.S. Department of Justice.

National Center for Mental Health and Juvenile Justice. (2005). *Juvenile mental health courts —Program descriptions: Processes and procedures.* Delmar, NY: Author.

National GAINS Center for People with Co-Occurring Disorders in the Justice System. (2004). *The prevalence of co-occurring mental and substance use disorders in jail settings.* Delmar, NY: Author.

Odegaard, A. M. (2007). Therapeutic jurisprudence: The impact of mental health courts on the criminal justice system. *North Dakota Law Review, 83,* 225–259.

Poythress, N., Petrila, J., McGaha, A., & Boothroyd, R. (2002). Perceived coercion and procedural justice in the Broward County Mental Health Court. *International Journal of Law and Psychiatry, 25,* 517–533.

Redlich, A. D. (2005). Voluntary, but knowing and intelligent: Comprehension in mental health courts. *Psychology, Public Policy, and Law, 11,* 605–619.

Redlich, A. D., Steadman, H. J., Monahan, J., Petrila, J., & Griffin, P. A. (2005). The second generation of mental health courts. *Psychology, Public Policy, and Law, 11,* 527–538.

Redlich, A. D., Steadman, H. J., Monahan, J., Robbins, P. C., & Petrila, J. (2006). Patterns of practice in mental health courts: A national survey. *Law and Human Behavior, 30,* 347–362.

Rottman, D., & Casey, P. (1999, July). Therapeutic jurisprudence and the emergence of problem-solving courts. *National Institute of Justice Journal,* 13–19.

Seltzer, T. (2005). Mental health courts: A misguided attempt to address the criminal justice system's unfair treatment of people with mental illness. *Psychology, Public Policy, and Law, 11,* 570–586.

Sickmund, M. (2004, June). *Juveniles in corrections.* Washington, DC: U.S. Department of Justice, Office of Justice Programs, Office of Juvenile Justice and Delinquency Prevention.

Sneed, Z., Koch, D. S., Estes, H., & Quinn, J. (2006). Employment and psychosocial outcomes for offenders with mental illness. *International Journal of Psychosocial Rehabilitation, 10,* 103–112.

Stafford, K. P., & Wygant, D. B. (2005). The role of competency to stand trial in mental health courts. *Behavioral Sciences and the Law, 23,* 245–258.

Steadman, H. J., Cocozza, J. J., & Veysey, B. M. (1999). Comparing outcomes for diverted and nondiverted jail detainees with mental illnesses. *Law and Human Behavior, 23,* 615–627.

Steadman, H. J., Davidson, S., & Brown, C. (2001). Mental health courts: Their promise and unanswered questions. *Psychiatric Services, 52,* 457–458.

Steadman, H. J., Redlich, A. D., Griffin, P., Petrila, J., & Monahan, J. (2005). From referral to disposition: Case processing in seven mental health courts. *Behavioral Sciences and the Law, 23,* 215–226.

Stefan, S., & Winick, B. J. (2005). A dialogue on mental health courts. *Psychology, Public Policy, and Law, 11,* 507–526.

Talesh, S. (2007). Mental health court judges as dynamic risk managers: A new conceptualization of the role of judges. *DePaul Law Review, 57,* 93–132.

Teplin, L. (1990). The prevalence of severe mental disorder among male urban jail detainees: Comparison with the Epidemiologic Catchment Area Program. *American Journal of Public Health, 80,* 553–669.

Teplin, L. (1994). Psychiatric and substance abuse disorders among male urban jail detainees. *American Journal of Public Health, 84,* 290–293.

Teplin, L., Abram, K., McClelland, G., Dulcan, M., & Mericle, A. (2002). Psychiatric disorders in youth in juvenile detention. *Archives of General Psychiatry, 59,* 1133–1143.

Thompson, M., Osher, F., & Tomasini-Joshi, D. (2007). *Improving responses to people with mental illnesses: The essential elements of a mental health court.* New York: Council of State Governments Justice Center.

Trupin, E. W., & Richards, H. J. (2003). Seattle's mental health courts: Early indicators of effectiveness. *International Journal of Law and Psychiatry, 26,* 33–53.

Wasserman, G., Ko, S., & McReynolds, L. (2004, August). Assessing the mental health status of youth in juvenile justice settings. *Juvenile Justice Bulletin,* 1–7.

Watson, A., Hanrahan, P., Luchins, D., & Lurigio, A. (2001). Mental health courts and the complex issue of offenders with mental illness. *Psychiatric Services, 52,* 477–481.

Wexler, D. B. (2001). Robes and rehabilitation: How judges can help offenders "make good." *Court Review, 38,* 18–23.

Wolff, N., & Pogorzelski, W. (2005). Measuring the effectiveness of mental health courts: Challenges and recommendations. *Psychology, Public Policy, and Law, 11,* 539–569.

7

Domestic Violence Courts: A Judicial Response to Intimate Partner Violence

ANGELA R. GOVER

Specialized domestic violence courts attempt to improve the judiciary's response to the crime of domestic violence by increasing coordination among criminal justice and social service agencies, by appropriately addressing victims' needs, and by holding defendants accountable for their behavior. Domestic violence courts are considered to be a type of problem-solving courts, similar to drug courts, youth courts, mental health courts, and community courts.[1,2] Problem-solving courts have a great deal of variation among their operational procedures, emphasis on program aspects, offender processing, and goals and objectives.[3] Indeed, domestic violence courts, as we will see, certainly follow suit in programmatic variation. As with other problem-solving courts, specialized domestic violence courts are a mechanism to encourage the court to focus on what is best for the victim, offender, and community.

The criminal justice system has come a long way from the days when emergency dispatchers would answer 911 calls and suggest to domestic violence victims that they stay at their mother's house for the night.[4] Today progress is realized when attention is placed on how domestic violence has been criminalized, mandatory arrest legislation has been passed, no-drop prosecution policies are common, civil protection orders have been implemented and expanded, and specialized domestic violence courts have been implemented across the United States, which is the focus of this chapter.

First, we need to understand the complexity of domestic violence. Subsequently, we will examine the history and development of domestic violence courts, their underlying philosophy and structure, concerns about the no-drop prosecution policy, and prospects for these courts in the future. The Lexington County Criminal Domestic Violence Court (CDVC), in Lexington County, South Carolina, is presented as an example of a domestic violence court. In addition to a description of the court, findings from a process and outcome evaluation of the CDVC are presented. The chapter concludes with a discussion of no-drop policies as a specific programming issue that specialized domestic violence courts have to consider and prospects for the future for domestic violence courts.

DEFINING DOMESTIC VIOLENCE

Domestic violence includes the acts of physical, emotional, or sexual abuse between intimate partners for purposes of establishing power and control over one's partner. Two additional forms of domestic violence are stalking and dating violence. Domestic violence is not distinct to any one culture, faith, age, and class; rather, domestic violence is prevalent in every demographic segment of society. Other terms used in the literature to refer to domestic violence include intimate partner violence, spousal abuse, wife assault, dating violence, and battering.

Unfortunately, states are not consistent in their statutes in terms of exactly how "intimate" is defined. Variations in definitions include different kinds of couples: married or unmarried couples, those that cohabitate or live separately, couples that had been formerly married or dated, and heterosexual or same-sex couples. In some states children, siblings, roommates, or other relatives living in the household also fall under the statutory definition of individuals who could be included in a domestic violence incident. In addition, the definition of an "intimate partner" does not necessarily require that the couple have an established intimate relationship. Regardless of the statutory definitions, the term "domestic violence" usually applies to a cyclic pattern of coercive actions where one intimate partner engages in various behaviors to establish power and control over his partner.

It is estimated that one out of every four women will be a victim of domestic violence at some point during her lifetime.[5] On an annual basis it is estimated that approximately 1.3 million women experience physical abuse by their intimate partners.[6] In one year, domestic violence victimizations resulted in approximately 2 million injuries with over 500,000 requiring medical attention.[7] In fact, one study reported that 44 percent of women who were murdered by their intimate partners had sought medical care at an emergency room within two years of their death, and 93 percent of the murdered women had previously visited an emergency room for an injury at least once.[8]

Both men and women are victims of domestic violence; however, the overwhelming majority of domestic violence involves women as victims and men as perpetrators.[9] Given this gender disparity, nearly all agencies and organizations that provide services to victims of domestic violence focus their attention and services primarily on violence against women and their children.

THE COMPLEXITY OF DOMESTIC VIOLENCE

Domestic violence is commonly referred to as "the cycle of violence," which is made up of three stages: (1) the tension building stage; (2) the explosive stage; and (3) the honeymoon stage.[10] During the tension building stage, the victim's fear increases as the batterer becomes more irritable and may begin verbally abusing the victim. During the explosive stage, the batterer perpetrates violence against his partner, and quite often the batterer actually believes that the victim is responsible for his violent behavior. The final stage is the honeymoon stage, which is when the batterer attempts to convince the victim that he is sorry for the violence, promising to never do it again, and perhaps even promising to seek professional help for his behavior, such as seeing a therapist or seeking religious counseling. This stage may involve gifts and/or material items to convince the victim that the violence will stop. Victims of domestic violence can be very emotionally dependent on their intimate partners, which explains why many women believe their batterers when they say the violence will stop. For victims who are successful at leaving their batterers by seeking services from a battered women's shelter, it is estimated that 60 percent return to their abusers within two months after their shelter stay.[11]

While it may be difficult to understand why an individual would stay with an abusive partner, there are many psychological, social, and emotional factors that keep women from *being able* to leave the relationship. Instead of asking the question, "why do women stay?," the question that should be asked is, "why are women abused?" Until society evolves to the point of having a true shift in the questions asked, victim advocates will continue with their efforts to explain why it is difficult for women to leave abusive relationships. It is important to understand that women who feel that they have no choice but to remain in their abusive relationships are not weak or ignorant, but that they have rational explanations for staying, including fear for their safety and their children's safety. It is extremely important for staff working in a specialized domestic violence court to be educated about the complexities of these dynamics because it can be frustrating for court staff to work with victims who initially want to leave their batterers but over time decide to remain in the relationships.

Many women remain in abusive relationships because they love their partners and do not want their relationships with their partners to end, despite the abuse. There are also very real emotional and economic dependency issues that make it difficult for women to leave abusive relationships.[12] Many women feel they cannot leave the relationship because of the economic predicament they are faced with if the relationship dissolves. Factors that may influence economic dependence include the following: young children in the home, a lack of alternative housing, and limited access to financial resources. Another form of economic dependency occurs when the abuser takes away privileges (e.g., use of the car, access to the bank account, etc.) or threatens the victim financially. In addition to economic dependency, emotional dependency occurs when the abuser's power over the victim makes her dependent for nurturance, protection, and support, even if the victim is capable of functioning autonomously.[13] Emotional dependency is common in many domestic violence situations and often creates feelings of helplessness, passiveness, and low self-esteem, which also adds to the difficulty of having the courage to leave the relationship.[14]

A growing body of literature has documented the acute and long-term physical and psychological consequences of domestic violence.[15,16,17] Studies that compare nonabused women to abused women find significantly higher rates of physical problems, depression, anxiety, drug and alcohol abuse, post-traumatic stress disorder, and suicide attempts.[18,19,20,21]

Children add to the complexity of domestic violence. It is estimated that 10 million children in the United States witness parental violence each year.[22] Previous research on the mental health consequences of intimate partner violence indicates that children do not have to be direct victims of childhood maltreatment to experience the detrimental effects of intimate partner violence. Studies have found that children who witnessed marital violence experienced negative long-term adjustment difficulties, experienced more violence in dating relationships, showed higher levels of antisocial behaviors, experienced depression, and showed a greater number of trauma symptoms than those who had not witnessed intimate partner violence.[23] Research has also found evidence of a relationship between being exposed to domestic violence and externalizing behavioral problems.[24] For example, McCloskey and Lichter found depression to be a mediating factor between children's exposure to family violence and aggression towards other peers.[25]

Examining the complexities of domestic violence demonstrates that this is an issue unlike any other crime. This is not a crime involving strangers. The nature of the crime, given that the parties involved are in a relationship, in and of itself, creates unique dynamics for the judicial system. The fact that one individual in the relationship is using violence as a means to establish power and control over the other partner adds another layer of complexity. Because children are often involved, the judicial system must also consider the potential consequences of witnessing parental violence. For these and other reasons, it is important that staff working in specialized courts are appropriately educated about the dynamics of domestic violence and the unique situations victims struggle with. The next section will provide an overview of the historical development of domestic violence courts.

THE HISTORICAL DEVELOPMENT OF DOMESTIC VIOLENCE COURTS

In 1967, Parnas described "domestic disturbances" as "verbal and brief, neither disturbing anyone's peace outside the family nor threatening or physically harming any of the disputants."[26] At that time, the law enforcement response to domestic violence was to avoid arrest at all costs. In fact, dispatchers would often dissuade victims from requesting law enforcement to respond by pointing out the negative repercussions such as a loss of family income from the alleged perpetrator's arrest. If offenders were no longer on the scene, dispatchers would often suggest that victims lock their doors or spend the night with their mothers.[27]

During this early time when courts were first starting to grant restraining orders, police intervention, or the involvement of the criminal justice system in family matters on any level, was not common. Instead, families with "these kinds of issues" were encouraged to enroll in family counseling programs. However, as the law enforcement response to domestic violence began to change, the judicial response did as well. It was not until the late 1970s that a woman could petition the court for an order of protection against her husband without also filing for divorce. Courts continued to resist involvement in family matters for years, until the 1980s and 1990s saw a proliferation of specialized prosecution units and specialized courts for domestic violence case processing.[28]

Recognition is certainly owed to the civil rights and women's rights movements of the late 1960s toward advancing the fight against domestic violence. Advocates within the grassroots "battered women's movement," also referred to as the "domestic violence movement," organized themselves and worked extremely hard to bring the issue out from behind closed doors.[29] As with other social movements during this era, the 1970s embraced the battered women's movement and attempted to educate the public about the negative consequences of domestic violence and the impact of this crime on victims, children, and society overall.[30,31,32] Finally, the term "domestic violence" started to overlap with the term "criminalization," and the legal system began to take domestic violence cases more seriously. Judges began to take notice of the same faces in their courtrooms again and again. As the crime of domestic violence moved more to the forefront of social consciousness, it became clear that the unique dynamics involved were not being adequately addressed within the framework of traditional courtrooms.

Although the criminal justice system began shifting its response to domestic violence, changes varied widely state by state in terms of statutory depth, responses by law enforcement agencies, responses by judicial systems, and the treatment provided for offenders. Sherman and Berk's landmark experiment that examined the deterrent effects of arrest on domestic violence in Minneapolis had immediate and *profound* impacts on state statutes and policies within individual law enforcement agencies and, in essence, can be linked to the development of specialized domestic violence courts.[33] Summarized briefly, Sherman and Berk's study indicated that individuals who were arrested for committing domestic violence and spent at least eight hours in jail had significantly lower recidivism rates compared with individuals who were either counseled or sent away from their homes for a specified period of time.[34] Not long after Sherman and Berk's findings were published,[35] nearly all urban police agencies had policies encouraging pro-arrest or mandating arrest,[36] yet the findings from the replication studies that followed the Minneapolis experiment were inconsistent.[37,38]

As expected, pro-arrest law enforcement policies and mandatory arrest laws had a major impact on the volume of domestic violence defendants, both male and female, entering the criminal justice system for processing. While some prosecutors' offices were flooded with domestic violence charges,[39] a small percentage of cases were actually prosecuted.[40] Prosecutors were initially very reluctant to prosecute cases involving intimate partners, simply because they feared the women would eventually stop cooperating with the process and change their minds about wanting the case prosecuted. Prosecutors felt like they were spending too much time and money on domestic violence cases that never ended up being prosecuted.[41] Still, women were highly discouraged to make such legal accusations and were encouraged to take a more therapeutic approach to the "problem" with counseling. When cases were prosecuted (in the early days), sentences were less severe and domestic violence was still referred to as domestic "disputes."

It is estimated that between 1984 and 1997 there was a 178 percent increase in domestic cases entering the state court systems across the country—a time that corresponded with the change in law enforcement's response to domestic violence.[42,43] Overall, in nearly all jurisdictions, prosecutor's offices were essentially faced with higher domestic violence caseloads after the hasty public policy actions taken following Sherman and Berk's study on mandatory arrest.[44] However, it should also be noted that domestic violence caseloads also increased during the 1990s due to the availability of civil protection orders after the passage of the 1994 federal Violence Against Women Act (VAWA). Most states' protection order legislation was already consistent with the VAWA, but there is extreme variation in accessibility of orders for victims of violence across states.[45]

The passage of VAWA contributed a great deal to the public's awareness about the issue of domestic violence in addition to making federal funding available for the development of specialized courts.[46] One of the main purposes of VAWA was to increase services for victims of domestic violence and to improve offender accountability. It would not have been possible to implement many specialized domestic violence courts without the initial funding appropriated from the VAWA that was made available to states through federal grant programs.

Thus far this chapter has discussed domestic violence in general, the complex nature of domestic violence, and the historical perspective that explains how far the criminal justice and judicial systems have come in their response to domestic violence. Staff working in traditional court systems that presided over nondomestic violence incidents are typically not specifically aware of these dynamics and would therefore not be able to fully understand the situation before the court. Since domestic violence is committed for reasons completely different from any other crime, it made logical sense that domestic violence cases should be handled differently by the justice system, and offenders should be processed, punished, and treated accordingly. The judicial system needed to make victim safety and offender accountability priorities, in addition to providing batterer intervention treatment that focused on the root cause of the need for one person to have power and control over another person. In addition, a larger issue was addressed simultaneously with the innovation of domestic violence courts: the perception of domestic violence within society and the criminal justice system. It became clear that domestic violence was not being taken lightly by the criminal justice system or by society. Compared to traditional courts, specialized courts try to address the underlying cause of the dispute between the parties. "Court officials see domestic violence courts as not just an effective method to process cases but a method to encourage offender accountability and discourage victims from assuming blame."[47] The following section will provide an overview of the philosophy of justice that has been incorporated within domestic violence courts.

DOMESTIC VIOLENCE COURT PHILOSOPHY

The predominant theoretical foundation for domestic violence courts is the therapeutic jurisprudence philosophy of justice.[48,49,50,51,52] Domestic violence courts have integrated various aspects of therapeutic jurisprudence into their court structure. Therapeutic jurisprudence was originally incorporated within mental health courts, but the concept has now been expanded to other specialized courts, such as domestic violence courts.[53] Compared to the more adversarial and punitive nature of a traditional court, a specialized court is considered to be structured around "problem solving" so that the best outcome is achieved for the offender, victim, and society.[54]

The basic principle of therapeutic jurisprudence is that the "law is a social force that has inevitable consequences for the mental health and psychological functioning of those it affects."[55] Therapeutic is defined very broadly to encompass any effects that improve the psychological, physical, or emotional health of a person.[56] Therefore, the goal of therapeutic jurisprudence is to enhance the positive therapeutic effects of the law.

The therapeutic jurisprudence approach requires those who are making case decisions to focus first on victim safety and second on offender accountability as they consider the potential benefits and consequences of their conclusions.[57] It has long been recognized that a multiagency, coordinated response to domestic violence is the most promising strategy for effective outcomes.[58] One comprehensive strategy to a coordinated community approach is to follow a model of therapeutic jurisprudence by incorporating the "therapeutic dimension of the law" into the court by requiring court-mandated batterer intervention programs as a sentencing option.[59]

In the case of therapeutic jurisprudence and domestic violence courts, the primary goal remains the same: victim safety. However, if possible, the domestic violence court staff, and especially the prosecutor and judge, will attempt to work through the root cause of the dispute (if both parties are willing) so that in addition to holding the alleged offender accountable, the court also attempts to prevent the situation from recurring. In other words, therapeutic jurisprudence can be conceptualized as the imposition of legal sanctions with an emphasis on treatment, if appropriate, on a case-by-case basis.

DOMESTIC VIOLENCE COURTS' PROGRAMMING COMPONENTS

Domestic violence courts were initially developed in the United States and have since been implemented in other jurisdictions such as Canada, Australia, and the United Kingdom.[60] Interestingly, one of the main reasons for the advent of specialized problem-solving courts was so that justice could be achieved in a speedier and quicker fashion.[61] From the time the first domestic violence court started in the early 1980s, it was estimated that by 2000 there were over 300 courts nationwide that had specialized domestic violence offender processing.[62,63] At the time MacLeod and Weber published their descriptive study of domestic violence courts in California in 2000, these courts were considered to be a relatively new judicial option.

Although research has identified common structural programmatic components that are common across courts, there has yet to be one court identified as the "model" court. One study that included a survey of 103 domestic violence courts around the country indicated that while these specialized courts were gaining momentum, the court community had yet to identify a comprehensive set of goals and objectives for these courts.[64] So on one level, it is not too surprising that a model court structure has not yet been developed, since these courts seem to be so individualized in structure. Currently, a universal domestic violence court model does not exist for new jurisdictions to follow when implementing a court.

When developing and implementing a domestic violence court, jurisdictions may attempt to replicate a specific court's operating procedures or may pick and chose programming components from various domestic violence courts already operating. Since the development and implementation of court programs depend on resources, some courts may incorporate structural programming components to the best of their abilities, based on their resources. Other courts may develop a specialized process that fits their needs, particularly in terms of investigation, charging, and prosecution.[65]

Domestic violence courts have been examined and evaluated in the literature in a number of ways. The published literature on domestic violence courts refers to court themes, crucial components, and main principles when describing structural aspects of domestic violence courts. All of these terms are interrelated and some are even overlapping aspects of the court structure, but they also provide different ways of examining domestic violence courts. The next sections will discuss crucial components of domestic violence courts according to the National Center for State Courts, two main principles of domestic violence courts as identified by the Center for Court Innovation, and two main structural court themes of domestic violence courts according to the Judicial Council of California. Three interrelated subtopics are then discussed: the domestic violence court's relationship with other agencies in the community, offender monitoring as an important component of the court's structure, and a major structural component of the court being the extent to which the victim is involved in the actual court process. This section will conclude with a discussion of the structural variation among domestic violence courts.

The National Center for State Courts suggests that the crucial components of specialized domestic violence courts include case coordination mechanisms, specialized intake units, specialized calendars, the designation of specialized judges, and consistent mechanisms for monitoring and enforcing batterer compliance with treatment.[66] In fact, Keilitz strongly advocates identifying and designating specialized judges with domestic violence as their only area of judgeship.[67] The Judicial Council of California also supports the notion that specialized judges are the key to the success of domestic violence courts.[68] However, Keilitz is careful to point out the criticism that specialized judges face the risk of becoming less neutral over time because they do, in fact, become more educated about the dynamics of domestic violence and are working more closely with staff in the domestic violence advocacy community.[69] Specialized dockets tend to lead to judge burnout, particularly domestic violence court dockets that are already at risk for high rates of burnout. This is an example of a real-world issue that a judicial system has to consider when implementing a domestic violence court.

The Center for Court Innovation in New York is well known for their innovative advances in the area of domestic violence courts. Ten years after New York implemented their first domestic violence court, Aldrich and Mazur evaluated the New York model as a means to suggest ways to apply key urban domestic violence court principles to courts in smaller, rural, and suburban jurisdictions.[70] The two main principles they identified were coordination with victim services and judicial monitoring. It is noted that it may be easier to implement these principles with a designated judge and specialized docket, but it is not an absolute prerequisite to the successful implementation of these two key principles.[71] The following includes recommendations from lessons learned in New York from existing domestic violence courts that were successful in linking victims to the services they needed: provide victims with immediate access to advocates, keep victims informed, schedule cases promptly, create "safe spaces" within the courthouse, and create strong linkages with a wide range of partners. In addition to the importance of providing services to victims, ongoing judicial monitoring has been touted as possibly the most effective technique for reducing recidivism.[72]

The Judicial Council of California conducted a survey of California's domestic violence courts and included courts that utilized court dockets that assigned domestic violence cases exclusively, regardless of whether an exclusive domestic violence docket was the final outcome.[73] The findings from this study indicated that the two main structural court themes included victim safety and offender accountability. In fact, the most common reasons reported for implementing these specialized courts included the need for improved assistance for victims, improved victim safety, and increased offender accountability. These findings are true of courts throughout the United States.

One structural issue unique to domestic violence courts includes their relationships with resources and services in the community that can assist in the comprehensive response required for domestic violence. Since every domestic violence case is different, services needed by the victim and/or perpetrator vary. There must be solid collaborative relationships between the court and other state, county, and community agencies and organizations so that the appropriate services can be delivered to victims and offenders. Oftentimes it is difficult for judicial systems to coordinate services with other agencies within the realm of state and county governments while continuing to keep up with their own dockets, cases, and other responsibilities and duties within their agencies.

Strongly related to the court's relationships with other agencies in the community are the departments of probation/corrections. Offender monitoring is an important component of the domestic violence court system. Domestic violence case monitoring involves a variety of agencies and key stakeholders such as court clerks, bailiffs, district attorneys, probation officers, batterer intervention programs, victim witness assistance providers, social service agencies, and judicial officers. To ensure strong communication between each of the stakeholders, many domestic violence courts hold regular meetings to review case files and discuss ways to improve their monitoring tactics.[74] Offender monitoring through communication across agencies will certainly become more technologically sophisticated during the twenty-first century.

The extent to which the victim is involved in the process is a major component of the court's structure. Many domestic violence courts are structured in a way that does not require the victim to attend the defendant's court hearing. The level of the victim's involvement directly leads to the issue of whether the victim wants the case prosecuted or not, which determines whether the victim is considered to be "cooperative" or "uncooperative."[75] Dawson and Dinovitzer examined the influence that victim cooperation played in the prosecution of cases in a specialized domestic violence court in Canada.[76] This court was specifically designed to minimize the reliance on victim involvement during prosecution. Even with the court structured in such a way, victim cooperation did, in fact, have a significant influence on the likelihood of prosecution. In fact, when the prosecutor perceived the victim to be cooperative, the odds of prosecution were seven times higher than if the prosecutor perceived the victim to be uncooperative.[77,78]

Domestic violence courts vary in structure for a variety of reasons, including the size of the jurisdiction, the number of cases typically assigned to the court's docket, and resource allocation such as facility space.[79] Some courts may schedule all of the domestic violence cases on a particular day of the week, or they may have one particular judge assigned to preside over the domestic cases. Case screening can pose a particular problem for domestic violence courts, simply because the technology resources may be very limited. This may lead to complications in hearings due to a lack of information exchange between various courts dealing simultaneously with issues involving the same family.

From a review of the literature, it is clear that victim safety and offender accountability are the predominant themes guiding domestic violence courts across the country. Court programs are being implemented to support these priorities to the best of the court's ability based on resource limitations and other bureaucratic issues that may arise when implementing specialized court programs.

THE LEXINGTON COUNTY DOMESTIC VIOLENCE COURT: A CASE STUDY

The Lexington County Criminal Domestic Violence Court (CDVC) was implemented in 1999 in Lexington, South Carolina, by the Lexington County Sheriff's Office to improve the county's law enforcement and judicial responses to domestic violence.[80,81] The court was established with funding from the 1994 Violence Against Women Act. To achieve this goal, the CDVC implemented a multiagency collaborative approach to processing domestic violence cases. Prior to the establishment of the specialized court, domestic violence cases were heard in one of eight magistrate level courts in Lexington County. The Sheriff's Department wanted to standardize the processing of all domestic violence cases in one court so that victims would receive the services and safety planning they needed, while offenders would be held accountable for their violent behavior and could also receive the treatment they needed.

The CDVC staff consisted of two full-time investigators and a full-time prosecutor who worked as a team on domestic violence cases. In addition, a full-time victim advocate was hired to assist domestic violence victims, and a court administrator was hired to handle the administrative tasks involved in running a separate court docket for domestic violence cases. Two magistrate level judges were assigned to specifically preside over the CDVC. The Lexington County Department of Mental Health dedicated a mental health counselor to diagnose and assign proper treatment plans for individuals who are charged with domestic violence, and a legal advocate from a local domestic violence shelter was assigned to the court to make contact with victims and to be present in court.[82] All of these individuals made up the unique court staff of the Lexington County CDVC. Much of the court's success can be attributed to the outstanding working relationships that the court staff established with one another and their commitment to the success and purpose of the CDVC. The CDVC court staff clearly worked together to process each case and to determine the best outcome for each victim and defendant.

All domestic violence cases were assigned to one of two dedicated domestic violence investigators. Investigators were responsible for providing follow-up on all cases by collecting additional evidence from victims and witnesses, serving as witnesses during prosecutions, often providing expert testimony, and serving warrants for arrests to defendants who were not present at the scene when the original responding officer arrived. Investigators would review in-house records to determine whether a history of violence existed between the individuals involved in the dispute and to determine whether previous calls for service had been made by the victim. Additionally, investigators would consult the National Crime Information Center database to search for federal, state, and local prior criminal history information on all defendants, and specifically evidence of prior domestic violence charges or convictions. Investigators obtained 911 tapes in all cases, which were found to be particularly useful in cases that involved an uncooperative victim. As mentioned earlier, investigators made a priority to make immediate contact with the victim in order to obtain more details in the case.

All magistrate level nonfelony cases of domestic violence that occurred in Lexington County were prosecuted in the specialized court. To hold offenders accountable for their violent behavior, the court imposed fines in a majority of the cases in addition to increasing the amount of time offenders spent in jail pretrial. Offender accountability was promoted by the CDVC with a strong emphasis on mandatory batterer treatment. To emphasize offender treatment, jail sentences were suspended for offenders who were eligible for and successfully completed a 26-week group-based cognitive therapy program for domestic violence batterers, financed by batterers themselves (similar to financial procedures followed by other batterer intervention programs).[83] Treatment program progress was monitored on a weekly basis; defendants who failed to comply with treatment conditions were issued bench warrants, and suspended jail sentences were imposed.

Various other operational changes in the Lexington County Sheriff's Department resulted in substantial progress as well. Deputies started using digital cameras for timely pictures of victims' injuries for evidence collection when responding to calls for service. Deputies were also trained in the importance of getting detailed statements from victims when initially responding to calls for service. Finally, investigators and other court staff participated in statewide and local domestic violence trainings sponsored by the South Carolina Coalition Against Domestic Violence, the South Carolina Attorney General's Office, and the South Carolina Victim Assistance Network.

Another unique component of the Lexington County CDVC is the use of criminal no-contact orders for alleged domestic violence offenders. After a defendant is arrested in Lexington County for criminal domestic violence, he/she is required to appear in bond court. In approximately 80 percent of cases, defendants are placed on a *criminal* no-contact order (NCO) as a condition of their bond (personal communication with the CDVC prosecutor). These orders are similar to civil protection orders in theory, but they are imposed by the court rather than requested by the victim. The NCO prohibits the alleged offender from contacting the victim in person, by phone, by text messaging, through a third party, by leaving messages, or in any way whatsoever during the period between the defendant's arraignment in bond court and sentencing.[84] Because the majority of situations involve victims and alleged offenders who share a residence, defendants are required to find alternative living arrangements. These bond restrictions are not lifted until the defendant appears in the CDVC and a disposition is made in the case, approximately 30 days after his/her bond hearing.

All representatives of the CDVC are present during case adjudication (the victim advocate, investigators, mental health personnel, etc.). Defendants are shown a video at the beginning of court that explains the four options that they have available to them: they may chose pretrial intervention if they are eligible, they can plead guilty, they can request a bench trial that will occur that day, or they can request a jury trial that will occur at a later date. Defendants are also given a paper document that again explains their available options, and then each defendant is individually called up to the front of the courtroom by name. The defendant is asked if he/she understands his/her options and what option he/she will exercise. The defendant is required to indicate his/her choice in writing and sign the document. After all defendants have been called before the judge, the bench trials begin.

Another unique aspect of the CDVC is the availability of the Pre-Trial Intervention Program (PTI) for eligible defendants. As a nonadjudicatory diversion program, PTI is available only to defendants who have not been previously convicted of a felony, have never been convicted of domestic violence, and are not currently on probation. Approximately 10 percent of the cases that are processed in the CDVC are referred to PTI, and approximately 50 percent of those defendants successfully complete the program (personal communication with the CDVC prosecutor). Defendants who participate in PTI's 26-week therapy program have not pled to anything nor have they been found guilty of a crime. If a PTI defendant fails to follow the conditions of his treatment, a bench warrant is issued for his arrest. These defendants have an opportunity when they are rearrested to plead guilty or to request a trial, at which time they may be found guilty. Some defendants who are arrested for a violation of their treatment agreement are detained in jail while they wait for their case to be heard in court. However, for defendants who successfully complete PTI, their domestic violence arrest is expunged from their criminal record. Nearly all individuals processed in the CDVC participate in the treatment program; the non-PTI offenders follow the same rules as the PTI offenders. In other words, the defendants who are attending treatment programming as a diversionary option are participating in the same treatment programs as individuals who either pled guilty or were determined by a judge or jury to be guilty of committing criminal domestic violence. A mental health counselor closely monitors each participant's progress on a weekly basis.

One important difference between the CDVC and the way that domestic violence cases are processed in traditional courts is the involvement of the court's dedicated victim advocate. Besides providing the victims with general information about courtroom procedures and attending court with the victims if she or he wishes, the CDVC advocate provides emergency crisis counseling to victims, provides education about their rights, and assists victims in their preparation to testify in court. Overall, the specialized court's success is heavily reliant on the work of the dedicated advocate's role.

PROCESS AND OUTCOME EVALUATION FINDINGS OF THE LEXINGTON COUNTY DOMESTIC VIOLENCE COURT

According to a study funded by the National Institute of Justice, positive results were reported from both process and outcome evaluations of the Lexington County Domestic Violence Court.[85,86,87] The process evaluation involves three forms of data collection: in-depth interviews with court staff, court observations, and interviews with a convenience sample of victims and defendants after their cases were heard in the domestic violence court. Interviews with the key court staff indicated that law enforcement and investigative procedures for domestic violence changed after the inception of the court. For example, every domestic violence case was assigned to a domestic violence investigator, who followed up with the victim in person. Investigators and responding officers were also more conscientious about taking pictures of injuries at the time of the incident and after the incident to capture pictures of injuries that do not immediately show.

Findings from the court observations indicated that a therapeutic jurisprudence philosophy of justice was incorporated into the workings of the court and that a well-established courtroom workgroup developed among the courtroom staff. Finally, the interviews with the victims and defendants/offenders were overwhelmingly positive in terms of the court's incorporation of elements of therapeutic jurisprudence.[88] Almost 70 percent of both victims and defendants/offenders viewed the outcomes of their cases as fair and just. An even higher percentage reported that they had been treated with respect and dignity by the court.

In summary, process evaluation findings indicated that the Lexington County court implemented their goals and objectives as planned. Based on the positive experience of the court, the court's operating budget was incorporated into the county's budget once the federal VAWA planning and implementation grant was completed. Court players indicated that they viewed and responded to domestic violence differently after the implementation of the court.[89] Overall, process evaluation findings indicated that the response to domestic violence changed in a positive way after the implementation of the specialized court.

Outcome evaluation findings also showed similar positive results in terms of official measures of recidivism in comparison to arrest rates before the implementation of the court.[90] Findings indicated that monthly arrests for domestic violence significantly increased after the implementation of the court. In addition, recidivism rates from a historical control group of randomly selected individuals who were processed in traditional magistrate courts were significantly higher than recidivism rates for randomly selected offenders who were processed in the specialized domestic violence court 18 months following their arrest. Specifically, the odds of being rearrested for a domestic violence for offenders processed in the domestic violence court compared to offenders processed in traditional magistrate courts decreased by 40 percent. So, while monthly arrest rates for domestic violence were significantly increasing, rearrest rates for domestic violence were significantly decreasing. These positive process and outcome evaluation findings show great promise for the integrated judicial process within the criminal justice system for holding domestic violence offenders accountable and enhancing victim safety.[91]

CURRENT CONCERN WITH DOMESTIC VIOLENCE COURTS: NO-DROP POLICIES

A current concern that both scholars and the practice community have with domestic violence courts has to do with whether the court adheres to a no-drop prosecution policy. A no-drop prosecution policy ensures that prosecutors move forward with a case even though the victim is unwilling to cooperate with the prosecution. The purpose of no-drop policies is to decrease the rate of domestic violence cases that are dismissed and increase the rate of cases prosecuted successfully. Proponents of no-drop policies point out that they provide stronger incentives for law enforcement officers and detectives to do a thorough job collecting evidence, such as taking pictures and using a video camera, which do not require the victim to be in court to testify. This approach means that the victim does not have a choice to drop the charges, because they did not file the charges; the charges are filed by the state, according to mandatory arrest policies. According to Bennett, Goodman, and Dutton, a survey of prosecutors' offices indicated that a majority of the offices were, in fact, operating according to a no-drop policy.[92]

No-drop policies for domestic violence courts have come under fire from many among the practice community, especially among advocates, who express concern that if the victim does not want the case prosecuted, it is very disempowering for the prosecutor to dismiss the victim's wishes by moving forward with the case. Indeed, many opponents believe that taking this decision out of victims' hands constitutes further victimization. This, in turn, could make victims less likely to contact the criminal justice system for future intervention.[93]

The no-drop issue is an unfortunate concern, because to some extent the controversy derails focus from the overall purpose and efficacy of the court. Regardless of whether a prosecutor is working cases according to a no-drop policy or not, all prosecutors deal with a high proportion of reluctant and uncooperative victims. Numerous studies have documented the high extent to which victims change their minds about prosecuting their batterers.[94,95]

DOMESTIC VIOLENCE COURTS: PROSPECTS FOR THE FUTURE

As MacLeod and Weber have pointed out, domestic violence courts are a quickly emerging area of judicial administration and scholarly research.[96]

Domestic violence courts have proliferated across the United States and have also been implemented in Leeds, England,[97] and in Perleu and Port of Spain, Trinidad.[98] These jurisdictions have similarly incorporated a multiagency approach to processing domestic violence defendants by making decisions based on input from law enforcement, social services, victim support services, and probation services.[99,100] Walsh summarizes the issue of domestic violence nicely by saying that it is a phenomenon that does not fit neatly into any one camp because it involves so many social services in society, including the health system, the criminal justice system, and the private and nonprofit system.[101] Given this overlap, a multidisciplinary response is necessary. Domestic violence courts fill the need for a multidisciplinary approach to defendant processing, if possible, with a rehabilitative approach that is combined with a focus on a therapeutic approach, rather than solely imposing a custodial sentence. Additionally, domestic violence courts support victim safety and offender accountability by putting the victims' needs first in addition to providing community-based treatment programs that focus on the root cause of domestic violence: the need for power and control over another human being. Finally, domestic violence courts provide a viable mechanism for collaboration between multiple agencies to deliver a more comprehensive response to victims and alleged offenders involved in family violence.[102]

Comparing domestic violence offenses to other crimes, comprehensively, is difficult given the intense emotional involvement between the victim and offender, and often the involvement of children. While recent years have shown promise in terms of collaborative efforts towards victim support and offender accountability, many domestic violence courts struggle with the major obstacle of obtaining resources for planning, implementation, and expansion. Additionally, many domestic violence courts continue to grapple with procedural issues such as obtaining police reports or fostering better communication between agencies. According to Butts there are still some very important questions that remain to be answered, but with continued scholarly focus and judicial attention on these issues the twenty-first century will have many answers to provide.[103]

NOTES

1. Mazur and Aldrich, 2003.
2. Mirchandani, 2005.
3. Butts, 2001.
4. Parnas, 1967.
5. Tjaden and Thoennes, 2000, p. 10.
6. National Center for Injury Prevention and Control, 2003, p. 14.
7. National Center for Injury Prevention and Control, 2003, p. 19.
8. Crandall et al., 2004, p. 906.
9. Buzawa and Buzawa, 2003.
10. Walker, 1979.
11. Brown, 1997, p. 6.

12. Bornstein, 2006.
13. Bornstein, 1992.
14. Bornstein, 2006.
15. Coker et al., 2000.
16. Kernic, Wolf, and Holt, 2000.
17. Rennison and Welchans, 2000.
18. Woods et al., 2005.
19. Downs and Rindels, 2004.
20. Lang et al., 2004.
21. Bennice et al., 2003.
22. Strauss, 1991.
23. Maker, Kemmelmeier, and Peterson, 1998.
24. Kernic et al., 2003.
25. McCloskey and Lichter, 2003.
26. Parnas, 1967, p. 914.
27. Parnas, 1967.
28. Tsai, 2000.
29. Schechter, 1982.
30. Bennett, Goodman, and Dutton, 1999.
31. Little, 2003.
32. Robinson and Cook, 2006.
33. Sherman and Berk, 1984.
34. Sherman and Berk, 1984.
35. Sherman and Berk, 1984.
36. Sherman, 1992, p. 2.
37. Ventura and Davis, 2005.
38. For an in-depth discussion of the findings from a comprehensive reanalysis of the replication studies, see Maxwell, C. D., Joel H. Garner, J. H., and Fagan, J. A. (2001). *Effects of arrests on intimate partner violence: New evidence from the spouse assault replication program.* Washington, DC: National Institute of Justice. (NCJ 188199.)
39. Cahn, 1992.
40. Dawson and Dinovitzer, 2001.
41. Fagan, 1996.
42. Ostrom and Kauder, 1999, p. 44.
43. The ten-year trend data are based on court filings between 1989 and 1998 from 10 states and partial data from 18 states (Keilitz, 2000).
44. Sherman and Berk, 1984.
45. DeJong and Burgess-Proctor, 2006.
46. Keilitz, 2000.
47. Mirchandani, 2006, p. 790.
48. Fritzler and Simon, 2000.
49. Ostrom, 2003.
50. Rottman and Casey, 1999.
51. Simon, 1995.
52. Wexler and Winick, 1996.
53. Tsai, 2000.
54. Ostrom, 2003.

55. Winick, 1997, p. 185.
56. Winick, 1997, p. 192.
57. Fritzler and Simon, 2000.
58. Hofford, 1991.
59. Tsai, 2000, p. 5.
60. Eley, 2005.
61. Mirchandani, 2005.
62. Eley, 2005.
63. Keilitz, 200.
64. Keilitz, 2000.
65. Eley, 2005.
66. Keilitz, 2000.
67. Keilitz, 2000.
68. McLeod and Webber, 2000.
69. Keilitz, 2000.
70. Aldrich and Mazur, 2005.
71. Aldrich and Mazur, 2005.
72. Newmark et al., 2001.
73. McLeod and Weber, 2000.
74. Mazur and Aldrich, 2003.
75. The term "cooperative victim" is commonly used by law enforcement and judicial personnel to refer to victims who are working with the criminal justice system through the investigation and prosecution stages and do not want to stay in a relationship with their batterers. The term "uncooperative victim" is commonly used by law enforcement and judicial personnel to refer to victims who are not working with the criminal justice system to process the offender and are staying in the relationship with the offender.
76. Dawson and Dinovitzer, 2001.
77. Dawson and Dinovitzer, 2001.
78. For an in-depth discussion of this issue, see Cretney, A., and Davis, G. (1997). Prosecuting domestic assault: Are victims failing courts, or courts failing victims? *The Howard Journal, 36,* 146–157.
79. MacLeod and Weber, 2000.
80. Gover, MacDonald, and Alpert, 2003.
81. Bureau of Census data from 2000 indicated that the majority of Lexington County is geographically dispersed into rural communities. The population at that time was approximately 220,000, and 84 percent of the residents were White. The county was predominately working class and the per capita income was approximately $22,000 a year.
82. Gover et al., 2003.
83. Cognitive behavioral therapy (CBT) is used with offenders to target character deficits related to antisocial attitudes, values, and beliefs, and antisocial personality factors (Cullen and Gendreau, 2000). Offenders accomplish this by learning to identify and challenge their high-risk thoughts, beliefs, and situations that support offending. CBT is a therapeutic technique designed to motivate and train offenders to change distorted cognitions related to thoughts, conceptualization of self and others, and assumptions, beliefs, or rules about behavior.
84. O'Connor, 1999.

85. Gover, MacDonald, and Alpert, 2003.
86. Gover, Brank, and MacDonald, 2007.
87. This investigation was supported by the National Institute of Justice, Office of Justice Programs, U.S. Department of Justice, to the University of South Carolina (Project No. 2000-WT-VX-0015). Points of view in this document are those of the authors and do not necessarily represent the official position of the Department of Justice.
88. Gover et al., 2007.
89. Gover, Brank, and MacDonald, 2007.
90. Gover, Brank, and MacDonald, 2007.
91. Gover, Brank, and MacDonald, 2007.
92. Bennett, Goodman, and Dutton, 1999.
93. According to Robinson and Cook (2006), "although the government seeks to reduce victim retractions, in some cases where victims retract the outcome can still be considered a success because they have benefited from the more positive concept of 'support retractions'" (208). This statement referred to victims in a study who had a support system, people to turn to for advice, various opportunities in terms of housing, welfare, education, and counseling, and other resources they would need to move beyond their violent experience and start anew.
94. Ford, 1983.
95. Rebovich, 1996.
96. MacLeod and Weber, 2000.
97. Walsh, 2001.
98. Lazarus-Black and McCall, 2006.
99. Fritzler and Simon, 2000.
100. Walsh, 2001.
101. Walsh, 2001.
102. Walsh recognizes that unlike specialized drug courts, the domestic violence court does not have an accurate way to monitor whether domestic violence offenders are complying with their treatment conditions (2001). Given that victims are routinely manipulated and intimidated by their abusers to report that they are not being reabused, Walsh recommends that domestic violence courts should expect to achieve a rehabilitative outcome when the abuse is "relatively minor" (2001, p. 30).
103. Butts, 2001.

REFERENCES

Aldrich, L., & Mazur, R. (2005). *Applying key principles of domestic violence courts in smaller jurisdictions.* New York: Center for Court Innovation and Bureau of Justice Assistance, U.S. Department of Justice.

Bennett, L., Goodman, L., & Dutton, M. A. (1999). Systemic obstacles to the criminal prosecution of a battering partner: A victim perspective. *Journal of Interpersonal Violence, 14,* 761–772.

Bennice, J. A., Resick, P. A., Mechanic, M., & Astin, M. (2003). The relative effects of intimate partner physical and sexual violence on post-traumatic stress disorder symptomology. *Violence and Victims, 18,* 87–94.

Bornstein, R. F. (1992). The dependent personality: Developmental, social, and clinical perspectives. *Psychological Bulletin, 112,* 3–123.

Bornstein, R. F. (2006). The complex relationship between dependency and domestic violence. *American Psychologist, 61,* 595–606.

Brown, J. (1997). Working toward freedom from violence: The process of change in battered women. *Violence Against Women, 3,* 5–22.

Butts, J. A. (2001). Introduction: Problem-solving courts. *Law & Policy, 23,* 121–124.

Buzawa, E. S., & Buzawa, C. G. (2003). *Domestic violence: The criminal justice response* (3rd ed.). Thousand Oaks, CA: Sage Publications.

Cahn, N. R. (1992). Innovative approaches to the prosecution of domestic violence crimes: An overview. In E. S. Buzawa & C. G. Buzawa (Eds.), *Domestic violence: The changing criminal justice response* (pp. 161–180). Westport, CT: Auburn House.

Coker, A. L., Smith, P. H., Bethea, L., King, M. R., & McKeown, R. E. (2000). Physical health consequences of physical and psychological intimate partner violence. *Archives of Family Medicine, 9,* 451–457.

Crandall, M. L., Nathens, A. B., Kernic, M. A., Hold,V. L., & Rivara, F. P. (2004). Predicting future injury among women in abusive relationships. *Journal of Trauma-Injury Infection and Critical Care, 56,* 902–912.

Cretney, A., & Davis, G. (1997). Prosecuting domestic assault: Are victims failing courts, or courts failing victims? *The Howard Journal of Criminal Justice, 36,* 146–157.

Cullen, F. T., & Gendreau, P. (2000). Assessing correctional rehabilitation: Policy, practice, and prospects. In Julie Horney (Ed.), *Policies, processes, and decisions of the criminal justice system* (*Criminal Justice 2000,* Vol. 3, pp. 109–175). Washington, DC: National Institute of Justice.

Dawson, M., & Dinovitzer, R. (2001). Victim cooperation and the prosecution of domestic violence in a specialized court. *Justice Quarterly, 18,* 593–622.

DeJong, C., & Burgess-Proctor, A. (2006). A summary of personal protection order statutes in the United States. *Violence Against Women, 12,* 68–88.

Downs, W. R., & Rindels, B. (2004). Adulthood depression, anxiety, and trauma symptoms: A comparison of women with nonabusive, abusive, and absent father figures in childhood. *Violence and Victims, 19,* 659–671.

Eley, S. (2005). Changing practices: The specialised domestic violence court process. *The Howard Journal of Criminal Justice, 44,* 113–142.

Fagan, J. (1995). The criminalization of domestic violence: Promises and limits. Paper presented at the annual conference on research and evaluation sponsored by the National Institute of Justice, the Bureau of Justice Assistance, and the Office of Juvenile Justice and Delinquency Prevention, Washington, DC, July 10.

Ford, D. A. (1983). Wife battery and criminal justice: A study of victim decision-making. *Family Relations, 32,* 463–475.

Fritzler, R. B., & Simon, L. M. J. (2000, Spring). Creating a domestic violence court: Combat in the trenches. *Court Review, 37,* 28–39.

Gover, A. R., MacDonald, J. M., & Alpert, G. P. (2003). Combating domestic violence: Findings from an evaluation of a local domestic violence court. *Criminology and Public Policy, 1,* 109–132.

Gover, A. R, MacDonald, J. M., Alpert, G. P., & Geary, I. A., Jr. (2004). Lexington County Domestic Violence Court: A partnership and evaluation. Report to the National Institute of Justice, U.S. Department of Justice and Lexington County Sheriff's Office from Department of Criminology and Criminal Justice, University of South Carolina.

Gover, A. R., Brank, E. M., & MacDonald, J. M. (2007). A specialized domestic violence court in South Carolina: An example of procedural justice for victims and defendants. *Violence Against Women, 13,* 603–626.

Hofford, M. (1991). Family violence: Challenging cases for probation officers. *Federal Probation, 55,* 12–17.

Keilitz, S. (2001). *Specialization of domestic violence case management in the courts: A national survey.* National Center for State Courts. Available at http://www.ncsconline.org/index.html (accessed May 15, 2008).

Kernic, M. A., Wolf, M. E., & Holt, V. L. (2000). Rates and relative risk of hospital admission among women in violent intimate partner relationships. *American Journal of Public Health, 90,* 1416–1420.

Kernic, M. A., Wolf, M. E., Holt, V. L., McKnight, B., Huebner, C. E., & Rivara, F. P. 2003. Behavioral problems among children whose mothers are abused by an intimate partner. *Child Abuse and Neglect, 27,* 1231–1246.

Klaus, P. (2005). *National crime victimization survey: Crime and the nation's households.* Bureau of Justice Statistics, U.S. Department of Justice. Available at http://www.ojp.usdoj.gov/bjs/pub/pdf/cnh05.pdf (accessed August 2, 2008).

Lang, A. J., Stein, M. B., Kennedy, C. M., & Foy, D. W. 2004. Adult psychopathology and intimate partner violence among survivors of childhood maltreatment. *Journal of Interpersonal Violence, 19,* 1102–1118.

Lazarus-Black, M., & McCall, P. L. (2006). The politics of place: Practice, process, and kinship in domestic violence courts. *Human Organization, 65,* 140–155.

Little, K. (2003, May). Specialized courts and domestic violence. *Issues of Democracy, 8*(1). Available at http://usinfo.state.gov/journals/itdhr/0503/ijde/littel.htm (accessed August 2, 2008).

MacLeod, D., & Weber, J. F. (2000). *Domestic violence courts: A descriptive study.* San Francisco, CA: Judicial Council of California, Administrative Office of the Courts.

Maker, A. H., Kemmelmeier, M., & Peterson, C. (1998). Long-term psychological consequences in women of witnessing parental physical conflict and experiencing abuse in childhood. *Journal of Interpersonal Violence, 13,* 574–589.

Mazur, R., and Aldrich, L. (2003). What makes domestic violence court work? Lessons from New York. *Judges Journal, 42,* 5–10.

McCloskey, L. A., and Litchter, E. L. (2003). The contribution of marital violence to adolescent aggression across different relationships. *Journal of Interpersonal Violence, 18,* 390–412.

Mirchandani, R. (2005). What's so special about specialized courts? The state and social change in Salt Lake City's domestic violence court. *Law & Society Review, 39,* 379–417.

National Center for Injury Prevention and Control. (2003). *Costs of intimate partner violence against women in the United States.* Atlanta GA: National Center for Injury Prevention and Control, Centers for Disease Control and Prevention, U.S. Department of Health and Human Services.

Newmark, L., Rempel, M., Diffily, K., & Mallik-Kane, K. (2001). *Specialized felony domestic violence: Lessons on implementation and impacts from the Kings County experience.* Washington, DC: The Urban Institute and the Center for State Courts for the National Institute of Justice, U.S. Department of Justice.

O'Connor, C. (1999). Domestic violence no-contact orders and the autonomy rights of victims. *Boston College Law Review, 40,* 937–967.

Ostrom, B. J. (2003). Domestic violence courts. *Criminology and Public Policy, 3,* 105–108.

Ostrom, B. J., & Kauder, N. B. (1999). *Examining the work of state courts, 1998: A national perspective from the court statistics project.* Williamsburg, VA: National Center for State Courts.

Parnas, R. I. (1967). The police response to the domestic disturbance. *Wisconsin Law Review, 2,* 914–960.

Rebovich, D. V. (1996). Prosecution response to domestic violence: Results of a survey of a large jurisdiction. In E. S. Buzawa & C. G. Buzawa (Eds.), *Do arrests and restraining orders work?* (pp. 176–191). Thousand Oaks, CA: Sage.

Rennison, C. M., & Welchans, S. (2000). *Intimate partner violence.* Washington, DC: Bureau of Justice Statistics, U.S. Department of Justice. (NCJ 178247.)

Robinson, A., & Dee Cook, D. (2006). Understanding victim retraction in cases of domestic violence: Specialist courts, government policy, and victim-centered justice. *Contemporary Justice Review, 9,* 189–213.

Rottmann, D., & Casey, P. (1999, July). Therapeutic jurisprudence and the emergence of problem-solving courts. *National Institute of Justice Journal,* 12–19.

Schechter, S. (1982). *Women and male violence: The victims and struggles of the battered women's movement.* Boston: South End Press.

Sherman, L. W. (1992). The influence of criminology on criminal law: Evaluating arrests for misdemeanor domestic violence. *The Journal of Criminal Law and Criminology, 83,* 1–45.

Sherman, L. W., & Berk, R. A. (1984). The specific deterrent effects of arrest for domestic assault. *American Sociological Review, 41,* 261–272.

Shurman, L. A., & Rodriguez, C. M. (2006). Cognitive-affective predictors of women's readiness to end domestic violence relationships. *Journal of Interpersonal Violence, 21,* 1417–1439.

Simon, L. M. J. (1995). A therapeutic jurisprudence approach to the legal processing of domestic violence cases. *Psychology, Public Policy, and Law, 1,* 43–79.

Strauss, M. A. (1991). Children as witness to marital violence: A risk factor for life long problems among a nationally representative sample of American men and women. Paper presented at Ross Roundtable on Children and Violence, Washington, DC, September 21–23.

Tjaden, P., & Thoennes, N. (2000). *Extent, nature, and consequences of intimate partner violence: Findings from the national violence against women survey, research report.* Washington, DC: National Institute of Justice, U.S. Department of Justice and the Centers for Disease Control and Prevention, U.S. Department of Health and Human Services. (NCJ 181867.)

Tsai, B. (2000). The trend toward specialized domestic violence courts: Improvements on an effective innovation. *Fordham Law Review, 68,* 1285–1327.

Ventura, L. A., & Davis, G. (2005). Domestic violence: Court case conviction and recidivism. *Violence Against Women, 11,* 255–277.

Walker, L. (1979). *The battered woman.* New York: Harper and Row.

Walsh, C. (2001). The trend toward specialization: West Yorkshire innovations in drug and domestic violence courts. *The Howard Journal of Criminal Justice, 40,* 26–38.

Wexler, D. B., & Winick, B. J. (1996). *Law in a therapeutic key: Developments in therapeutic jurisprudence.* Durham, NC: Carolina Academic Press.

Winick, B. J. (1997). The jurisprudence of therapeutic jurisprudence. *Psychology, Public Policy, and Law, 3,* 184–206.

Woods, A. B., Page, G. G., O'Campo, P., Pugh, L. C., Ford, D., & Campbell, J. C. (2005). The mediation effect of posttraumatic stress disorder symptoms on the relationship of intimate partner violence and IFN-e levels. *American Journal of Community Psychology, 36,* 159–176.

8

Problem-Solving in Community Courts: Who Decides the Problem?

VICTORIA MALKIN

Community courts have been defined as "neighborhood focused courts that attempt to harness the power of the justice system to address local problems."[1] This is a broad mandate for a court, and perhaps the broadest to date for any of the problem-solving courts in operation. Problem-solving courts aim to address a "broken system" symbolized by a "revolving door" through which repeat offenders continually circulate while underlying problems remain ignored.[2] But the problem addressed by community courts is perhaps the most amorphous of any of these new courts. It remains to be defined by a place or neighborhood as opposed to being a particular issue that is managed in a standardized way across all the courts. This approach advocates a degree of flexibility and discretion that initially seems appealing as local courts are left to decide what they determine to be their focus according to community needs. However, it also means that at this time these courts' operating models, goals, and methods of evaluation continue to remain open and somewhat unspecified.[3]

For advocates, the decentralization of a court system into a local neighborhood permits the possibility of more effective institutional and administrative practices. Moreover, community courts are advertised as part of a community revitalization effort where these institutions can address local problems and generate social change. But how should we understand the transformation of a court into an institution that by proxy seems to be incorporated into a component of community development, thus departing from our traditional idea of the role of a court and the criminal justice system? To understand community courts and their new role, one should consider their emergence alongside the underlying ideologies and the societal changes that accompany their creation, in particular the deterioration of different urban neighborhoods and increasing inequality from the 1970s onwards, and the corresponding changes in urban social welfare policies and policing practices.

Two popular visions of crime reduction and social change underlie a community court's operations. First is a loosely defined idea that community participation will facilitate local problem solving and thus social change. Second is the popular "Broken Windows" theory of crime control. This theory argues that public disorder is a precursor to higher levels of crime. Using the example of Red Hook Community Justice Center, which opened in Brooklyn, New York, in 2000, I will consider the potential conflicts and possibilities these ideas present when put into practice.[4] Communities certainly need effective courts, but it is not clear whether involving courts in community development allows for a synergy that can encourage community participation in social action, or whether the court actually sets the terms of the debates in such a way that portions of the community remain silenced or disempowered.

THE ORIGINS AND DEVELOPMENT OF COMMUNITY COURTS

The first community court opened in Midtown Manhattan in 1993. It was planned by the Center for Court Innovation with backing from the New York State Courts system alongside strong support from the Times Square Business Community, which hoped to benefit from having the court operate inside its precinct. Following its success, the Center for Court Innovation worked to open a community court in Red Hook, Brooklyn, and Harlem. These first three projects put the ideas behind community courts into practice, opening neighborhood-based courts that addressed low-level crimes that were a cause for community concern. In all three courts, cases were adjudicated and offenders were ordered to complete sanctions. These sanctions could include community restoration projects and/or social service evaluations and treatment programs selected by a judge in consultation with social workers to address an individual's designated problems.

Other jurisdictions have followed with their own examples. But what exactly counts as a community court? Currently there are some 32 in the United States with more slated to open.[5] Unlike other problem-solving courts where specific operational models and sanctions are continually refined and replicated across courtrooms to improve the treatment of individuals experiencing particular problems (such as drug addiction, mental health problems, or domestic violence), community courts began as a diverse group. Initially they were proposed as a mechanism to respond to a perceived crisis between courts and communities, as articulated in a Bureau of Justice Assistance workshop that tried to define the model:

> Observers have noted that justice has become remote from communities and the people who live in them. Community residents have reported feeling out of touch with courts. They want courts to address low-level crime that is part of daily life.[6]

In this same workshop, 11 representatives of community courts discussed the "evolving model" (of community courts) and found that the courts differed in their operational models, organization, and programs. In two cases, the "community courts" were not even decentralized courts operating within a particular neighborhood and addressing its specific problems, but rather were specialized courtrooms located in the downtown centralized court building where quality-of-life crimes were heard and adjudicated. The range of models empirically observed led to an expansive definition of goals and operations:

> The community court approach was recognized as a promising solution to quality-of-life problems by many different communities.... All the planners and many community members describe common goals such as establishing community norms and creating an environment supporting revitalization efforts, but the focal point of the programs vary with neighborhoods and the problems confronting individual communities.[7]

It appears therefore that what is unique to the community courts' mandate is their appeal to flexibility. But this comes with its own problems. Fifteen years after the first community court opened in Midtown Manhattan, these courts have no standardized operations, nor are there easy ways to evaluate and compare them given this flexibility. In fact, in 2008, the Center for Court Innovation compared shared goals and concerns across community courts and highlighted how they are in flux as the model refines.[8] Nevertheless, while operating models, strategies, and specific goals may differ, this report, coupled with observations of promotional materials from community courts around the country, indicates that a common denominator for many of the community courts in operation is the focus on issues that affect a neighborhood's quality of life.

While sanctions and programs for offenders may differ among the existing community courts, they all search for some version of restorative justice that can hold defendants in the courtroom "accountable to a community" and remind them that there are "no victimless crimes."[9] Most commonly, defendants in court are sentenced to community service groups and other forms of classes and therapeutic interventions selected to address an individual's underlying problems (as defined by the court). Such a model encourages a broad amount of discretion: neither the defendant's problem nor the community's quality-of-life issues should be predetermined. Ideally, they remain open questions to be defined by each community court in a particular neighborhood. As opposed to specific strategies or goals, the model has been summarized as a set of "principles" by the Center for Court Innovation. These principles include: (1) Holding offenders to a greater level of accountability for quality-of-life crimes (now quality of life is no longer a description of a lifestyle, but a new category of crime that includes minor violations and misdemeanors, which I discuss further below); (2) increasing communication between the community and the criminal justice system; (3) improving community perceptions of safety; (4) increasing case processing efficiency; and (5) reducing certain crimes in certain neighborhoods.[10]

In this scenario, community courts are now advocated as an efficient way to address quality-of-life crimes and public safety. The process is also supposed to benefit from communication between courts and community, although the form this should take remains unspecified in practice but echoes a general call for community participation in crime control.[11] This initial concept is certainly intriguing, offering possibilities and flexibility for a court that lie outside of its usual parameters: not only does the court take a community's concerns into consideration, the community court's mandate has expanded the role of a court considerably, more so than other problem-solving courts to date. The court is no longer primarily there to adjudicate guilt and innocence, nor even to rehabilitate and work therapeutically with an *individual* offender.[12] The court is now an institution that communicates with the public, takes public opinion into account *and* is included in part of a larger package of crime reduction and community revitalization.[13] While problem-solving courts have usually operated by addressing an individual's "problem" with the goal of reducing recidivism and closing a revolving door, community courts expand this goal to include the transformation of a community's quality of life, thus contributing to community revitalization efforts

COMMUNITY COURTS AND COMMUNITY PARTICIPATION

The progression of a court from an institution whose purpose is to deliberate and apply the law to an institution dedicated to community development and social change is better understood when examined alongside other social changes taking place in the United States. Community courts emerged in the wake of fiscal policies that led to a decline in local government programs, interventions, and basic services. Centralized planning and social services were dominant policy objectives up until the dismantling of New Deal politics and the welfare state that began in the Reagan era and was finalized by Bill Clinton in the 1990s. Since then the pendulum has swung to emphasize decentralization, local control, and the privatization of government responsibilities into the private sector. Communities are now encouraged to pursue community revitalization programs via neighborhood development organizations, Business Improvement Districts, nonprofit organizations, and public-private partnerships.[14] Rhetorically the power of the community flourishes as the liberal welfare state shrinks. Neighborhoods, no longer guaranteed basic social services, investment in education, or affordable housing, compete in a free market to become vital economic centers where civic associations form and problem-solve neighborhood issues and the impact of budget cuts among other things.

Community courts follow this trend. They arrive promoting effective government via decentralization. Promotional materials for problem-solving courts highlight how innovations such as community courts can appeal to local businesses and nonprofit groups, which may support the court's programs on the basis of their contribution to a local community.[15] This semiprivatization echoes reforms taking place throughout government agencies. Meanwhile, the role and function of the court is now expanded, and this is justified in the name of a community. The court emerges with the creation and welfare of the community in tow. This approach follows current trends where government now acts "through community" as opposed to intervening across society.[16] Communities are fabricated and become objects for intervention by experts and policy makers without even knowing if the individuals placed inside these boundaries are held together through the bonds of shared interest and reciprocity, just some of the many practices that underpin an idea of community. Community courts alongside other problem-solving courts continually appeal to "communities," with communities of neighborhoods, victims, addicts, sufferers, and others, all of whom are assumed to share common interests.[17]

The community court approach was not only promoted to enable a court that is there for a community, but the court advocates some form of community participation to direct its focus onto local problems. However, when the dust settles, the precise role and the nature of the authority allocated to the community remain murky and unspecified. What is argued to be one of the most important pieces of the court's mandate is the piece that is most difficult to pin down and standardize, perhaps because of the vague definition of just what a community is. Indeed, the danger remains that as opposed to being a direct actor in determining the court's focus, the community becomes an imagined group served by the court. In effect, the community becomes the object as opposed to the subject of the actions taking place in its name.

The Red Hook Community Justice Center is a community court in a lower income neighborhood in Brooklyn, New York, and provides one example of the benefits and limits of community participation.[18] In Red Hook, unemployment and poverty are high.[19] The majority of the residents live in public housing. Drug dealing and addiction remain a problem. Previously the local economy revolved around the nearby waterfront and shipyards, but since their disappearance, along with other economic changes, inequality and poverty have increased. During the planning stages and afterwards, the Center for Court Innovation consulted with different stakeholders, primarily social service providers and community activists who were active at public meetings. Concerns included lack of social services, jobs, and youth activities. Many had suffered the immediate impact of drugs and experienced firsthand how it affected their daily lives. Other factions of the neighborhood (more gentrified parts) focused more on traffic and public disorder.

While a court and local residents may both share the desire to improve the quality of life and reduce disorder and crime, in the case of Red Hook the solutions and policies prescribed to achieve this goal were dictated by the court. Administrators took seriously the worry over the decline in youth activities and added some youth programs in the court. They also were mindful of residents' concerns over lack of social services. Over time, projects and programs were changed, added, and removed, depending on funding, enthusiasm, and logistics. The court and its operations were continually promoted to residents (and also in its press materials and fund-raising efforts) as a "one stop service center" that should increase public safety and the local quality of life.

The neighborhood location of the court did allow for several informal modes of communication that improved the administrative decisions and management. Several employees became more involved with community issues and different attempts were made to address local issues such as abandoned cars in alleys and an unkempt park. While these initiatives were a positive outcome of having the court in the neighborhood, they were not a mandated part of the court's operating procedures and such outcomes are dependent on the goodwill of individuals as opposed to a programmatic intent of the court to prioritize civic action. As operations continued, different court actors, including the lawyers, prosecutors, judge, and the court director, regularly attended different community meetings to both listen to community issues and advocate for the court and its programs. In these meetings the court can also hear about local complaints and issues, which it then can incorporate into its courtroom procedures.

Residents were aware of the court in their midst, and for many this is something they hoped would make a direct impact on the neighborhood. But the provision of local social services via the criminal justice system and inside a court building was anathema to many who were uncomfortable walking through a security system to see a social service provider. Moreover, many complained they would not want others in the neighborhood to see them go in. As the director of the center for court innovation himself would say, "Red Hook is a moving target." The flexibility inherent in the court's mandate might be necessary to devise programs and build community support, but it maintains a certain amount of ambiguity.[20] It becomes hard to evaluate an institution whose primary goal is to improve a neighborhood's quality of life. Moreover, it is unclear how the court could take direct responsibility for changes in the neighborhood, most of which residents ascribed to police activity, as discussed below.

The Red Hook Community Justice Center was planned to focus on neighborhood problems but there was no clear mandate for what role the community should play either in the formulation of the problem to be solved or in the strategies and policies chosen to address these goals. A Community Advisory Board was created after the court opened and meetings were planned on a quarterly basis when possible. At these meetings the court presented its programs, asked for feedback, and reported on case processing. Generally, interactions with the community were focused more on building consensus and support for the court than as a mechanism meant to lead to more power sharing or devise common goals. In this scenario, community participation did not translate into community authority or power and should not be mistaken for this as was frequently the assumption in popular rhetoric. The community was envisioned as a participant in its capacity to help the court become more effective, but the tactics and strategies for achieving change were set by the court. In this sense, the community provided information that the court lacked, correcting for deficiencies in the information available to the experts and administrators.[21]

Unlike some participatory models where goals and/or strategies are decided together through a deliberative process between different groups, the community court lacks the flexibility or discretion to allow for co-governing. For this to take place, the different participating groups would need both the authority and the flexibility to change certain taken-for-granted ways of doing things. As Archon Fung describes, this requires the creation of a type of "accountable autonomy" where an institution and its players have the power to reset their agenda so long as the broader goal can be measured, as in some of the more successful attempts at community policing in Chicago where police were allowed to significantly readjust their actions along with the community, but the broader goal of crime reduction could be tracked over time.[22] In community courts, not only would one have to come up with an efficient way to assess a community's quality of life as a measure of the overall goal, institutional restrictions and procedures would need to be lifted in order to enable new forms of power sharing to develop with a community. In Red Hook, actors inside the court are not allocated the flexibility needed to reset an agenda allowing for community (partial) control. Lawyers, judges, and police still remain accountable to their centralized governing bodies where evaluation still takes place through the numbers of arrests, charges, and convictions. No incentives for autonomy were in place that could have permitted the community to become a full participant with authority in the court's strategic development. The limitations to community participation mean that the main focus and power of a community court are exercised within the courtroom where the solutions prescribed are determined by the judge, the lawyers, and the court. Although they may be better informed than traditional courts about the neighborhood in which they work, they do not share this authority with the community, nor can they speak for the community.

QUALITY OF LIFE IN THE COURTROOM AND BEYOND

While community involvement is one backbone of a community court, a larger question remains: how and why should a court address a neighborhood's quality-of-life issues through courtroom procedures? It is impossible to consider this question without realizing how the term "quality of life" has been transformed from the desire for an ideal environment to a legal category subject to law enforcement. This change emerged alongside the increase in public disorder and the decline in the American city beginning in the 1970s and continuing up through the 1990s. For example, in New York City, economic restructuring and the decline in middle-class jobs led to massive urban transformations affecting particular groups and neighborhoods in different ways.[23] Meanwhile, increasing poverty, drug addiction, and violence, as well as middle-class white flight, led to urban downtown deterioration and urban decline in selected residential neighborhoods. Analyses of these urban changes swing between those who attribute more importance to the structural changes in economic and employment opportunities that dislocated some communities from jobs and economic growth and those who stress behavioral and cultural traits that generated a culture of poverty that resulted in the marginalization of specific groups and the generation of an underclass.[24] While the root causes of the changing American city can be debated, the result was a perception of more insecure streets and public disorder.

In New York City, homelessness, panhandling, indigent individuals, and urban decay of public spaces led to public discontent; up until the 1990s the prevalent response was to advocate for more centralized expert planning and social services to address individuals in crisis, often with little attention given to the local impacts and community perceptions. The failure of centralized government policies to address local concerns led to complaints across different segments of the city. While business and real-estate interests faltered, local residential neighborhoods also felt abandoned as their surroundings deteriorated.[25] Business Improvement Districts formed and raised money to restore public services such as policing, sanitation, and local green spaces, as well as to lobby local politicians to address quality-of-life concerns that were impacting downtown businesses.

Efforts were made by mayoral administrations in New York City and the police to address community complaints and increasing urban decline, but it was the election of Mayor Rudy Giuliani in 1994 that catapulted quality of life into a law enforcement category and policing strategy.[26] Giuliani combined a series of ideas into policy as he attributed urban disorder to "declining civility and decency in the city"[27] and announced that certain behaviors would no longer be tolerated: illegal street vendors; panhandling; squeegee men; fare hopping; and general loitering in areas where the public might feel threatened, such as around ATM machines or public housing lobbies. These actions were now subject to law enforcement either through existing laws or through the passage of new legislation. By 1994, *Police Strategy No. 5. Reclaiming the Public Spaces of New York* was published by the mayor and the New York City Police Department.[28] This report solidified the move towards public order policing, placing it on front and center stage in relation to crime control through the "Broken Windows" theory of crime.[29] Broken Windows argues that allowing signs of urban disorder to continue generates serious crime by sending the message that crime is tolerated. In this narrative public disorder is no longer solely a disturbance or concern for local residents, it is the precursor to (and causation of) larger crimes. Quality-of-life violations were now realigned into a larger strategy of crime prevention, legitimizing the rigid use of law enforcement and coercive social control (policing and the law) to be applied to certain behaviors when they occurred in the wrong place. Quality of life is now reconstructed as a policy and expressed in the idea of quality-of-life policing and quality-of-life crimes. Whereas police had previously resisted arresting homeless people, illegal vendors, and even prostitutes on the grounds that such actions were beyond their purview, the new strategy argued that these behaviors were what must be stopped to reduce crime levels.[30] Police issued summonses or arrested people on applicable misdemeanor charges or violations when an individual was considered to be a potential risk to urban order. Budgets and manpower were dedicated to quality-of-life policing, as well as stop-and-frisk policies in particular neighborhoods, disproportionately targeting Black and Latino residents.[31]

Currently the jury is still out as to whether this type of aggressive pursuit of low-level crime was behind the decline in crime in New York City and other places.[32] Nor is it clear whether this type of policing eradicates the particular problem (such as homelessness, graffiti, or prostitution) or moves it to another neighborhood. Nevertheless, one observable result is the increase in low-level arrests, alongside the appropriation of quality-of-life issues into quality-of-life crime and hence politics. Whereas this was once a subjective category, or a lived experience, quality-of-life politics has redefined and expanded the meaning of the term. It now is a legal category that judges social behaviors and presents some as a risk to public order and crime, transforming complaints about local level neighborhood problems and disorder such as noise, trash, poor services, and urban blight into a larger moral category that judges individual behavior.[33] Larger questions about urban change take second place as individual behavior is prioritized as the cause of urban decline in particular neighborhoods.

Policing is now a major force in the restoration of public order and the reversal of local decline, and community courts emerged as a new partner in this landscape. Advocates proposed that community courts process a range of crimes and address these arrests in the context of the local neighborhood, thus becoming a partner in urban revitalization and social change. In this new approach, defendants were mandated to participate in a range of sanctions, including community service sanctions, drug treatment programs, and even an innovative variety of job training and educational programs, if these could be understood to be *meaningful sanctions* that could address an individual's underlying problems and the local quality of life.[34]

In Red Hook, the community court arrived into a neighborhood where drug addiction and drug-related violence had been high through the 1990s, although by the time the court opened in 2000, this had abated with the decline of crack wars and drug-related violence throughout the city. A number of the streets were being slowly gentrified. A small number of middle-class residents and artists had taken advantage of the real estate prices and the waterfront views and remained hopeful that economic development and revitalization was forthcoming. The court operated in this complex social landscape where it tried to determine which quality-of-life issues mattered and negotiate through different social fields that were the product of race, class, and socioeconomic changes.[35] Gentrifying middle-class residents worried about traffic laws, disgruntled residents in public housing complained about the lack of police response when they requested it, and older residents remembered a time when more social service agencies and youth activities were available for individuals in need or young people with not enough to do to stay out of trouble.

Given this variety, constructing a coherent vision of how to address community quality of life is no simple program. In Red Hook, the search for quality of life was tackled through the courtroom in various ways. The court heard misdemeanor cases and quality-of-life violations from different neighborhoods encompassed by three police precincts. Most misdemeanor cases came in under criminal trespass, drug-related arrests, assaults, public disorder, and some domestic violence. Available sanctions included "readiness for treatment groups," referrals for detoxification and longer term drug treatment, an anger management class, a health education class for prostitutes, community service, a general social service evaluation, an alternative mediation process, driving school, and attendance at a job program talk, among others. Social workers and some programs took place on site. Individuals were also referred to programs elsewhere as applicable (depending on the mandate, insurance, and availability of programs). The court also sent defendants to community service groups that performed tasks around a neighborhood as needed, from cleaning streets and the park to painting over graffiti and shoveling snow. In all community courts, the community service group is the primary mode of retribution. Indeed, the cost-saving element of these groups and the services they provide are frequently used to promote these courts in a community as one of their key benefits and an important mechanism for accountability.

Aside from the community service groups, community courts are following a path similar to other problem-solving courts, treating individuals for particular problems as designated by the court. While police are instructed to take minor violations seriously, community courts are now there to provide an appropriate sanction to this ever-growing group of defendants as they arrive in court. In Red Hook, defendants with minor violations that might have merited a "time served" in the downtown court (after spending up to 48 hours in a cell waiting to go to court) were assessed and monitored by the court. Those with long rap sheets were sent to drug treatment when applicable, and in many cases kept under supervision for long periods of time. While many took this opportunity to avoid jail, a few benefited from the intervention to actually address their drug addiction. Case processing was more efficient, an experience valued by defendants who objected to long waits in inhospitable environments downtown, but defendants were rarely released without a sanction or intervention regardless of the outcome of their case. While mandating defendants who appear in court to social services is ideally one way to address and manage some of their particular problems, it is unclear how this strategy will necessarily improve a neighborhood's quality-of-life problems, outside of providing treatment for individuals who lack access to these services through other agencies.

In Red Hook, the court justified its focus on drugs in the courtroom both as a response to the caseload coming in and as a way to address the local quality of life as residents complained about drug dealing and its associated problems. While residents frequently decried what they felt was the lack of real motivation on the part of the police to remove drug dealers and provide constant police on the beat to stop dealers reappearing, the community court began to follow a drug court model as a small but persistent group of defendants repeatedly came through the court on drug-related crimes. However, alongside these cases, the largest amount of traffic in the courtroom was the minor violations and quality-of-life summonses, including, but not limited to, being in a park after dark, walking a dog without a leash, graffiti, drinking, and urinating in public. Defendants filled up court on Tuesday mornings (the designated quality-of-life summonses day). During one Community Advisory Board meeting in 2001 the court director announced that over 11,000 summonses had been heard at the court, representing almost two-thirds of the court caseload in numbers. On these days, individuals were given two options: to wait and appear in front of the judge or to go directly upstairs to a quality-of-life class and receive an adjournment contemplating dismissal on their case. This meant that if the individual stayed out of court for six months the summons would be dismissed and not included on any further court records. If individuals skipped the court appearance date cited on their tickets, a warrant was issued for their arrest. These procedures worked in tandem with quality-of-life policing, ensuring that the court clearly signaled the seriousness with which it took these cases and underlining the fact that the court was not "business as usual" (a phrase repeatedly used by court actors in court and elsewhere).

In the courtroom and the quality-of-life classes, the judge and class leaders highlighted the court's concern with community issues. In court, the judge often added a personal note on his view of a case, mentioning that he had heard that a particular park was of a concern to residents, or telling people how he would attend community meetings and how this helped him understand how upset the community was about certain issues, for example, drug dealing, unleashed dogs, and traffic. In the classes, leaders also stressed their interest in community views, underscoring how residents complained about quality-of-life issues, such as "drinking in public" and/or "public urination." This was sometimes further legitimized with the presentation of an annual (unscientific) survey conducted by the AmeriCorps group associated with the Red Hook Community Justice Center.[36] Classes were then invited to consider these issues. Leaders openly pushed a Broken Windows framework as they told the class how lack of "public order encourages more crime and creates a bad impression of the neighborhood." Finally individuals were informed about the court and its services.

In these quality-of-life classes, individuals might frequently agree with the problems presented without endorsing or imagining the solution presented to them. In particular, they were not as likely to embrace the "quality-of-life" as a law enforcement category. Residents had a myriad of complaints about their quality-of-life issues, but they had not participated in designing the solution presented by the court. They also noticed how quality-of-life policing could encroach on their everyday life. Moreover, many were also aware of an ambiguous moral message in their class as they were now held responsible for the physical deterioration and problems in their community. One interview with a social worker who worked in Red Hook highlighted these contradictions. This young man had been ticketed for drinking in public during an annual father's day barbecue in a public housing complex.

Interview: Did you actually have a beer in your hand?

Alfred: Yeah, I had a beer. . . . See I was guilty. You know I figure it's Father's Day, Fourth of July, that sort of thing. . . . So they put me in the class and some things I understood about quality-of-life, you know they were right about it. But some things they just exaggerate about it, you know. They would say like, let me use an example, they said, how would you like someone sitting in front of your grandmother's window drinking all night, making noise? I said I wouldn't like that at all. I said, but we weren't in front of nobody's window drinking and making noise. It was Father's Day. We have this barbecue annually. It was like one or two in the afternoon. We were in a group, people sitting, playing basketball, you know, guys sitting around talking, had the kids there. . . . I mean, people live in public housing. . . . We don't have a porch or backyard. So the grounds is our porch and our backyard. So I feel if we're having an organized you know gathering, with permission, whatever, the cops shouldn't be ticketing us. They shouldn't be you know giving us tickets just to meet a quota.

One guy [in the class] was really upset. . . . He was this guy was in Bay Ridge. He was in his front porch drinking a beer. But the law says that you're not allowed to drink an alcoholic beverage, even if it's on your property. . . . You can drink one in the back of your house, but not in the front. So everybody had issues. . . . To me, I mean that quality-of-life law, I think that applies to like say if you're in a public area like a tourist area, like 42nd Street, or a public park. I mean I don't think it should apply to public living areas. I mean granted you know people do get out of hand and leave messes at times. . . . You don't have a place where you can, how can I say? Get together, recreationally. I think that's going too far. And that's a way of targeting minorities. So all they gotta do when they want to get quotas is run right up in the projects and get all the tickets they want to get. I mean and they constantly harass people in public housing anyway, for everything.

In classes and interviews with residents, "quality of life" was frequently used as a term describing an experience of their urban environment, but they were reluctant to identify with the violations they received as being the primary cause of crime and community deterioration. Defendants brought up the issue of poor services (no public restrooms, for example) as well as the lack of public or private space in which to relax. Race and class issues also arose as individuals felt powerless to protest their arrest while many saw the social hierarchy confirmed as police overtime and quotas generated more summonses and arrests. Class leaders most often responded to these critiques by reframing the question as a problem about an individual's behavior as opposed to a larger social structural problem.

They also would present examples to counteract the complaint, such as asking why men were more likely to receive tickets for public urination than women, or whether a child should see someone drunk. Active discussions about the cause for deterioration in quality of life as experienced by residents were circumvented and participants were reminded that the purpose of the class was to delineate the law, reminding the group that their chance to complain should have been taken in front of the judge. The class was constantly returned to the fact that the community considered these issues to be a problem. Residents might try to contest the argument or reframe the debate, but the message of the court was that change lay in the individual and individuals must be held accountable for quality-of-life crimes. While this process began with the violation and arrest, it continued in the community court where individuals were assessed for the potential to become repeat offenders and public nuisances and warned about the risk they themselves presented for community development.

The courtroom and classes propel a particular narrative of community problems, which leaves no room to incorporate a vision of the harm policing may cause when not exercised with the type of discretion asked for by the community residents nor of the discontent residents experience over the lack of social and/or government services. The frequent argument heard from that court that it "treats the problems, not just the symptoms" constructs the problem and the solution within its own terms. In the quality-of-life class a popularized version of a culture of poverty thesis is repackaged and presented as a moral argument. Individuals are blamed for the social problems they experience. Not only is an individual's behavior an individual's problem, it is now the cause behind urban blight and just behind this, crime, poverty, and other social ills. Individuals in court are not only a potential drain on limited resources, they become symbolic of what holds the neighborhood down, or closes it off, from its true market potential.

COMMUNITY COURTS AND CIVIC ACTION

Community courts offer the possibility of more efficient courtroom processing through their smaller size and specialized caseload. They also combine restorative punishment (community service) with rehabilitative goals (social services). While these features represent improvements in the institutional and operational management, given their anticipated community focus, one large question remains, which is how a community might take advantage of this new resource in their midst. So far, community courts have had a mixed reception. Some appreciate the benefits they offer in terms of social services or community service; others complain that these courts essentially criminalize poverty as the criminal justice system is now redesigned to be the new gatekeeper into social services.[37]

Significant effort was made at the Red Hook Community Justice to communicate the value of the court and its programs to surrounding residents, reassuring residents that the court was there to solve problems and reminding them of the resource they had in their midst. The court prioritized building harmonious consensus both inside and outside of the courtroom. Essentially it asked that questions of justice and inequity be exchanged for the pursuit of common goals among different actors. Defendants and lawyers were reminded that even more important than an individual's crime was whether the court could provide help and treatment to a person in need.[38]

In Red Hook, many activists hoped the court could help bring change to the neighborhood. Most residents, however, were indifferent to its arrival, assuming it had little to do with their daily reality and remaining unclear as to its actual purpose. This confusion among residents was unsurprising given the somewhat mixed messages that emerges from community courts: it is a court that is a resource, it is a court whose purpose is to address quality-of-life issues, it is a court that takes its cues from the community, but, in the end, for most, it is a court whose functioning and caseload depends on police activity and not the community, although court officials continually reassure residents that they are there for the community.

Residents of Red Hook had a range of explanations for the court's arrival and goals and many were hopeful it could be a positive force for the neighborhood. Many also began to appropriate the court for their own purposes. In parallel with the importance a good relationship with the judge had inside the courtroom as he ruled over case processing, treatment options, and appropriate mandates for defendants, the residents imagined the advantages they believed a relationship with a judge might afford them outside of the courtroom.[39] In many ways, the judge's presence and actions came to symbolize the community court, its effectiveness, and its goals in many residents' minds. At a variety of community meetings, from tenants' association meetings in the public housing to police precinct meetings, residents requested his attendance and assumed his presence had the most impact, over and above other court employees who might also attend. Once he was there they frequently addressed and entreated him to solve a particular situation. And it was the judge who often gave his word at meetings and promised individuals to take their complaints seriously—from getting a special drug counselor for the local school to investigating whether the police actually do show up to check out tenant patrol groups. For residents the most meaningful resource provided by the community court was access to what they understood to be a direct line of power. Residents understood the judge as the actor in their midst that might reverse situations they felt were unfair. Just as the court held individuals accountable for their own behavior and its impact on community growth, residents looked for an individual, and in this case the judge, to hold accountable to local concerns.

While access to a judge was certainly positive in terms of access to information, dependence on one person to solve a problem highlighted the experience of powerlessness felt by residents in Red Hook to address questions of justice and equity. For example, time and again in tenants' meetings and elsewhere, residents decried inappropriate law enforcement. For many, the lack of police beats in the neighborhood (as opposed to drug sweeps and raids) was equated with a general feeling of abandonment. At the same time as residents asked for police presence, they did not want unnecessary arrests. Even the most active and illustrious residents had often had to negotiate the arrest of someone in their family. Frequently this was achieved by picking up the phone and using personal contacts to find someone who might help connect you to the powers that protect. One community activist described how her son managed to avoid arrest only by citing his mother's name and showing that he knew other community leaders. Meanwhile, this woman's daughter also advocated for more police presence to enforce the laws, in particular the loitering laws in public housing, as she remained concerned about the drug activity. At the same time, she was aware that this could make herself and her brother more vulnerable, but she also relied on her knowledge of people in the system to protect her.

> Even I've been stopped. . . . And when I felt uncomfortable enough I say to the officer, I happened to know the Captain's name at the time. And I said to him, well, you know we can do this, but we can do this in front of the 76 Precinct because I'm feeling rather uncomfortable right now. My brother was in the car and the officer said to him, "Get out the car! We need to search.". . . And when I started saying names, "How do you know them?" Right away, then, I must have been in trouble [before], that's how I know them. Not that I know them because my mother happens to be on [the community board's] public safety [group] since '86, whatever. . . .

For individuals in Red Hook, protection and action were tied to whom you knew. This same logic was applied to their appreciation of the Red Hook Community Justice Center. When they did envision it as a resource, it was frequently tied into a conceptualization of a judge as the source of power. Their focus was on how power was personified and exercised by an individual. A connection to the judge was the most consequential relationship a resident might have. Residents often sought out the judge to solve a community problem. As opposed to the idea of collective civic action to solve problems, residents demanded action from the government and sought out the person who had sufficient power and who could be held personally accountable. For this reason, many would feel disappointed if the judge failed to appear at their particular meeting, not appreciating the arrival of a proxy sent on his behalf. The judge remained aware that his role had expanded, but he had also accepted the blanket of personal responsibility for maintaining the correct boundaries and remaining accountable:

> [P]eople give me information and . . . I try to refer them as quickly as possible to the DA's office, . . . *But, I will make sure that the information goes to the DA's office.* And the one thing I said to all the lawyers in the beginning was that if I learn something about a case, I would tell them immediately and we would send the case downtown. There's actually been a couple cases where I've told the lawyers, if this case goes to trial, just send it downtown. . . . Simply by the nature of the building, from being in the community, people will see you and tell you things. The building is designed you have to walk around the building. I like to do it anyway, I like to see people.

> But, people will, literally, talk to you. . . . It's also, I guess, part of going to meetings and people seeing you all the time is that they become more comfortable approaching you, which is fine with me. So that's just what's gonna happen. (author's italics)

For residents, the judge was their conduit to power and influence, which was a rational conclusion given the status accorded to judges in general and to the judge in a community court in particular. The judge's dispositions, his treatment of defendants, and his community role resonated more with many residents than the variety of programs and community service groups offered by the court. Although the court was organized to be much more than one person, in many instances it had come to be refracted through the potential power of the judge's position. This was a logical response from individuals who had managed to get whatever power and resources they had through their personal connections to a center of power. Just as the court emphasized that change started with the individual and his or her behavior, so the residents assumed that it was the individual in power who had the ability to get things done and bring change to the situations of injustice and inequity many experienced in their daily life.

CONCLUSION

Community courts have advanced the problem-solving-court model one step further by proposing that courts are focused on specific local spaces and neighborhoods. The decentralization of community courts and their focus on low-level crimes can permit more efficient case processing and provide an array of useful sanctions and community service groups. I have not tried to evaluate the operations of community courts. Instead, I have tried to consider their overall approach, and in doing so, I argue that currently it appears impossible to really assess community courts in general, or compare them against each other, given the absence of a clear strategy. Indeed, community courts began as a flexible model that focused on local neighborhoods and problem solving, but in practice they appear to have morphed into "quality-of-life" courts in the majority of cases, with varying degrees of community input and participation. We can understand this development only by looking at their evolution within the context of urban social changes and government policies that prioritize the decentralization of social services and rely on local community organizations for community development. In the current political climate, it appears that the most direct form of government intervention in urban neighborhoods is delivered through the criminal justice system. Quality-of-life policing has taken the front stage in urban revitalization, and community courts intervene by providing the social interventions and services individuals lack in their neighborhoods.

Just as quality-of-life policing is argued to be for the benefit of a local neighborhood and larger community, the coercive power of community courts is now envisioned as for the public good. The court is now a force that can be used to bring social change to poor underserved neighborhoods. In spite of a rhetoric that suggests that community courts are there for the community and are part of the community, the principal model of change offered by the courts appears to focus primarily on the individual. Certain individual behaviors are categorized as disruptive and tied to neighborhood decline. In contrast to previous models of social change that begin with collective action and protest, the model presented through community courts are that change begins with the individual who can provide moral redemption for a community that needs to be transformed.

Community courts, as with other problem-solving courts, need to define how and where problems (and therefore their solutions) begin. They can only do so by considering all the different spheres and registers of social experience.[40] In the community court, the most salient narrative for problem solving and social change begins with the individual (not so different from the idea that education begins with the parents) leaving out other areas of social experience and understandings of social life. Nevertheless, the appeal to the individual and the focus on individual behavior resonates with many residents who attempt to use this to their own advantage. In Red Hook, for example, this same message was taken and redirected at the community court judge as residents asked him to intervene and help in their search for more responsive and effective government. The expansion of the power of the court and its representation in the figure of the judge again suggest more of a cult of the individual rather than the power of the collective.

The arrival of these courts and the expansion of power they represent in specific communities needs to be seriously debated. In Red Hook, the flexibility and discretion given to the judge inside the courtroom extended his power and the influence of the court inside and outside of the courtroom. But it remains unclear what problem community courts really seek to solve. Is it a community's quality of life? Is it a lack of social services in underserved communities? Is it individual behavior in a local space? Is it the lack of civic engagement and collective action in particular neighborhoods? All of these problems have specific and different possible solutions. Nor is the provision of social services through a criminal court necessarily the most effective way to bring social services into an underserved community. Community courts permit state involvement in particular neighborhoods where the state is "needed," but it now arrives through the criminal justice system, which currently seems to be the only expanding domain of government where public security and public order are the favored policy interventions.[41] A court focused on low-level crimes does not merit being called a community court without a clear mechanism in place that prioritizes how and why these courts are there for the community. Currently, the expansion of power these courts represent along with the focus on individual behavior as opposed to collective action seems to suggest that for a court that came in seeking to help and empower a community, it remains with a community very much in the hands of power.

NOTES

1. Karafin, 2008, p. 1.

2. Berman, 2000, p. 80; Berman & Feinblatt, 2001.

3. Karafin, 2008.

4. This Research was conducted while the author was a staff associate at the Center for Violence Research and Prevention, Mailman School of Public Health, Columbia University, and supported by Grant 2000-MU-AX-0006 from the National Institute of Justice. The author wishes to thank all the individuals who gave their time. Special thanks go to the staff at the Red Hook Community Justice Center and Red Hook residents for the openness. Opinions expressed here are the sole responsibility of the author.

5. Karafin, 2008, p. 1.

6. Lee, 2000, p. 5.

7. Lee, 2005, p. 5.

8. Karafin, 2008.

9. Campbell, 2000.

10. Feinblatt & Berman, 2001; Karafin, 2008, pp. 15–16.

11. Kurki, 2000; Moore, 1999; Sampson, 2001.

12. Winick, 2003.

13. Fagan & Malkin, 2003.

14. Stoutland, 1999.

15. Feinblatt & Berman, 2001, p. 5.

16. Rose, 1998.

17. Malkin, 2006, pp. 366–368.

18. This research took place from October 2000 to December 2001. Ethnographic work included participant observation in the court, community meetings, and other local community events. I attended operations meetings within the court and some community service and other treatment program groups. Alongside participant observation I (transcribed) recorded interviews with 59 individuals representing court employees, defendants, community residents, and activists, as well as 13 community service crews in the court.

19. For a comprehensive overview of Red Hook demographics and its social services in general, see the Center for New York City Affairs, New School University, *Consider the future: Strengthening children and family services in Red Hook, Brooklyn* (2003). Available at http://www.newschool.edu/milano/nycaffairs/pubs/considerthefuture.pdf (last visited October 22, 2003).

20. Malkin, 2003.

21. Fung, 2006, p. 66.

22. Fung, 2006a.

23. Waldinger, 1996; Vitale, 2008, pp. 144–183.

24. Wilson, 1990.

25. Gregory, 1998; Vitale, 2008, pp. 70–92.

26. Erzen, 2001.

27. Gregory, 1998, p. 234.

28. Guiliani & Bratton, 1994.

29. Wilson & Kelling, 1982; also Kelling & Coles, 1998.

30. Vitale, 2008.

31. McArdle & Erzen, 2001.
32. cf. Erzen, 2001; Johnson et al., 2003, 2002.
33. Gregory, 1998, pp. 231–235.
34. Bureau of Justice Assistance, 1998, p. 2.
35. While the Red Hook Community Justice Center is located in the neighborhood of Red Hook, Brooklyn, the court arraigns cases from three surrounding police precincts. This actually complicates what "community" the court actually serves, but for the purpose of this chapter I have focused on the surrounding neighborhood of Red Hook, and, in fact, much of the court's community outreach and planning has focused on this neighborhood.
36. The survey is conducted annually by AmeriCorps workers in September. It is one form of internal monitoring by the court who uses the survey to get another understanding of what the community perceives to be neighborhood problems. Some 1,000 surveys are collected annually, the majority from Red Hook, with about one-third from other neighborhoods. On it, a list of "crime and public safety" issues are presented to respondents who are asked to respond to whether this is a problem.
37. cf. Yeung, 2008.
38. Malkin, 2006; Winick, 2003.
39. Malkin, 2006, pp. 373–381.
40. Greenhouse et al., 1994.
41. Hornqvist, 2004, pp. 35–39.

REFERENCES

Berman, G. (2000). What is a traditional judge anyway? Problem solving in the State Courts. *Judicature, 84*(2), 78–85.

Berman, G., & Feinblatt, J. (2001). Problem-solving-courts: A brief primer. *Law and Policy, 23*(2), 125–140.

Bratton, W., & Guliani, R. (1994). *Police strategy no. 5: Reclaiming the public spaces of New York.* New York: City of New York.

Bureau of Justice Assistance. (1998). *Overcoming obstacles to community courts: A summary of workshop proceedings.* Community Justice Series (prepared by the Center for Court Innovation). Washington DC: U.S. Department of Justice.

Campbell, R. (2000). *There are no victimless crimes.* New York: Center for Court Innovation.

Erzen, T. (2001). Turnstile jumpers and broken windows policing. Disorder in New York City. In A. McArdle and T. Erzen (Eds.), *Zero tolerance: Quality-of-life and the new police brutality in New York City* (pp. 19–49). New York: New York University Press.

Fagan, J., & Malkin, V. (2003). Theorizing community justice through community courts. *Fordham Urban Law Journal, 30*(3), 897–953.

Feinblatt, J., & Berman, G. (2001). Community courts: A brief primer. *United States Attorney's Bulletin, 49,* 33–40.

Fung, A. (2006, December). Varieties of participation in complex governance. *Public Administration Review, 66,* 66–75.

Fung, A. (2006a). *Empowered participation. Reinventing urban democracy.* Princeton, NJ: Princeton University Press.

Greenhouse, C., Yngvesson, B., & Engel, D. (1994). *Law and community in three American towns.* Ithaca, NY: Cornell University Press.

Gregory, S. (1998). *Black Corona: Race and the politics of place in an urban community.* Princeton, NJ: Princeton University Press.

Hornqvist, M. (2004). The birth of public order policy. *Race and Class, 46*(1), 30–52.

Johnson, B., Golub, A., Taylor, A., & Eterno, J. (2003). *Does quality-of-life policing widen the net?* Report submitted to the U.S. Department of Justice. Retrieved September 24, 2008, from http://www.ncjrs.gov/pdffiles1/nij/grants/198996.pdf.

Johnson, B., Golub, A., Taylor, A., & Eterno, J. (2002). *Quality-of-life policing: Do offenders get the message?* Report submitted to the U.S. Department of Justice. Retrieved September 24, 2008, from http://www.ncjrs.gov/pdffiles1/nij/grants/196673.pdf.

Karafin, D. L. (2008). *Community courts across the globe. A measure of goals, performance, measures and operations.* A Report Submitted to the Open Society Institute. Open Society Foundation

Kelling, G. L., & Coles, C. M. (1998). *Fixing Broken Windows: Restoring order and reducing crime in our communities.* New York: Free Press.

Kurki, L. (2000). Restorative and community justice. *Crime and Justice Research: A Review of Research, 27,* 235–303.

Lee, E. (2000). *Community courts, an evolving model.* Community Justice Series #2, Bureau of Justice Assistance. Washington, DC: U.S. Department of Justice.

Malkin, V. (2006). The end of welfare as we know it. What happens when the judge is in-charge. *Critique of Anthropology, 25*(4), 361–388.

Malkin, V. (2003). Community courts and the process of accountability. Consensus and conflict at the Red Hook Community Justice Center. *American Criminal Law Review, 40,* 1573–1593.

Moore, M. (1990). Security and community development. In R. Fergusen and W. Dickens (Eds.), *Urban problems and community development* (pp. 299–321). Washington, DC: Brookings Institution Press.

McArdle, A., & Erzen, T. (2001). *Zero tolerance. Quality of life and the new police brutality in New York City,* New York: New York University Press.

Rose, N. (1996). The death of the social: Refiguring the territory of government. *Economy and Society, 25,* 327–356.

Rottman, D. (1996). Community courts: Prospects and limits. *National Institute of Justice Journal, 231,* 46–51.

Sampson, R. (2001). Crime and public safety: Insights from community-level perspectives on social capital. In S. Saegert, J. Thompson, & M. Warren (Eds.), *Social capital and poor communities* (pp. 89–114). New York: Russell Sage Foundation.

Stoutland, S. (1999). Community development corporations: Mission strategy and accomplishments. In R. Fergusen and W. Dickens (Eds.), *Urban problems and community development* (pp. 193–241). Washington, DC: Brookings Institution Press.

Vitale, A. (2008). *City of disorder: How the quality-of-life campaign transformed New York City politics.* New York: New York University Press.

Waldinger, R. (1996). *Still the promised city? New immigrants and African-Americans in post-industrial New York.* Cambridge, MA: Harvard University Press.

Wilson, J. Q., & Kelling, G. L. (1982, March). Broken Windows: The police and neighborhood safety. *Atlantic Monthly,* 29–38.

Wilson, W. J. (1990). *The truly disadvantaged: The Inner city, the underclass, and public policy.* Chicago: University of Chicago Press.

Winick, B. (2003). Therapeutic jurisprudence and problem-solving-courts. *Fordham Urban Law Journal, 30*(3), 1055–90.

Yeung, B. (2008, July). Succor. Succor in the court. *Miller McCune.* Retrieved September 24, 2008, from http://www.miller-mccune.com/article/491.

9

Youth Courts: Youth Empowerment in Problem Solving

TRACY GODWIN MULLINS

Youth courts, although not official courts per se, often are included within the problem-solving justice movement. This is due, in large part, to their extensive focus on holding youth accountable for their actions by engaging the community—particularly its youth—in the justice process through active deliberation concerning problem behaviors manifested by their peers. So, if not a traditional court, what are youth court programs?

Youth courts are primarily juvenile diversion programs in which youth are sentenced by their peers for minor delinquent and status offenses and other problem behaviors, although there are some youth courts that serve as dispositional alternatives for juvenile or municipal court judges. Other names by which youth courts are known include teen court, peer court, and student court. Though their primary purpose is to serve as a means for holding youthful offenders accountable for their actions through a peer-imposed sentence aimed at problem solving, another major focus of youth courts is to provide a forum for youth who serve as volunteers for the program to learn about the justice system and attain valuable life skills (e.g., public speaking, critical thinking, listening, problem solving). This dual focus and ability to affect such a wide range of young people in a community is what sets youth courts apart from other juvenile diversion programs and youth service programs, as well as from the traditional court system.

There is not a single recipe to follow on how to develop and operate a youth court program. One of their biggest advantages lies in their flexibility and adaptability to community interests, needs, and resources. There are, however, some commonalities among programs and some basic concepts upon which youth courts adhere that can provide a blueprint for development and implementation efforts. A grassroots program at their core, youth courts have garnered national attention and resources over the past 10–15 years that have contributed to their remarkable growth and proliferation. Respecting their history, understanding their present, and considering their future will help propel the youth court movement into the next decade and beyond.

HISTORY OF YOUTH COURT MOVEMENT

There are conflicting reports in the literature as to when and where the first youth court originated. One of the earliest recorded accounts can be traced to an article in the May 16, 1949, edition of the *Mansfield News Journal* about a youth-operated "Hi-Y" bicycle court in which teen judges imposed sanctions on juvenile defendants charged with minor traffic violations involving bicycles.[1] Another account was found in a December 26, 1965, issue of *The Rapid City Sunday Journal* that discussed the implementation of a new youth jury program in Rapid City, South Dakota.[2] There are also anecdotal reports of programs that were established in Horseheads, New York, in 1968 and Naperville, Illinois, in 1972.[3]

While the youth court concept is not new, the number of youth courts in the United States has exploded over the past 15 years, and the grassroots movement to establish youth courts on a local level seems to grow stronger each year. In 1994, the American Bar Association reported locating 78 youth courts in operation.[4] By 1998, the number of youth courts known to be operating had increased to approximately 450 in 44 states.[5] As of October 2006, the number of youth courts in the United States had risen to an impressive 1,127 programs in 49 states and the District of Columbia,[6] and it is projected that more than 1,255 programs are in operation today.[7]

While it is not possible to pinpoint the exact cause of this overwhelming increase, there are several key factors that are unique to the youth court movement that have contributed to its recent and relatively rapid growth. The first time attention was focused on youth courts on a national level was spearheaded by Natalie Rothstein, who founded the Odessa Teen Court Program in Texas in 1983. She was a strong advocate of holding youth accountable for their actions before they develop a pattern of lawbreaking behavior. Concerned that the delinquency problem in Odessa was being exacerbated by the juvenile justice system's unresponsiveness to juvenile offenders, she developed the Odessa Teen Court as a diversion program.[8] Before her death in 1993, Ms. Rothstein actively promoted the teen court concept locally and nationally by publishing articles about the program in national journals and making presentations at national conferences related to juvenile justice. Considering that youth courts are often isolated in communities and do not get much attention outside of their specific locales, her contributions and work in this area led to the Odessa Teen Court becoming one of the most widely known programs in the United States and sparked initial interest in the youth court concept in many jurisdictions.

Another driving force behind the youth court growth spurt can be attributed to the support and focus on the youth court concept provided by the federal government over the past 15 years. Prior to the federal government's initiatives to provide training and resources, there was limited information about the youth court concept and even less information available on how to get a youth court program started. Most literature reviewed focused on descriptions of specific programs and their operations, with a few reports providing insight into the varying structures of these programs. In 1994, the National Highway Traffic Safety Administration (NHTSA) saw youth courts as a viable alternative for law enforcement officers searching for diversion programs to which they could refer youth for alcohol-related offenses. NHTSA, through funds provided to the American Probation and Parole Association, spearheaded the development of an implementation guide designed to provide baseline information on developing, implementing, and enhancing teen court programs within their jurisdictions. Training and technical assistance followed to help get the word out to communities about these programs and provide assistance in program development efforts.

In the late 1990s, the Office of Juvenile Justice and Delinquency Prevention (OJJDP) joined forces with NHTSA and funneled additional resources aimed at helping communities establish these programs to address minor delinquent and status offenders. OJJDP established the National Youth Court Center (NYCC), operated by the American Probation and Parole Association from 1998 to 2006, to serve as a central point of contact for youth court programs across the nation. The NYCC served as an information clearinghouse, provided training and technical assistance, and developed resource materials on how to develop and enhance youth court programs in the United States. Over the years of its operation, with funds from OJJDP, the NYCC also partnered with the American Bar Association, Street Law, Inc., the Constitutional Rights Foundation in Los Angeles and Chicago, and the American Youth Policy Forum for the development of additional programmatic resources for youth court programs.

At the same time the federal government was focusing its attention on youth courts, local youth court programs began to see the benefits that networking and partnerships can provide and began organizing on a state level as a means to foster more support for the concept.[9] This reinforced the momentum initiated by the federal government agencies and contributed to the development of even more local programs.

As of 2008, there were 21 states with state associations and networking groups.[10] Some of the specific benefits youth courts derive from organizing on a state level include the ability to unify and network with others working in youth courts, plan and organize education and training events for youth court staff and youth court volunteers to help them enhance services and their skills, and assist in the development of new programs. State associations and networks also have an enhanced ability to promote the youth court concept and to work toward gaining more political and financial support within the state. There is also a more structured opportunity for increased interaction among youth courts and other stakeholder groups (e.g., judges, state agencies, law enforcement, schools), which can help break down barriers between these groups and improve communication. Networking on a state level makes it easier for local programs to stay informed about current issues that may affect youth courts in the state such as proposed youth court legislation or funding opportunities.[11]

In late 2006 and throughout 2007, the Office of Juvenile Justice and Delinquency Prevention refocused its resources, through funds provided to the National Council of Juvenile and Family Court Judges and Phi Alpha Delta Public Service Center, on building capacity of state youth court associations and networking groups to develop a self-governing national association for youth court programs. As a result of these efforts, the National Association of Youth Courts (NAYC) was incorporated as a self-governing nonprofit organization on May 23, 2007. Its primary purpose is to support and promote the work of teen courts, peer courts, youth courts, and student courts across the United States. The goals of the NAYC are the following:

- To encourage the development and expansion of youth courts and state associations of youth courts;
- To provide a forum for training of youth and adult volunteers, the sharing of ideas, best practices, and resources for the operation of youth courts;
- To provide support for local education, prevention, and intervention services to the youth;
- To share information on grants and other funding streams, assisting local courts in grant applications;
- To become a pass-through agency for funds received from governmental agencies or private sector grants;
- To enhance connections and relationships with government agencies and community-based programs or organizations; and
- To educate public and private agencies, businesses, and individuals on the benefits of youth courts.[12]

HOW YOUTH COURTS OPERATE

As mentioned earlier, youth courts by definition are programs in which youth sentence their peers for minor delinquent and status offenses and problem behaviors. However, where youth courts are located, how they get their authority to operate, and how they carry out their basic functions differ widely among programs throughout the nation.

Youth court programs are located in rural, suburban, and urban areas, as well as in small and large communities. Within these communities, some are located in justice agencies such as law enforcement, probation, juvenile court, or prosecutors' offices. Others are incorporated as a nonprofit agency or are operated in the community by established nonprofit organizations such as Boys and Girls Clubs, YMCAs, and Youth Service Bureaus. A handful of youth courts are operated by municipalities or other types of government organizations.

Finally, a growing number of youth courts are operated and administered by schools. While some school-based youth courts will accept delinquency or status offense referrals from the justice system, many school-based youth courts are established to address school disciplinary infractions that occur on the school campus that would not be eligible for a court referral. Youth participating in school-based youth courts are often able to avoid being suspended by participating in and completing the program successfully.

The authority of youth courts to operate generally can arise from legislation or through an agreement (contract). As of early 2006, 25 states had some form of legislation regarding youth courts.[13] State youth court legislation varies from the vague (whereby it basically grants permission for youth courts to operate) to the specific (e.g., where it stipulates whether youth courts can function as dispositional-only programs or whether they can serve as fact-finding courts, it specifies the age range of respondents and volunteers that can participate, it designates the types of offenses and behaviors it can address, it describes the types of dispositions the program can offer, and it addresses whether the program can charge a fee). Therefore, local programs need to conduct research to determine whether their state has legislation and review it carefully to determine what, if any, provisions are included with which they must comply.

There are a variety of reasons that states may choose to legislate youth courts. Some do so to increase consistency and establish minimal standards for the programs' operations in their state. Others see legislation as a means for legitimizing the youth court program for local community stakeholders. Legislation also can provide funding, mandate state support, and provide limited immunity from civil liability.[14]

On the flip side, there can be some downsides to and arguments against legislation. Most of these arguments relate to stipulations made in legislation that may inhibit local programs from being able to adapt the program's practices to meet their unique needs and resources. For example, what works in a youth court operating in an urban area may not work for one in a rural area. The types of problems communities and youth face may be different and the type of resources available to address these varying needs also is very different. States that pass youth court legislation "should ensure that teen courts will maintain their individuality, while providing broad mandates to help all teen court programs maintain acceptable standards."[15]

Primary Function of Youth Courts

The vast majority (92 percent) of youth courts are established to serve as sentencing-only programs; therefore, youth admit their wrongdoing or agree not to contest the charges against them and are sent to youth court for sentencing. The remaining 8 percent do allow youth to plead not guilty and use the youth court to determine guilt or innocence in addition to determining an appropriate sentence. Typical age ranges served by these programs (youth volunteers and respondents) are 12–18 years—although younger youth have been served by some programs if the case and situation warrants.[16]

All youth courts have an incentive for participation. If youth complete the program successfully, most youth courts have provisions that allow for the case to be dismissed. Other programs state the youth's record will be expunged, although this can be difficult to guarantee in many jurisdictions due to the variety of entities that may have a record of the juvenile on file (e.g., law enforcement, county attorney, probation, juvenile court). Once a youth has completed the program, youth court staff must ensure that complete information is provided to the entities responsible for ensuring whatever end result has been promised.

Types of Offenses

In a study conducted by the American Youth Policy Forum in 2005, it was estimated that youth courts collectively handle more than 110,000 to 125,000 cases each year.[17] Nationally, common types of delinquent offenses referred to youth courts include but are not limited to theft, shoplifting, traffic violations, possession of drug paraphernalia, simple assault, and vandalism. Some typical status offenses (i.e., offenses considered illegal for youth but do not apply to adult offenders) include truancy, curfew violations, and a minor's possession of alcohol. Youth courts also address problem behaviors that would not necessarily invoke a response by the justice system such as school disciplinary cases. Most respondents are first-time offenders, and by having their case diverted to a youth court they are given the opportunity to have the charges against them dismissed if they complete the program successfully. Many youth courts will accept youth with prior offenses if the offense is eligible and they feel the young person can benefit from the program's services.

When viewed from a national perspective, youth courts address a wide range of delinquent and status offenses and problem behaviors, but there is considerable variation in terms of what local programs will accept. It is important to remember when making decisions around issues related to the types of referrals to accept that, "Youth courts take young people, not cases, and each respondent who is being considered for referral to youth court must be individually screened."[18] Making sure that referrals are within the bounds of statutory or agency mandates or restrictions, are related to the goals and objectives of the program, and are ones for which the program can provide adequate sentencing options or services are necessary steps to targeting appropriate cases for the program and serving respondents' needs more effectively.

Referrals to youth courts are made from myriad sources including judges, juvenile probation, law enforcement, prosecutors, and schools. Some youth courts receive referrals from only one source, while others will accept referrals from multiple agencies.[19] Locally, youth courts have to make their own decision about what type of cases they should accept and from where they should receive their referrals. Some of the issues that must be considered when making these types of decisions include, but are not limited to, the types of problems that the community is experiencing that are not being adequately addressed by some other entity, state laws that may govern youth courts, availability of appropriate dispositions to address the needs of potential youth court respondents, and safety concerns of respondents and volunteers.[20]

It is widely recognized that a swift and certain response is among the elements needed for successful intervention with juvenile offenders. A shorter time frame between the commission of the offense or problem behavior and the imposition of a consequence enhances the ability of the young person to connect his or her actions to the consequences that were imposed. Long delays or ambivalent responses by the system send a message to the youth that what he or she did is not important. When the system is perceived as not viewing the offense or behavior as important, then the young person will be more likely to view his or her behavior that way too. Furthermore, the respondent's life circumstances and/or behavior may have changed since the incident, and delayed actions may be perceived as capricious or overly punitive. This may result in an unintended consequence of negative backlash behavior by the youthful offender.[21]

A strength of many youth court programs, as compared to many traditional court systems, is its ability to intervene quickly soon after an incident or offense has occurred. Approximately 25 percent of youth courts report that they are able to hold a youth court hearing within one to two weeks of the date of the offense or incident.[22]

Once a youth court receives a referral, the youth court coordinator conducts an intake interview with the parent/guardian and the youth respondent to explain the program, ensure the referral is appropriate and that the youth and his or her parent/guardian are agreeable to the terms of participation in the program, receive signatures on the necessary consent and waiver forms, and schedule the case for a youth court hearing.

Youth Court Program Models

Problem-solving courts reach out to the community and find ways for community members to be involved in the justice process.[23] In this area, youth courts excel. The justice process centers around, and is totally dependent on, participation of community members.

There are four primary models of youth court proceedings[24] that operate throughout the country—adult judge, youth judge, youth tribunal, and peer jury. The models reflect the ways in which youth court hearings are structured and what volunteer roles each type of program utilizes to carry out the basic court functions. These models are not meant to be absolute; some local communities implement variations and hybrids of these models to meet their unique needs and resources. The main element that must be present, regardless of the model or variation of a model used, is that youth court hearings must be youth-focused and youth-driven and operated in a manner that empowers the youth participating in the hearing.[25] The following provides a brief summary of each of the four primary models.

Adult Judge

In the adult judge model, youth volunteers serve in the roles of youth prosecuting and defense attorneys, clerks, bailiffs, and jurors. An adult volunteer (often a local attorney) serves as the youth court judge. The role of the adult judge is not to render a decision. Rather, the judge presides over the hearing and follows a protocol to keep the process on task.

Youth Judge

In the youth judge model, youth volunteers serve in the roles of youth prosecuting and defense attorneys, clerks, bailiffs, and jurors. As the name indicates, a youth volunteer also serves as the youth court judge. Typically, youth judges are older, have volunteered with the program for more than a year, and through their dedicated service have earned the distinction of serving as the judge. It bears saying, however, that although there are no formal roles for adults in this model, there is always an adult in the courtroom during hearings to monitor the proceedings and intervene when absolutely necessary.

Youth Tribunal

Youth prosecuting and defense attorneys bring out the facts and circumstances of the case. In this model, there is not a separate peer jury. The hearing is presided over by a panel of three youth judges who also make the disposition recommendation.

Peer Jury

The primary difference in peer jury model programs is that there are no youth prosecuting and defense attorneys. In this model, a panel of jurors (often six to eight youth) engages in a dialogue directly with the respondent and other witnesses to gain an understanding of the facts and circumstances of the case. The peer jury then deliberates and determines an appropriate disposition for the respondent. In some programs, youth advocates and community advocates may be used to make opening and closing statements on behalf of the respondent and community respectively; however, these advocates do not question the respondent directly.

During the youth court hearings, the facts and circumstances of the case are reviewed and information regarding mitigating and aggravating circumstances is revealed so that the youth volunteers can render an appropriate disposition recommendation. In youth court programs that are designed to determine a disposition and not determine guilt or innocence, the role of the prosecuting and defense attorney is to bring out mitigating and aggravating circumstances of the case so the most appropriate disposition can be rendered. Most youth courts rely on the police report and oral testimony from the respondent during the hearing to bring out this information during the proceeding. However, other programs allow input (either from oral testimony or from written statements) from parents/guardians, victims, and other key witnesses to gain a better understanding of the far-reaching impact of the respondent's actions. For the small percentage of youth courts that allow youth to plead not guilty, a similar process is followed to bring forth information for the youth volunteers to consider in determining guilt or innocence. If the youth court respondent is found guilty, the youth court also imposes the disposition.

Youth Court Dispositions

Once the case has been heard, the youth jurors or judge panel retire to deliberate and determine an appropriate disposition recommendation and problem resolution. Common youth court disposition options include community service, apologies to parents/guardians or victims, educational classes related to the needs of the respondent or to the type of offense, essays, and, if the program model supports it, youth court jury duty.

Almost all (98 percent) youth courts require that a minimum number of community service hours be ordered as part of the recommended disposition.[26] Historically, community service has revolved around menial assignments, while little attention has been paid to the advantages that community service can provide toward influencing respondents' attitudes and providing public benefits.[27] In the education system, community service is often used as a learning tool to help link the skills and knowledge that students learn in class to issues, needs, or problems they identify in their school or community. In the past several years, youth courts have begun to apply aspects of the service-learning strategies used in schools to the community service component of the program in order to provide respondents with an opportunity to make recompense and reparation to the community and victims through their community service obligation.[28] For some youth courts, this means designing local service projects (e.g., repairing playground equipment at a local park, working at a soup kitchen as a group to prepare and serve a meal to the homeless, plant and tend a vegetable garden for a local nursing home) that address local needs and problems and provide lasting benefits to the community they serve. This approach can be more time intensive, but is an additional strategy for involving communities in the justice process.

Beyond a requirement of community service hours, most youth judge or jury panels include one or more of the other more common dispositions or some other creative option (e.g., mediation, drug testing, home curfew) as part of the disposition. Some youth courts offer jurors and judge panels a great deal of flexibility when making sentencing decisions. Other programs provide stringent and specific guidelines on the dispositions that can be imposed for particular offenses. In general, the *National Youth Court Guidelines* encourage youth courts to implement sentencing guidelines that will protect the accountability and integrity of the program, yet will also allow for juror or judge panel discretion and flexibility.[29]

In the models that have a separate jury, serving as a youth court juror on future youth court cases is often used as a disposition option for youth court respondents. This requirement can increase the educational value of the program for respondents and help ensure that other respondents are being sentenced by a jury of their true peers. It also enhances the positive peer influence aspect of the program because the respondents have more opportunities for interaction with youth who volunteer with the program and learn problem-solving skills. According to a study by the American Youth Policy Forum, approximately one in five youthful offenders who participate as jurors choose to continue volunteering with the program after their program requirements are completed.[30] Take, for example, the following account from the Youth Court Coordinator for the Placer County Peer Court in California:[31]

> I currently have a girl who came through Peer Court 3 years ago and had such a bad attitude, was uncooperative and completed her sentence only because we dragged her kicking and screaming through. Her Mom was nice but had little control. Following completion, suddenly she started asking to be on the jury and then signed up and went through the teen attorney training. This year she has done a number of cases both prosecution and defense and has just completed an application to be on the Board of Directors. Her grades and school attendance have done a 360 and we don't even recognize her as the same person!

Volunteer Roles and Recruitment Strategies

Youth courts rely extensively on youth volunteers serving in a variety of roles that may include prosecuting attorneys, defense attorneys, jurors, clerks, bailiffs, and sometimes judges. The involvement of youth volunteers in the program also can extend to roles including serving on the board of directors or advisory committees and helping with marketing, recruiting, and training new volunteers. It is estimated that more than 100,000 youth volunteer for youth courts each year.[32] Schools serve as a primary location for recruiting youth volunteers; however, other sources for recruiting youth volunteers include former youth court respondents, Boy's and Girl's Clubs, Boy and Girl Scout programs, Explorer Posts, faith-based organizations, organizations that serve homeschooled youth, and other youth-serving organizations in the community.

There are a number of youth in a community who are automatically attracted to volunteering for youth courts—particularly those who have a desire to pursue a career in the legal field. However, the key in any youth court recruitment effort is to encourage and solicit involvement from a mix of young people who are diverse in terms of representation from different ethnic, social, and economic backgrounds, and are also diverse in relation to their life experiences (e.g., suburban versus inner-city, good grades versus bad grades, pro-social versus at-risk). This diversity among volunteers enables youth courts to respond to the needs of the individuals they serve more effectively. Positive peer influence is touted as a major benefit of youth court. Having a group of peers imposing judgment on a respondent who is reflective and representative of the respondents' peer group and is someone who the respondent feels has an appreciation for what he or she is going through elevates the power of the peer influence aspect of youth courts.[33]

Most youth courts have at least one staff to oversee program operations, but with the vast tasks associated with starting and operating youth court programs, staff cannot do it alone. Therefore, adult volunteers in the community also play a key role in the success and sustainability of youth courts. Some ways in which adult volunteers assist youth courts include providing clerical or administrative support, serving as members of boards of directors and advisory committees, raising funds for the program, marketing the program, recruiting and training youth volunteers, serving as legal advisors to youth attorneys or mentors to other youth involved in the program, and serving as a youth court judge. Places youth courts target for recruitment efforts aimed at adult volunteers include retired and senior citizen programs, civic and social organizations, local universities and colleges, faith-based organizations, parent-teacher associations, and local bar associations.

It cannot be stressed enough, however, that youth empowerment is a central tenet of youth court programs. Adults working and volunteering with the program must be aware of how their actions can affect youths' feelings and sense of empowerment. Essentially, adults should serve as a guide by the side of youth volunteers involved in the program. Adults who attempt to control or force their views and values on youth volunteers or exert too much power during the youth court proceedings inhibit the growth and learning experience that youth court programs provide.[34]

Volunteer Training

Once youth and adults choose to volunteer, they must be oriented and trained to perform their role(s) proficiently and effectively. Training also provides youth volunteers with an opportunity for personal growth and enrichment. This is important to youth courts because, in addition to holding youthful offenders accountable for their behavior, another major goal of youth courts is to educate youth about the legal system and to assist them in building competent life skills that will aid them when confronted with challenging choices and problems in life. Training in youth court programs is not a one-shot process; rather it is an ongoing process. Frequent and consistent training reinforces knowledge and skill development that are necessary to achieve the positive program outcomes.

Some of the topics addressed in training programs provided by youth courts include information on the U.S. legal and judicial system and the ways youth courts differ from traditional courts; trial, advocacy, and case preparation skills; ethics, respect, appropriate courtroom demeanor, and confidentiality; listening, problem solving, and critical thinking (particularly with respect to the questioning and deliberation processes); goals of sentencing in youth courts; effects of crime on victims, communities, offenders, and offenders' families; and the types of sentencing options the program has available. Youth courts also introduce youth to concepts of restorative justice, cultural diversity, causes of crime, and issues related to the types of offenses the program accepts (e.g., substance abuse awareness). On-the-job and in-service training sessions are used to complement initial training as a way to continue and enhance the learning and skill-building processes.[35]

YOUTH COURT EFFECTIVENESS

Youth court effectiveness can be defined in many ways. Although as a program designed, in part, to address delinquent and problem behavior in youth, the ultimate measure of effectiveness often centers on recidivism rates. Though the number of youth courts has grown exponentially in the past 15 years, there has been little research conducted on the program's effectiveness in terms of reducing recidivism. When asked about recidivism rates, most local programs report low, but often widely varying, percentages based on very different definitions of recidivism. The studies that have been published often focus on one program or a few programs within a state, lack rigorous methodologies, and have had mixed results.[36]

To date, there has been only one national evaluation on youth court programs designed to assess its effectiveness. Using a quasi-experimental design, the Urban Institute, with funds from the Office of Juvenile Justice and Delinquency Prevention, studied the Anchorage Youth Court in Anchorage, Alaska; teen courts operated by the Arizona Superior Court in Maricopa County, Arizona; Montgomery County Teen Court in Rockville, MD; and the Independence Youth Court in Independence, Missouri. They compared more than 500 cases from the four sites with similar cases handled by traditional juvenile justice systems in those jurisdictions. In addition to collecting baseline data on the youth and their parents or guardians, they tracked the youth for six months to measure the extent to which recidivism rates differed between those youth who went through the teen court programs and those who were processed through alternate means in the formal juvenile justice system.[37]

The results from the Anchorage Youth Court and the Independence Youth Court indicated that youth who went through the youth court were significantly less likely to be referred to the juvenile justice system for new offenses within six months of their initial offense. In the teen courts in Maricopa County, Arizona, the results showed that there was a reduced probability of youth to reoffend and be referred to the juvenile justice system within six months of the initial charge; however, the results were not statistically significant. In Rockville, Maryland, the comparison group used was a more proactive, police diversion program that provided similar services to those provided by the teen court. The recidivism rates for the Montgomery County Teen Court were actually slightly higher than the police diversion program; however, the reoffending rates for both groups were under 10 percent and did not reach a level of statistical significance.[38] Though the Urban Institute's findings did suggest that "teen courts represent a promising alternative for the juvenile justice system," they also raised additional questions to examine and indicated the need for more rigorous evaluation on effectiveness of these programs. [39]

Because of the wide variations in program operations and the independent nature of the way youth courts operate nationally, future research should be designed to look more closely at what is going on in different youth courts that may contribute to different outcomes.[40]

THE EVOLUTION OF YOUTH COURTS

A noticeable difference between the standard operating procedure of many youth courts in the 1990s compared to that of many of the youth courts operating today can be attributed to the implementation of program practices based on restorative justice principles. Restorative justice recognizes that crime breaks relationships between the offender and his or her family, friends, victims, and community. The Balanced and Restorative Justice Model outlines a problem-solving approach that enables offenders to make amends to their victims and communities; builds on offenders' strengths and increases offenders' competencies; and protects the public through a process in which the individual victims, community, and offender are all active stakeholders.[41]

Historically, many youth courts focused their hearings on the offender and learned facts about the incident and based decisions from the police report and from oral testimony provided by the respondent. Consideration of and opportunity for victim impact information were not viewed as major objectives of the programs. As an awareness of the tenets of restorative justice has risen among persons operating youth courts, there has been a shift in focus from viewing the goal of teen court as responding to a crime or problem behavior by punishing the juvenile to that of focusing on the negative result that was created by the problem behavior or crime and assisting the juvenile in making amends for his or her behavior and the resulting injury.

Within the restorative justice construct there is also a focus placed on helping the young person rebuild relationships with others (e.g., family, friends, victims, community) that have been damaged as the result of the crime or problem behavior. This is a crucial distinction (i.e., punishment versus reparation) many youth court program staff and organizers now recognize that has made them more successful in their attempts to move toward more problem-solving and restorative justice-based practices.[42] For example, the youth court coordinator for the Cattaraugus County Youth Court in New York states, "My team members are told in training that we do not even use the word 'punishment' during hearings."[43]

The implications of this shift in program philosophy among the programs that choose to implement restorative practices is significant and the ways in which programs can choose to augment or implement their practices to support this philosophical shift are numerous. The most obvious change that has occurred as a result of this philosophical shift is that more and more youth courts recognize the valuable role that victims can play in providing input and impact information on how the crime or behavior affected them and in soliciting their opinions on the best way in which the harm can be repaired. Many youth courts now offer victims an opportunity to provide impact information to the program. Most of the time this is done through the use of written victim impact statements; however, there are youth courts that will allow victims to provide oral testimony or provide their impact information through other electronic methods (e.g., audio or video statements).[44]

Some youth court programs have also expanded their capacity to address victim issues through the implementation of a victim advocate for the youth court. For example, in the Colonie Youth Court Program in Latham, New York, a trained youth volunteer victim advocate represents the rights and interests of the victim, is responsible solely to the needs of the victim, and acts as a liaison between the victim and the youth court process. Patrice Lockart, a founding member of the board of directors for the Colonie Youth Court who helped establish this position in the program, states,

> I do feel that in our court the added role has enhanced the process. It has also provided much needed education and awareness about victims of crimes and what they go through to both the respondent and the youth member/volunteers/jury. Hopefully we put a face to the victim for the youth to see. By doing so, it connects their behavior to actual harm to the victim that was done while providing a way for them to repair the harm (taking into consideration the wishes of the victim how that should be done).[45]

Although the introduction of victim impact information may increase the amount of time it takes to conduct a youth court hearing, when this type of information is provided to youth court judge panels or juries it personalizes the case in a much more dramatic way and enables them to impose an individualized disposition that can help the youth court respondent understand how his actions have affected others and make amends and repair the harm to the extent possible.

THE FUNDING CHALLENGE

Though some programs report periodic challenges in finding, maintaining, and training volunteers and staff or finding appropriate community service sites or other services for youth court respondents, by and large the most often reported challenge shared by the majority of youth courts is attaining and maintaining adequate funding for the program. Most youth courts exist on very small annual operating budgets (less than $50,000)[46] and are considered to be cost-effective programs,[47] but it is not uncommon for youth courts to be developed and implemented using grant funds that are typically designated for start-up efforts and classified as seed money. These funds are typically limited in duration and are not designed to be a sustainable funding base.[48]

While most youth courts receive their funding from a single source, many others have two to five sources of funding. As a result, program coordinators often have to spend an inordinate amount of time seeking funds for the program, which can detract from the time they have to manage and focus on the day-to-day activities of the program (e.g., volunteer recruitment, training, intake sessions, case management).[49] Youth court administrators are constantly on the lookout for ways in which they can create a lasting funding stream for their programs. When that magic source or sources are not located, often the program has to reduce or terminate services.

The Colonie Youth Court experience offers one example of how a youth court addressed its funding challenge to create its sustainable funding base. The Colonie Youth Court Program was established in Latham, New York, in 1994 as a nonprofit 501 3(c) organization. Overall, through the first 10 years of its operation the program was fairly successful in attaining grant funding for its operations, but as the years went on, the challenge of finding grant funds became more difficult and time consuming for staff. However, through the years it had been operating, the program had been very deliberate in its education and involvement of community stakeholders in the program. Referral agencies received regular updates on the status of their referrals, stakeholders were invited to attend and speak at the program's volunteer training graduation events and other high profile events, and key stakeholders from a variety of agencies in the community held seats on the program's board of directors. Rather than only seeking stakeholder assistance and involvement in times of dire need, the program gladly shared its success with all stakeholder agencies and truly embodied the spirit of ongoing interagency collaboration and communication. It is these and other efforts the program made to encourage meaningful participation of its stakeholders that played a huge role in the program's ultimate success in persuading the local police department to absorb the program within its agency in 2004 and add it as a line item in its budget to create a sustainable funding base for the program.

Other states, such as Florida, Illinois, and West Virginia, have attempted to address some of their funding concerns by seeking and having legislation passed that allocates funding for their youth court programs through assessments made on certain types of convicted adult offenders.[50] Florida was the first state to get this type of legislation passed. In the early 1990s, local teen court advocates in the state began building the foundation for this type of legislation by expanding the programs throughout the State of Florida and working toward the establishment of the Florida Association of Teen Courts in 1997. The networking and support for teen courts throughout the state was rewarded in 1997 when Governor Lawton Chiles signed a bill into law (F.S.S. 938.19) that gave local county governments the authority to adopt an ordinance to assess a $3 fee on approved court cases and traffic tickets that was designated for the operation and administration of teen courts on a county level.[51]

Funding by legislation requires constant vigil. Appropriations can be changed or eliminated, particularly in times of economic stress and tight budgets.[52] Florida was faced with the possibility of their funding through legislation being withdrawn when a state constitutional revision that was to take effect in July 2004 (Article V, Revision 7) shifted funding for the court system in Florida from the county level to the state. Although most of the teen courts in Florida are not operated as a court function, they were incorporated into the court reorganization process. The ramification was that all teen court funding was to be eliminated by July 2004. Through the networking they had through their state association, the teen courts in Florida were able to rally and advocate for new legislation that would protect funding for teen courts. As a result, the Article V "Glitch Bill" was created and passed, which allows counties to collect a $65 fee for any misdemeanor or felony criminal or traffic court case in the state. It requires that 25 percent of the fee be allocated for juvenile crime prevention programs, which includes teen courts. The development of a strategic plan, establishment of state standards for youth courts, and creation of a common message are among the recommendations that Kathleen Self, the former president of the Florida Association of Teen Courts, makes to other states who want to organize and seek legislation on a state level.[53]

The funding challenge is not unique to youth courts. Effective strategies to raise funds for programs require planning, research, outreach, and cultivation of potential donors and funders. Similar to the advice you hear when participating in a personal financial planning program, whenever possible, youth courts —especially those that rely on grant funds—should have a diversified funding stream. This will provide some protection when one or more of the sources of funding are reduced or eliminated.

THE FUTURE OF YOUTH COURTS

So far, the number of communities implementing and operating youth courts does not appear to be decreasing. However, tighter economic times are leading to closer scrutiny for limited funds. Policy makers and funders are calling for agencies to implement programs that use evidence-based practices. With that being said, for youth courts to continue with the momentum they have enjoyed over the past 15 years, it is imperative that more work be done to help youth courts determine the factors that are most successful at contributing to increased program completion and reductions in recidivism, as well as satisfaction, participation, and learning among youth volunteers. In doing so, youth courts will be better equipped to implement and provide more effective services for the youth they serve. With more reliable research, combined with national advocacy and support (such as that provided through the newly developed National Association for Youth Courts), more inroads can be made toward professionalizing the youth court field and positioning it to play a major role in the juvenile justice system in the next 15–20 years.

NOTES

1. Sentences meted out, 1949, as cited in Butts, Buck, & Coggeshall, 2002.
2. Martley, 1965.
3. National Association of Youth Courts, n.d.(a),
4. Paula Nessel, personal communication with the author, 1994.
5. Godwin, Fulton, & Steinhart, 1998.
6. National Association of Youth Courts, n.d.(b).
7. National Association of Youth Courts, n.d.(b).
8. Knepper, 1994.
9. Godwin Mullins & Dunlap, 2004.
10. Kathleen Self, email message sent to the author, August 22, 2008.
11. Godwin Mullins & Dunlap, 2004.
12. Katie Self, email message sent to author, June 21, 2008.
13. Heward, 2006.
14. Heward, 2006.
15. Heward, 2006, p. 2.
16. National Youth Court Center Database, 2006.
17. Pearson & Jurich, 2005.
18. Fisher, 2006, p. 4.
19. Godwin, Fulton, & Steinhart, 1998.
20. Fisher, 2006.
21. Howell, 1995.
22. Federal Youth Court Database, 2006, as cited in Fisher, 2006.
23. Berman & Feinblatt, 2005.
24. Godwin, Fulton, & Steinhart, 1998.
25. Godwin, Heward, & Spina, 2000.
26. National Youth Court Center Database, 2006.
27. Maloney & Bazemore, 1994.
28. Degleman, Doggett, & Medina, 2006.
29. Godwin, Heward, & Spina, 2000.
30. Pearson & Jurich, 2005.
31. Karen Green, email message sent to author, May 9, 2008.
32. Pearson & Jurich, 2005.
33. Godwin, Heward, & Spina, 2000.
34. Godwin, Heward, & Spina, 2000.
35. Godwin, Heward, & Spina, 2000.
36. Povitisky, 2005.
37. Butts, Buck, & Coggeshall, 2002.

38. Butts, Buck, & Coggeshall, 2002.
39. Butts, Buck, & Coggeshall, 2002, p. 34.
40. Schneider, 2008.
41. Pranis, 1998.
42. Godwin, 2001.
43. Laurie Peterson, email message sent to author, May 8, 2008.
44. Godwin, 2001.
45. Patrice Lockart, email message sent to author, August 21, 2008.
46. Schneider, 2008.
47. Pearson & Jurich, 2005.
48. Godwin, Heward, & Spina, 2000.
49. Schneider, 2008.
50. Heward, 2006.
51. Pearson, 2004.
52. Heward, 2006.
53. Pearson, 2004.

REFERENCES

Berman, G., & Feinblatt, J. (2005). *Good courts: The case for problem solving justice.* New York: The New Press.

Butts, J. A., Buck, J., & Coggeshall, M. B. (2002). *The impact of teen courts on young offenders.* Washington, DC: The Urban Institute.

Degleman, C., Doggett, K., & Medina, G. (2006). *Giving back: Introducing community service learning.* Washington, DC: Office of Juvenile Justice and Delinquency Prevention.

Fisher, M. (2006). *Youth cases for youth courts: Desktop guide. A guide to the typical offenses handled by youth courts.* Chicago, IL: American Bar Association.

Godwin Mullins, T., & Dunlap, K. (2004, May). A comparison of statewide youth court associations and networking groups. In T. Godwin Mullins (Ed.), *Selected topics on youth courts: A monograph.* Washington, DC: Office for Juvenile Justice and Delinquency Prevention.

Godwin, T., Heward, M., & Spina, T. (2000). *National Youth Court Guidelines.* Lexington, KY: American Probation and Parole Association.

Godwin, T. (2001). *Restorative justice in teen courts: A preliminary look.* Lexington, KY: American Probation and Parole Association.

Godwin, T., Fulton, B. A., & Steinhart, D. (1998). *Peer justice and youth empowerment: An implementation guide for teen court programs.* Washington, DC: Office of Juvenile Justice and Delinquency Prevention, National Highway Traffic Safety Administration.

Heward, M. E. (2006, September). *An update on teen court legislation.* Washington, DC: Office of Juvenile Justice and Delinquency Prevention.

Howell, J. C., (Ed.). (1995, May). *Guide for implementing the comprehensive strategy for serious, violent, and chronic juvenile offenders.* Washington, DC: Office of Juvenile Justice and Delinquency Prevention.

Knepper, P. (1994, June). *The Kentucky guide to teen/youth courts.* Highland Heights, KY: Northern Kentucky University.

Maloney, D., & Bazemore, G. (1994, December). Making a difference: Community service helps heal troubled youths. *Corrections Today, 56*(7), 74–84, 149.

Martley, E. (1965, December 26). Juvenile offenders tried by jury of peers. *The Rapid City (South Dakota) Sunday Journal.*

National Association for Youth Courts. (n.d.)(a). *Facts and stats.* Retrieved June 20, 2008, from http://www.youthcourt.net/content/view/35/49//.

National Association of Youth Courts. (n.d.)(b). *Youth court list by state.* Retrieved August 15, 2008, from http://www.youthcourt.net/content/view/7/14/.

National Youth Court Center Database. (2006). Unpublished data.

Pearson, S. S. (2004, September). *Policymakers support youth court growth: Voices and recommendations from the field.* Lexington, KY: National Youth Court Center, American Probation and Parole Association. Retrieved September 2, 2008, from http://www.youthcourt.net/content/view/74.

Pearson, S. S., & Jurich, S. (2005). *Youth court: A community solution for embracing at-risk youth. A national update.* Washington, DC: American Youth Policy Forum.

Povitisky, W. (2005). *Teen court: Does it reduce recidivism?* Unpublished master's thesis, University of Maryland, College Park. Retrieved August 14, 2008, from http://www.lib.umd.edu/drum/bitstream/1903/3274/1/umi-umd-3102.pdf.

Pranis, K. (1998, December). *Guide for implementing balanced and restorative justice.* Washington, DC: Office of Juvenile Justice and Delinquency Prevention.

Schneider, J. (2008). *Youth courts: An empirical update and analysis of future organizational and research needs.* Washington, DC: Hamilton Fish Institute.

Sentences meted out. (1949, May 16). *Mansfield (Ohio) News Journal.*

Selected Bibliography

Abuwala, R., & Farole, D. J., Jr. (2008). *The effects of the Harlem Housing Court on tenant perceptions of justice.* New York: Center for Court Innovation.

Acquaviva, G. L. (2006). Mental health courts: No longer experimental. *Seton Hall Law Review, 36,* 971–1013.

Aldrich, L., & Mazur, R. (2005). *Applying key principles of domestic violence courts in smaller jurisdictions.* New York: Center for Court Innovation and Bureau of Justice Assistance, U.S. Department of Justice.

Arrendondo, D., Kumli, J., Soto, L., Colin, E., Ornellas, J., Davilla, R., Edwards, L., & Hyman, E. (2001). Juvenile mental health court: Rationale and protocols. *Juvenile and Family Court Journal, 52*(4), 1–19.

Bakht, N., & Bentley, P. (2004). *Problem solving courts as agents of change.* Ontario, Canada: National Justice Institute.

Belenko, S. R. (2000). *Drugs and drug policy in America: A documentary history, Primary documents in American history and contemporary issues.* Westport, CT: Greenwood Press.

Belenko, S. (2001). *Research on drug courts: A critical review: 2001 update.* New York: National Center on Addiction and Substance Abuse at Columbia University.

Belenko, S. (2002). Drug courts. In C. G. Leukefeld, F. Tims, & D. Farabee (Eds.), *Treatment of drug offenders: Policies and issues* (pp. 301–318). New York: Springer.

Belenko, S., DeMatteo, D., & Patapis, N. (2007). Drug courts. In D. W. Springer & A. R. Roberts (Eds.), *Handbook of forensic mental health with victims and offenders: Assessment, treatment, and research* (pp. 385–423). New York: Springer Publishing Co.

Bennice, J. A., Resick, P. A., Mechanic, M., & Astin, M. (2003). The relative effects of intimate partner physical and sexual violence on post-traumatic stress disorder symptomology. *Violence and Victims, 18,* 87–94.

Bentley, P. (2005, Fall). An international take on drug treatment courts. *NADCP News,* 28.

Berman, G. (2000). What is a traditional judge anyway?: Problem solving in the state courts, *Judicature, 84,* 78–80.

Berman, G., & Feinblatt, J. (2001). Problem-solving-courts: A brief primer. *Law and Policy, 23*(2), 125–140.

Berman, G., & Feinblatt, J. (2005). *Good courts: The case for problem-solving justice.* New York: The New Press.

Bernstein, R., & Seltzer, T. (2003). The role of mental health courts in system reform. *University of the District of Columbia Law Review, 7,* 143–162.

Bhati, A., Roman, J. K., & Chafin, A. (2008). *To treat or not to treat: Evidence on the prospects of expanding treatment to drug-involved offenders.* Washington, DC: Justice Policy Center, Urban Institute.

Boldt, R. C. (1998). Rehabilitative punishment and the drug treatment court movement. *Washington University Law Quarterly, 76,* 1205–1306.

Boldt, R., & Singer, J. (2006). Juristocracy in the trenches: Problem-solving judges and therapeutic jurisprudence in drug treatment courts and unified family courts. *Maryland Law Review, 65,* 82–99.

Boothroyd, R. A., Mercado, C. C., Poythress, N. G., Christy, A., & Petrila, J. (2005). Clinical outcomes of defendants in mental health court. *Psychiatric Services, 56,* 829–834.

Boothroyd, R. A., Poythress, N. G., McGaha, A., & Petrila, J. (2003). The Broward mental health court: Process, outcomes, and service utilization. *International Journal of Law and Psychiatry, 26,* 55–71.

Bornstein, R. F. (2006). The complex relationship between dependency and domestic violence. *American Psychologist, 61,* 595–606.

Bouffard, J., & Taxman, F. (2004). Looking inside the "black box" of drug court treatment services using direct observations. *Journal of Drug Issues, 34*(1), 195–218.

Braithwaite, J. (1989). *Crime, shame and reintegration.* Cambridge, UK: Cambridge University Press.

Braithwaite, J. (2002). Restorative justice and therapeutic jurisprudence. *Criminal Law Bulletin, 38,* 244–262.

Bratton, W., & Guliani, R. (1994). *Police strategy no. 5: Reclaiming the public spaces of New York.* New York: City of New York.

Brewster, M. P. (2001). An evaluation of the Chester County (PA) Drug Court Program. *Journal of Drug Issues, 31*(1), 177–206.

Brown, J. (1997). Working toward freedom from violence: The process of change in battered women. *Violence Against Women, 3,* 5–22.

Bureau of Justice Assistance. (1998). *Overcoming obstacles to community courts: A summary of workshop proceedings.* Community Justice Series (prepared by the Center for Court Innovation). Washington DC: U.S. Department of Justice.

Bureau of Justice Assistance Drug Court Clearinghouse. (2001, June). *Juvenile drug court activity: Update.* Washington, DC: American University. Available at http://www.american.edu/justice.

Bureau of Justice Assistance. (2003). *Juvenile drug courts: Strategies in practice.* Washington, DC: Office of Justice Programs, U.S. Department of Justice (NCJ 197866).

Bureau of Justice Assistance, Drug Court Clearinghouse Project (BJA). (2004). *Recidivism and other findings reported from selected evaluations of adult drug court programs published: 2000–present.* Washington, DC: School of Public Affairs, American University.

Bureau of Justice Assistance Drug Court Clearinghouse. (2008). *Recidivism and other findings reported in selective evaluation reports of juvenile drug court programs: 2000–present.* Last Update: August 22, 2008, available at http://www.american.edu/justice.

Butts, J. A. (2001). Introduction: Problem-solving courts. *Law & Policy, 23,* 121–124.

Butts, J. A., Buck, J., & Coggeshall, M. B. (2002). *The impact of teen courts on young offenders.* Washington, DC: The Urban Institute.

Cannato, V. (2001). *The ungovernable city: John Lindsay's New York and the crisis of liberalism.* New York: Basic Books.

Campbell, R. (2000). *There are no victimless crimes.* New York: Center for Court Innovation.

Casey, P. M., & Rottman, D. B. (2003). *Problem-solving courts: Models and trends.* Williamsburg, VA: National Center for State Courts.

Casey, T. (2004). When good intentions are not enough: Problem-solving courts and the impending crisis of legitimacy. *Southern Methodist University Law Review, 57,* 1459–1519.

Chiodo, A. (2002). Sentencing drug-addicted offenders and the Toronto Drug Court. *Criminal Law Quarterly, 45,* 53–100.

Christy, A., Poythress, N. G., Boothroyd, R. A., Petrila, J., & Mehra, S. (2005). Evaluating the efficiency and community safety goals of the Broward County mental health court. *Behavioral Sciences and the Law, 23,* 1–17.

Cocozza, J. J., & Shufelt, J. L. (2006). *Juvenile mental health courts: An emerging strategy.* Available from the National Center for Mental Health and Juvenile Justice at http://www.ncmhjj.com/pdfs/publications/JuvenileMentalHealthCourts.pdf.

Coker, A. L., Smith, P. H., Bethea, L., King, M. R., & McKeown, R. E. (2000). Physical health consequences of physical and psychological intimate partner violence. *Archives of Family Medicine, 9,* 451–457.

Cooper, C. (2003). *Drug court activities update: Summary information on all programs and detailed information on adult drug courts* [Internet]. Office of Justice Programs; Drug Court Clearinghouse and Technical Assistance Project 2001 [cited February 26, 2003]. Available at http://spa.american.edu/justice/docuements/1933.pdf (accessed January 29, 2008).

Cosden, M., Ellens, J., Schnell, J., Yamini-Diouf, Y., & Wolfe, M. (2003). Evaluation of a mental health court with assertive community treatment. *Behavioral Sciences and the Law, 21,* 415–427.

Cosden, M., Ellens, J., Schnell, J., & Yamini-Diouf, Y. (2005). Efficacy of a mental health treatment court with assertive community treatment. *Behavioral Sciences and the Law, 23,* 199–214.

Council of State Governments. (2005). *Mental health courts: A national snapshot.* Available at http://consensusproject.org/mhcp/national-snapshot.pdf.

Cullen, F. T., & Gendreau, P. (2000). Assessing correctional rehabilitation: Policy, practice, and prospects. In Julie Horney (Ed.), *Policies, processes, and decisions of the criminal justice system* (*Criminal Justice 2000,* Vol. 3, pp. 109–175). Washington, DC: National Institute of Justice.

Dawson, M., & Dinovitzer, R. (2001). Victim cooperation and the prosecution of domestic violence in a specialized court. *Justice Quarterly, 18,* 593–622.

DeMatteo, D. S., Marlowe, D. B., & Festinger, D. S. (2006). Secondary prevention services for clients who are low risk in drug court: A conceptual model. *Crime & Delinquency, 52*(1), 114–134.

Degleman, C., Doggett, K., & Medina, G. (2006). Giving back: Introducing community service learning. Washington, DC: Office of Juvenile Justice and Delinquency Prevention. Available at http://www.ndci.org/pdf/Guiding_Principles_of_DWI_Court.pdf.

Dill, P., & Wells-Parker, E. (2006). Court-mandated treatment for convicted drinking drivers. *Alcohol Research and Health, 29,* 41–48, 43–44.

DWI Resource Center. (2006). *Court monitoring handbook.* Albuquerque, NM: DWI Resource Center. Available at http://www.dwiresourcecenter.org/downloads/naap/CourtHandbook.pdf.

Eley, S. (2005). Changing practices: The specialized domestic violence court process. *The Howard Journal of Criminal Justice, 44,* 113–142.

Erickson, S. T., Campbell, A., & Lamberti, J. S. (2006). Variations in mental health courts: Challenges, opportunities, and a call for caution. *Community Mental Health Journal, 42,* 335–344.

Erzen, T. (2001). Turnstile jumpers and broken windows policing. Disorder in New York City. In A. McArdle and T. Erzen (Eds.), *Zero tolerance: Quality-of-life and the new police brutality in New York City* (pp. 19–49). New York: New York University Press.

Fagan, J., & Malkin, V. (2003). Theorizing community justice through community courts. *Fordham Urban Law Journal, 30*(3), 897–953.

Farole, D. J. (2006). *The challenge of going to scale: Lessons from other disciplines for problem-solving courts.* Available from the Center for Court-Innovation at http://www.courtinnovation.org/_uploads/documents/Lessons.pdf.

Farole, D., Rempel, M., Byrne, F., & Chang, Y-W. (2008). *Problem-solving and the American bench: A national survey of trial court judges.* New York: Center for Court Innovation.

Feinblatt, J., & Berman, G. (2001). Community courts: A brief primer. *United States Attorney's Bulletin, 49,* 33–40.

Festinger, D. S., Marlowe, D. B., Lee, P. A., Kirby, K. C., Bovasso, G., & McLellan, A. T. (2002). Status hearings in drug court: When more is less and less is more. *Drug and Alcohol Dependence, 68,* 151–157.

Finigan, M., Carey, S. M., & Cox, A. (2007). *Impact of a mature drug court over 10 years of operation: Recidivism and costs.* Washington, DC: National Institute of Justice, Office of Research and Evaluation.

Fischer, B. (2003). "Doing good with a vengeance": A critical assessment of the practices, effects and implications of drug treatment courts in North America. *Criminal Justice, 3*(3), 227–248.

Fisher, M. (2006). *Youth cases for youth courts: Desktop guide. A guide to the typical offenses handled by youth courts.* Chicago, IL: American Bar Association.

Fisher, M., Geiger, B., & Highes, M. E. (2007). Female recidivist speak about their experience in drug court while engaging in appreciative inquiry. *International Journal of Offender Therapy and Comparative Criminology, 51*(6), 703–722.

Freeman-Wilson, K. (2006). *DWI Courts and DWI/Drug Courts: Reducing recidivism, saving lives* [Internet]. National Drug Court Institute 1999 [cited June, 29 2006]. Available at www.ndci.org/dui.pdf.

Fritzler, R. B., & Simon, L. M. J. (2000, Spring). Creating a domestic violence court: Combat in the trenches. *Court Review, 37* 28–39.

Godwin, T., Heward, M., & Spina, T. (2000). *National Youth Court guidelines.* Lexington, KY: American Probation and Parole Association.

Godwin, T. (2001). *Restorative justice in teen courts: A preliminary look.* Lexington, KY: American Probation and Parole Association.

Godwin Mullins, T., & Dunlap, K. (2004). A comparison of statewide youth court associations and networking groups. In T. Godwin Mullins (Ed.), *Selected topics on youth courts: A monograph.* Washington, DC: Office for Juvenile Justice and Delinquency Prevention.

Goldkamp, J., & Irons-Guynn, C. (2000). *Emerging Judicial strategies for the mentally ill in the criminal caseload: Mental health courts in Fort Lauderdale, Seattle, San Bernardino, and Anchorage.* Washington, DC: Bureau of Justice Assistance, U.S. Department of Justice.

Goldkamp, J. (1999). Challenges for research and innovation: When is a drug court not a drug court? In W. C. Terry (Ed.), *The early drug courts: Case studies in judicial innovation.* Thousand Oaks, CA: Sage Publications.

Goldkamp, J. S., White, M. D., & Robinson, J. B. (2001). Do drug courts work? Getting inside the drug court black box. *Journal of Drug Issues, 31*(1), 27–72.

Gottfredson, D. C., & Exum, M. L. (2002). The Baltimore City Drug Treatment Court: One-year results from a randomized study. *Journal of Research in Crime and Delinquency, 39*(3), 337–356.

Gover, A. R., Brank, E. M., & MacDonald, J. M. (2007). A specialized domestic violence court in South Carolina: An example of procedural justice for victims and defendants. *Violence Against Women, 13,* 603–626.

Gover, A. R., MacDonald, J. M., & Alpert, G. P. (2003). Combating domestic violence: Findings from an evaluation of a local domestic violence court. *Criminology and Public Policy, 1,* 109–132.

Gover, A. R, MacDonald, J. M., Alpert, G. P., and Geary, I. A., Jr. (2004). Lexington County Domestic Violence Court: A partnership and evaluation. Report to the National Institute of Justice, U.S. Department of Justice and Lexington County Sheriff's Office from Department of Criminology and Criminal Justice, University of South Carolina.

Government Accountability Office (GAO). (2005). *Adult drug court: Evidence indicates recidivism reductions and mixed results for other outcomes.* Washington, DC: United States Government Accountability Office.

Gregoire, T. K., & Burke, A. C. (2004). The relationship of legal coercion to readiness to change among adults with alcohol and other drug problems. *Journal of Substance Abuse Treatment, 26,* 35–41.

Griffin, P. A., Steadman, H. J., & Petrila, J. (2002). The use of criminal charges and sanctions in mental health courts. *Psychiatric Services, 53,* 1285–1289.

Guerin, P., and W. Pitts. (2002). *Evaluation of the Bernalillo County Metropolitan DWI/Drug Court: Final report.* Albuquerque, NM: University of New Mexico, Institute for Social Research.

Haimowitz, S. (2002). Can mental health courts end the criminalization of persons with mental illness? *Psychiatric Services, 53,* 1226–1228.

Hanson, D. (2008). DWI courts are effective in reducing DWI/DUI. *Alcohol: Problems and solutions.* Available at http://www.alcoholinformation.org.

Hedlund, J., & Fell, J. (2007). *Repeat offenders and persistent drinking drivers in the U.S.* Washington, DC: National Highway Traffic Safety Administration.

Heward, M. E. (2006). *An update on teen court legislation.* Washington, DC: Office of Juvenile Justice and Delinquency Prevention.

Herinckx, H. A., Swart, S. C., Ama, S. M., Dolezal, C. S., & King, S. (2005). Rearrest and linkage to mental health services among clients of the Clark County Mental Health Court Program. *Psychiatric Services, 56,* 853–857.

Hoffman, M. (2002). Therapeutic jurisprudence, neo-rehabilitationism, and judicial collectivism: The least dangerous branch becomes most dangerous. *Fordham Urban Law Journal, 29*(5), 2063–2098.

Huddleston, C. W., Wilson-Freeman, K., Marlowe, D. B., & Roussell, A. (2005). Painting the picture: A national report card on drug courts and other problem solving court programs in the United States. Alexandra, VA: National Drug Court Institute.

James, D. J., & Glaze, L. E. (2006). *Mental health problems of prison and jail inmates.* Washington, DC: U.S. Department of Justice, Office of Justice Programs, Bureau of Justice Statistics.

Judicial Council of Georgia. (n.d.). *Research results: Georgia's DUI courts work.* Available at http://www.ndci.org/pdf/GA_DUI_Court_Recidivism_032707.pdf.

Karafin, D. L. (2008). *Community courts across the globe. A measure of goals, performance, measures and operations.* A Report Submitted to the Open Society Institute. Open Society Foundation.

Kassebaum, G., & Okamoto, D. K. (2001). The drug court as a sentencing model. *Journal of Contemporary Criminal Justice, 17,* 89–104.

Keele, C. E. (2002). Criminalization of the mentally ill: The challenging role of the defense attorney in the mental health court system. *University of Missouri at Kansas City Law Review, 71,* 193–210.

Keilitz, S. (2001). *Specialization of domestic violence case management in the courts: A national survey.* National Center for State Courts. Available at http://www.ncsconline.org/index.html (accessed May 15, 2008).

Kings County Bar Association Drug Policy Project. (2005). *Effective drug control: Toward a new legal framework: State-level regulation as a workable alternative to the "war on drugs."* Seattle, WA: Kings County Bar Association Drug Policy Project.

Kluger, J. H. (2000). Judicial roundtable: Reflections of problem-court justices. *New York State Bar Association Journal, 72*(5), 11.

Kuehn, B. M. (2007). Mental health courts show promise. *Journal of the American Medical Association, 297,* 1641–1643.

Kurki, L. (2000). Restorative and community justice. *Crime and justice research: A review of research, 27,* 235–303.

LaPrairie, C., Gliksman, L., Erickson, P., Wall, R., & Newton-Taylor, B. (2002). Drug treatment courts: A viable option for Canada? Sentencing issues and preliminary findings from the Toronto Drug Treatment Court. *Substance Use and Misuse, 37*(12–13), 1529–1566.

Lazarus-Black, M., & McCall, P. L. (2006). The politics of place: Practice, process, and kinship in domestic violence courts. *Human Organization, 65,* 140–155.

Lederman, C. (2000). What is a traditional judge anyway? Problem solving in state courts. *Judicature, 84*(2), 80–82.

Lee, E. (2000). *Community courts, an evolving model.* Community Justice Series #2, Bureau of Justice Assistance. Washington DC: U.S. Department of Justice.

Little, K. (2003, May). Specialized courts and domestic violence. *Issues of Democracy: The Changing Face of U.S. Courts, 8*(1), 26–31.

Longshore, D., Turner, S., Wenzel, S., Morral, A., Harrell, A., McBride, D., Deschenes, E., & Iguchi, M. (2001). Drug courts: A conceptual framework. *Journal of Drug Issues, 31* (1), 7–26.

Mackinem, M., & Higgins, P. (2007). Tell me about the test: The construction of truth and lies in drug court. *Journal of Contemporary Ethnography, 36*(3), 223–251.

Mackinem, M. B., & Higgins, P. C. (2008). *Drug court: Constructing the moral identity of drug offenders.* Springfield, IL: C. C. Thomas.

MacLeod, D., & Weber, J. F. (2000). *Domestic violence courts: A descriptive study*. San Francisco, CA: Judicial Council of California, Administrative Office of the Courts.

Malkin, V. (2003). Community courts and the process of accountability: Consensus and conflict at the Red Hook Community Justice Center. *American Criminal Law Review, 40*(4), 1573–1593.

Marlowe, D. B. (2002). Effective strategies for intervening with drug abusing offenders. *Villanova Law Review, 47,* 989–1025.

Marlowe, D. B. (2003, August). Integrating substance abuse treatment and criminal justice supervision. *Science & Practice Perspectives,* 5–14.

Marlowe, D. B., DeMatteo, D. S., & Festinger, D. S. (2003). A sober assessment of drug courts. *Federal Sentencing Reporter, 16,* 113–128.

Marlowe, D. B., Festinger, D. S., Dugosh, K. L., & Lee, P. A. (2005). Are judicial status hearings a "key component" of drug court? Six and twelve months outcomes. *Drug and Alcohol Dependence, 79,* 145–155.

Marlowe, D. B., Festinger, D. S., & Lee, P. A. (2003). The role of judicial status hearings in drug court. *Offender Substance Abuse Report, 3,* 33–46.

Marlowe, D. B., Festinger, D. S., & Lee, P. A. (2004). The judge is a key component of drug court. *Drug Court Review, 4*(2), 1–34.

Marlowe, D. B., Festinger, D. S., Lee, P. A., Dugosh, K. L., & Benasutti, K. M. (2006). Matching judicial supervision to clients' risk status in drug court. *Crime & Delinquency, 52*(1), 52–76.

Mazur, R., & Aldrich, L. (2003). What makes domestic violence court work? Lessons from New York. *Judges Journal, 42,* 5–10.

McArdle, A., & Erzen, T. (2001). *Zero tolerance. Quality of life and the new police brutality in New York City,* New York: New York University Press.

McCoy, C. (2003). The politics of problem-solving: An overview of the origins and development of therapeutic courts. *American Criminal Law Review, 40,* 1513–1534.

McNiel, D. E., & Binder, R. L. (2007). Effectiveness of a mental health court in reducing criminal recidivism and violence. *American Journal of Psychiatry, 164,* 1395–1403.

Meekins, T. M. (2007). Risky business: Criminal specialty courts and the ethical obligations of the zealous criminal defender. *Berkeley Journal of Criminal Law, 12,* 75.

Miethe, T. D., Lu, H., & Reese, E. (2000). Reintegrative shaming and recidivism risks in drug court: Explanations for some unexpected findings. *Crime & Delinquency, 469* (4), 522–541.

Miller, J. M., and Shutt, J. E. (2001). Considering the need for empirically grounded drug court screening mechanisms. *Journal of Drug Issues, 31*(1), 91–106.

Mirchandani, R. (2005). What's so special about specialized courts? The state and social change in Salt Lake City's domestic violence court. *Law & Society Review, 39,* 379–417.

Moore, M. E., & Hiday, V. A. (2006). Mental health court outcomes: A comparison of re-arrest and re-arrest severity between mental health court and traditional court participants. *Law and Human Behavior, 30,* 659–674.

Morissey, J., Meyer, P., & Cuddeback, G. (2007). Extending assertive community treatment to criminal justice settings: Origins, current evidence, and future directions. *Community Mental Health, 43,* 527–544.

Naples, M., & Steadman, H. J. (2003). Can persons with co-occurring disorder and violent charges be successfully diverted? *International Journal of Forensic Mental Health, 2,* 137–143.

National Association for Youth Courts. (n.d.). *Facts and stats*. Retrieved June 20, 2008, from http://www.youthcourt.net/content/view/35/49//.

National Association of Youth Courts. (n.d.). *Youth court list by state*. Retrieved August 15, 2008, from http://www.youthcourt.net/content/view/7/14/.

National Association of Drug Court Professionals. (1997). *Defining drug courts: The key components*. Washington, DC: Office of Justice Programs, U.S. Department of Justice.

National Center for Injury Prevention and Control. (2003). *Costs of intimate partner violence against women in the United States*. Atlanta, GA: National Center for Injury Prevention and Control, Centers for Disease Control and Prevention, U.S. Department of Health and Human Services.

National Center for Mental Health and Juvenile Justice. (2005). *Juvenile mental health courts —Program descriptions: Processes and procedures*. Delmar, NY: Author.

National GAINS Center for People with Co-Occurring Disorders in the Justice System. (2004). *The prevalence of co-occurring mental and substance use disorders in jail settings*. Delmar, NY: Author.

National Institute of Justice (NIJ). (2006). *Drug courts: The second decade*. Washington, DC: Department of Justice, National Institute of Justice/NCJRS (Eds.).

Newmark, L., Rempel, M., Diffily, K., & Mallik-Kane, K. (2001). *Specialized felony domestic violence: Lessons on implementation and impacts from the Kings County experience*. Washington, DC: The Urban Institute and the Center for State Courts for the National Institute of Justice, U.S. Department of Justice.

Nolan, J. L., Jr. (2002, January/February). Therapeutic adjudication. *Society*, 29–38.

Nolan, J. L., Jr. (2003). Redefining criminal courts: Problem-solving and the meaning of justice. *American Criminal Law Review, 40*, 1541–1565.

NPC Research. (2008). *Michigan DUI courts outcomes evaluation final report*. Portland, OR: NPC Research. Available at http://www.npcresearch.com/Files/MI_DUI_Outcome_Evaluation_EXECUTIVE_SUMMARY_Re-Release_March_2008.pdf.

Odegaard, A. M. (2007). Therapeutic jurisprudence: The impact of mental health courts on the criminal justice system. *North Dakota Law Review, 83*, 225–259.

Ostrom, B. J. (2003). Domestic violence courts. *Criminology and Public Policy, 3*, 105–108.

Pearson, S. S. (2004). *Policymakers support youth court growth: Voices and recommendations from the field*. Lexington, KY: National Youth Court Center, American Probation and Parole Association. Retrieved September 2, 2008, from http://www.youthcourt.net/content/view/74.

Pearson, S. S., & Jurich, S. (2005). *Youth court: A community solution for embracing at-risk youth. A national update*. Washington, DC: American Youth Policy Forum.

Peters, R. H., Hass, A. L., & Hunt, W. M. (2001). Treatment "dosage" effects in drug court programs. *Journal of Offender Rehabilitation, 33*(4), 63–72.

Peters, R. H., & Murrin, M. R. (2000). Effectiveness of treatment-based drug courts in reducing criminal recidivism. *Criminal Justice and Behavior, 27*(1), 72–96.

Popovic, J. (2006). Court process and therapeutic jurisprudence: Have we thrown the baby out with the bathwater? *eLaw Journal*, Special Series 1, 60–77.

Povitisky, W. (2005). "Teen court: Does it reduce recidivism." Unpublished master's thesis, University of Maryland, College Park. Retrieved August 14, 2008, from http://www.lib.umd.edu/drum/bitstream/1903/3274/1/umi-umd-3102.pdf.

Poythress, N., Petrila, J., McGaha, A., & Boothroyd, R. (2002). Perceived coercion and procedural justice in the Broward County Mental Health Court. *International Journal of Law and Psychiatry, 25*, 517–533.

Pranis, K. (1998). *Guide for implementing balanced and restorative justice.* Washington, DC: Office of Juvenile Justice and Delinquency Prevention.

Quinn, M. C. (2000). Whose team am I on anyway? Musings of a public defender about drug treatment court practice. *N.Y.U. Review of Law and Social Change, 26*(37), 37–75.

Redlich, A. D. (2005). Voluntary, but knowing and intelligent: Comprehension in mental health courts. *Psychology, Public Policy, and Law, 11,* 605–619.

Redlich, A. D., Steadman, H. J., Monahan, J., Petrila, J., & Griffin, P. A. (2005). The second generation of mental health courts. *Psychology, Public Policy, and Law, 11,* 527–538.

Redlich, A. D., Steadman, H. J., Monahan, J., Robbins, P. C., & Petrila, J. (2006). Patterns of practice in mental health courts: A national survey. *Law and Human Behavior, 30,* 347–362.

Rempel, M., Kralstein-Fox, D., Cissner, A., Cohen, R., Labriola, M., Farole, D., Bader, A., & Magnani, M. (2003). *The New York State drug court evaluation.* New York: Center for Court Evaluation.

Rennison, C. M., & Welchans, S. (2000). *Intimate partner violence.* Washington, DC: Bureau of Justice Statistics, U.S. Department of Justice (NCJ 178247).

Robinson, A., & Cook, D. (2006). Understanding victim retraction in cases of domestic violence: Specialist courts, government policy, and victim-centered justice. *Contemporary Justice Review, 9,* 189–213.

Robinson, L. O. (2005). Community court and community justice commentary. *American Criminal Law Review, 40,* 1535–1539.

Rottman, D., & Casey, P. (2000). Therapeutic jurisprudence and the emergence of problem-solving courts. *Alternatives to incarceration,* 27–30.

Sanford, J. S., & Arrigo, B. A. (2005). Lifting the cover on drug courts: Evaluation findings and policy concerns. *International Journal of Offender Therapy and Comparative Criminology, 49*(3), 239–259.

Schneider, J. (2008). *Youth courts: An empirical update and analysis of future organizational and research needs.* Washington, DC: Hamilton Fish Institute.

Seltzer, T. (2005). Mental health courts: A misguided attempt to address the criminal justice system's unfair treatment of people with mental illness. *Psychology, Public Policy, and Law, 11,* 570–586.

Sneed, Z., Koch, D. S., Estes, H., & Quinn, J. (2006). Employment and psychosocial outcomes for offenders with mental illness. *International Journal of Psychosocial, 10,* 103–112.

Spinak, J. M. (2003). Why defenders feel defensive: The defender's role in problem solving courts. *American Criminal Law Review, 40*(4), 1617–1622.

Spohn, C., Piper, R. K., Martin, T., & Davis Frenzel, E. (2001). Drug courts and recidivism: The results of an evaluation using two comparison groups and multiple indicators of recidivism. *Journal of Drug Issues, 31*(1), 149–176.

Stafford, K. P., & Wygant, D. B. (2005). The role of competency to stand trial in mental health courts. *Behavioral Sciences and the Law, 23,* 245–258.

Steadman, H. J., Davidson, S., & Brown, C. (2001). Mental health courts: Their promise and unanswered questions. *Psychiatric Services, 52,* 457–458.

Steadman, H. J., Redlich, A. D., Griffin, P., Petrila, J., & Monahan, J. (2005). From referral to disposition: Case processing in seven mental health courts. *Behavioral Sciences and the Law, 23,* 215–226.

Stefan, S., & Winick, B. J. (2005). A dialogue on mental health courts. *Psychology, Public Policy, and Law, 11,* 507–526.

Sviridoff, M., Rottman, D. B., Ostrom, B., and Curtis, R. (2000). *Dispensing justice locally: The implementation and effects of the midtown community court.* New York: Harwood Academic Publishers.

Talesh, S. (2007). Mental health court judges as dynamic risk managers: A new conceptualization of the role of judges. *DePaul Law Review, 57,* 93–132.

Terry, W. C. (1999). *The early drug courts: Case studies in judicial innovation. Drugs, health, and social policy series, 7.* Thousand Oaks, CA: Sage Publications.

Thompson, A. T. (2002). Courting disorder: Some thoughts on community courts. *Washington University Journal of Law and Policy, 10,* 63–99.

Thompson, K. M. (2002). *The impact of North Dakota's juvenile drug court on school achievement. Department of Sociology. North Dakota State University. Fargo, ND 58105.*

Thompson, K. M. (2004). *An adult recidivism outcome evaluation of North Dakota's juvenile drug court. Department of Sociology. North Dakota State University. Fargo, ND 58105.*

Thompson, M., Osher, F., & Tomasini-Joshi, D. (2007). *Improving responses to people with mental illnesses: The essential elements of a mental health court.* New York: Council of State Governments Justice Center.

Tribal Law and Policy Institute. (2002). *Tribal healing to wellness courts: Treatment guidelines for adults and juveniles.* Published by the Tribal Law and Policy Institute under a cooperative agreement with the Drug Courts Program Office, Office of Justice Programs, U.S. Department of Justice in 2002.

Trupin, E. W., & Richards, H. J. (2003). Seattle's mental health courts: Early indicators of effectiveness. *International Journal of Law and Psychiatry, 26,* 33–53.

Tsai, B. (2000). The trend toward specialized domestic violence courts: Improvements on an effective innovation. *Fordham Law Review, 68,* 1285–1327.

Vitale, A. (2008). *City of disorder: How the quality-of-life campaign transformed New York City politics.* New York: New York University Press

Ventura, L. A., & Davis, G. (2005). Domestic violence: Court case conviction and recidivism. *Violence Against Women, 11,* 255–277.

Walsh, C. (2001). The trend toward specialization: West Yorkshire innovations in drug and domestic violence courts. *The Howard Journal of Criminal Justice, 40,* 26–38.

Wasserman, G., Ko, S., & McReynolds, L. (2004). Assessing the mental health status of youth in juvenile justice settings. *Juvenile Justice Bulletin,* 1–7.

Watson, A., Hanrahan, P., Luchins, D., & Lurigio, A. (2001). Mental health courts and the complex issue of offenders with mental illness. *Psychiatric Services, 52,* 477–481.

Webster, J. M., Rosen, P. J., Krietemeyer, J., Mateyoke-Scrivner, A., Staton-Tindall, M., & Leukefeld, C. (2006). Gender, mental health, and treatment motivation in a drug court setting. *Journal of Psychoactive Drugs, 38*(4), 441–448.

Wexler, D. B. (2001). Robes and rehabilitation: How judges can help offenders "make good." *Court Review, 38,* 18–23.

Winick, B. J., & Wexler, D. B. (2003). *Judging in a therapeutic key: Therapeutic jurisprudence and the courts.* Durham, NC: Carolina Academic Press.

Winick, B. J., & Wexler, D. B. (2002). Drug treatment court: Therapeutic jurisprudence applied. *Touro Law Review, 18,* 479–485.

Winick, B. (2003). Therapeutic jurisprudence and problem-solving-courts. *Fordham Urban Law Journal, 30*(3), 1055–90.

Wolf, R. V., & Berman, G. (2007). *Drug courts: Personal stories—narratives from across New York State.* New York: Center for Court Innovation.

Wolff, N., & Pogorzelski, W. (2005). Measuring the effectiveness of mental health courts: Challenges and recommendations. *Psychology, Public Policy, and Law, 11,* 539–569.

Zeilbauer, P. (2003, November 9). Court treatment system is found to help drug offenders stay clean. *New York Times,* Metro section, New York edition.

About the Contributors

Greg Berman is the director of the Center for Court Innovation, a nonprofit think tank that helps courts reduce crime, aid victims, and improve public trust in justice. Part of the founding team responsible for creating the Center, he has helped guide the organization from start-up to an annual budget of $17 million. The Center has received numerous awards for its work including the Innovations in American Government Award from the Ford Foundation and Harvard's John F. Kennedy School of Government. Greg is the co-author of *Good Courts: The Case for Problem-Solving Justice* (The New Press, 2005). He has contributed to several other books including *Documenting Results, Judicial Politics, A Problem-Solving Revolution,* and *Judging in a Therapeutic Key.* In addition, his written work has appeared in *The Guardian* (U.K.), *ABA Judges Journal* (guest editor), *Law and Policy, National Law Journal, Judicature, New Statesman* (U.K.), *New York Sun, Justice System Journal, Court Review, American Criminal Law Review,* and other publications. Greg is the co-founder and executive editor of the *Journal of Court Innovation.*

Richard C. Boldt is professor of law at the University of Maryland School of Law. He teaches courses in constitutional law, criminal law, mental disability law, and torts. Professor Boldt writes about criminal responsibility, contemporary blaming practices, and the intersection of the criminal justice and public health systems, with a special emphasis on the legal issues surrounding alcohol and other drug use disorders. His work includes "Rehabilitative Punishment and the Drug Treatment Court Movement," which was published by the *Washington University Law Quarterly*, and "The Construction of Responsibility in the Criminal Law," published by the *University of Pennsylvania Law Review.* Boldt practiced law at the Legal Action Center, a public interest law firm specializing in the legal issues faced by ex-offenders and persons with substance use disorders. He has held faculty positions at the Northern Illinois University College of Law and the City University of New York Law School at Queens College, and was a visiting professor at Brooklyn Law School.

Caroline S. Cooper is Associate Director of American University's Justice Programs Office and a member of the Research Faculty of AU's School of Public Affairs. She is a graduate of Smith College, Howard University (M.A.), and the Washington College of Law. For a number of years, she has been involved with the provision of technical assistance, evaluation, and training services to courts and other justice agencies. She has also been a practicing attorney, has served as an assistant public defender, and has written numerous publications addressing a variety of judicial system issues relating to the management of criminal, civil, juvenile, and family matters; drug courts; and court emergency preparedness. She is the Director of the BJA Drug Court Clearinghouse and Associate Director of the BJA Criminal Courts Technical Assistance Project conducted by the School of Public Affairs at American University.

David DeMatteo, J.D., Ph.D., is an Assistant Professor in the Department of Psychology at Drexel University, and Co-Director of the J.D./Ph.D. Program in Law and Psychology offered by Drexel University and Villanova University School of Law. Prior to joining the Drexel faculty, Dr. DeMatteo spent four years as a Research Scientist at the Treatment Research Institute at the University of Pennsylvania, where he conducted randomized controlled trials examining judicially based treatment programs for drug-involved offenders in drug courts. Dr. DeMatteo's research has been funded by the National Institute on Drug Abuse, Pennsylvania Department of Health, and American Psychology-Law Society. He has published several articles and book chapters relating to drug courts and related topics.

Angela R. Gover, Ph.D., is an Associate Professor in the School of Public Affair's Program on Domestic Violence at the University of Colorado at Denver. Dr. Gover's research focuses on intimate partner violence, childhood maltreatment, victimization, and evaluation research. Some of her published work has appeared in *Violence and Victims, Criminology and Public Policy, Violence Against Women,* and *Journal of Interpersonal Violence.* Dr. Gover spent eight years working with colleagues at the University of South Carolina and the Lexington County Sheriff's Department on two Department of Justice funded research projects involving the county's law enforcement and judicial responses to domestic violence. Her recently completed project examined the impact of proactive enforcement of no-contact orders issued by the Lexington County Criminal Domestic Violence Court on victim safety and repeat victimization.

Patricia A. Griffin, Ph.D., is a senior consultant for the National GAINS Center for Persons with Co-Occurring Disorders in the Justice System, the TAPA Center for Jail Diversion, and the Philadelphia Department of Behavioral Health. Her areas of writing and research include policy and system issues for offenders with co-occurring mental illness and substance use disorders, diversion of persons with severe mental illness from the criminal justice system, mental health courts, community forensic treatment services, and linkages between institutions and the community. She has worked as Director of Forensic Services for Virginia and State Coordinator for Community Forensic Services in Florida. She is co-author with Mark Munetz, M.D., of the recent publication "Use of the Sequential Intercept Model as an Approach to Decriminalization of People with Serious Mental Illness."

David J. Hanson, Professor Emeritus of Sociology of the State University of New York College at Potsdam, has researched the subject of alcohol and drinking for 40 years, beginning with his Ph.D. dissertation. He has received alcohol research grants from federal and state agencies, published over a dozen chapters in books on alcohol, prepared articles for a half-dozen encyclopedias, and published two books on alcohol. His publications and scholarly papers number over 300 and textbooks in over a dozen fields of study report his research. Dr. Hanson has served as alcohol consultant to the Canadian government and testified on Capitol Hill; his research has repeatedly been reported in the *New York Times* and other major newspapers, where he is frequently quoted; and he has appeared as an alcohol expert on the *NBC Nightly News with Tom Brokaw,* the BBC's *The World Tonight,* the *Dr. Laura* television program, the Fox News Channel, the CBC, *CNN Saturday,* National Public Radio's *All Things Considered* and *To the Best of Our Knowledge,* the ABC national radio news, and over 60 radio programs across the country.

Paul Higgins, Ph.D., is a professor of sociology at the University of South Carolina, Columbia. He has published more than a dozen books and monographs about deviance, disability, and sociology, including works about deaf communities, rehabilitation professionals, educating together deaf and hearing students, and thinking about deviance. He and Mitch Mackinem have written and published *Drug Court: Constructing the Moral Identity of Drug Offenders* with C. C. Thomas.

Mitchell B. Mackinem became an Assistant Professor of Sociology at Claflin University after 20 years of experience in the addictions treatment field. He has worked as a frontline addictions counselor, planned and implemented a residential treatment program, and was founder and director of the Richland County Drug Court Programs, where he worked for 10 years. Mitch Mackinem has provided training on numerous addictions topics including diagnostics, group therapy, starting drug courts, and drug testing, as well as presentations to the Society for the Study of Social Problems, American Society of Criminology, and the Academy of Criminal Justice Sciences. Paul Higgins and Mitch Mackinem have written two books, *Drug Court: Constructing the Moral Identity of Drug Offenders* and *Thinking About Deviance 2nd edition.* Mitch uses his varied experiences to inform his publications and continuing research on problem-solving courts, court alternatives, and deviance.

Victoria Malkin has a Ph.D. in social anthropology from University College, London. Her previous research focused on transnational migration between the United States and Mexico. She also worked on a Russell Sage funded project that investigated the contemporary situation of second-generation immigrants in New York City. Her research on Community Courts was part of a National Institute of Justice funded research study in 2000–2002 with Jeffrey Fagan, at the Center for Violence Research and Prevention, Mailman School of Public Health. She currently is a Foundation Anthropologist at the Wenner-Gren Foundation for Anthropological Research in New York City.

Tracy Godwin Mullins is a Senior Research Associate for the Council of State Governments (CSG)/American Probation and Parole Association (APPA) in Lexington, Kentucky. She has been with CSG/APPA for 14 years where she has worked on several federally funded projects focusing on juvenile justice, victim services, and offender issues. From 1994 through 2006, Tracy served as the Project Director for several federally funded national youth court initiatives, including the National Youth Court Center, sponsored by the Office of Juvenile Justice and Delinquency Prevention and administered by the CSG/APPA. She has written and served as a co-author on more than a dozen publications on a variety of youth court issues including *Peer Justice and Youth Empowerment: An Implementation Guide for Teen Court Programs* and the *National Youth Court Guidelines.*

Index